Capitalism
Crises and Alternatives

Acknowledgements

Resistance Books and the International Institute for Research are grateful to all those who helped in the production of this book, in particular Jay Blackwood, Iain Bruce, Terry Conway, Peter Cooper, Steph Grant, Geoff Ryan, Susan Pashkoff and Richard Willsem

The individual articles in this book are copyright © of the authors and/or the original publishers.

Published February 2012 by Resistance Books and the International Institute for Research and Education as Issue 52 of Notebooks for Study and Research.

Edited by Özlem Onaran and Fred Leplat

Cover design by Lauren Plum

ISBN: 978-0-902869-63-9

Printed in Britain by Lightning Source

Capitalism
Crises and Alternatives

Michel Husson, Andy Kilmister,
Susan Pashkoff, Sean Thompson, John Rees,
Özlem Onaran, Eric Toussaint,
Sandra Ezquerra, Catherine Samary,
Jean Sanuk, and Claudio Katz

Edited by Özlem Onaran and Fred Leplat

Resistance Books
London

International Institute for Research & Education
Amsterdam, Islamabad & Manila

Contents

Preface, Özlem Onaran 9
WHERE IS THE CRISIS GOING?
Michel Husson 11
THE CRISIS IN BRITAIN
Andy Kilmister 41
AUSTERITY AND THE LIES THAT IMPOVERISH
Susan Pashkoff 59
A GREEN INDUSTRIAL REVOLUTION
Sean Thompson 77
MARXISM AND THE CRISIS
John Rees 101
A FISCAL CRISIS OR A CRISIS OF DISTRIBUTION?
Özlem Onaran 113
THE DEBT IN THE NORTH: SOME ALTERNATIVE PATHS,
Eric Toussaint 149
WOMEN'S CRISES
Sandra Ezquerra 179
EASTERN EUROPE FACED WITH THE CRISIS OF THE
SYSTEM, Catherine Samary 189
CHINA'S RISE AMIDST THE CRISIS
Jean Sanuk 219
LATIN AMERICA'S CRISIS
Claudio Katz 233
IN THE EYE OF THE STORM: THE DEBT CRISIS IN THE
EUROPEAN UNION, Eric Toussaint 249
About Resistance Books and the IIRE 275

Contributors

Michel Husson is an economist at IRES (a trade union-linked institute) in Paris. He is member of the Fondation Copernic, a left-wing think tank, and of the Scientific Council of ATTAC. He has published Un pur capitalisme, Lausanne 2008, Éditions Page Deux. You can consult his writings on http://hussonet.free.fr

Andy Kilmister teaches economics at Oxford Brookes University and is a member of Socialist Resistance. He is the editor of *Debatte: Journal of Contemporary Central and Eastern Europe* and the co-author (with Gary Browning) of *Critical and Post-Critical Political Economy* (Palgrave/Macmillan, 2006).

Susan Pashkoff has an MA and PhD in Economics from the New School for Social Research, Graduate Faculty, NY. A former senior lecturer in Economics, she is a regular blogger and lifelong political activist.

Sean Thompson is a Marxist and has been concerned with ecosocialist ideas since the late nineteen seventies. He is a member of the Green Party (and of Green Left, its ecosocialist wing) and a contributor to *Socialist Resistance*.

John Rees books include *The Algebra of Revolution, Imperialism and Resistance, Strategy and Tactics* and, most recently, *The People Demand - a Short History of the Arab Revolutions* (with Joseph Daher). He is on the editorial board of Counterfire and is co-founder of the Stop the War Coalition.

Özlem Onaran is a lecturer in Economics. She has published extensively in the areas of globalization, crisis, employment, wages, and inequality.

Eric Toussaint teaches at the University of Liege. He is President of the Committee for Cancellation of Third World Debt and is a member of the International Committee of Fourth International. His books include *The World Bank - A Critical Primer* (Pluto Press, London, 2008) and *Your Money or your Life - The Tyranny of the Global Finance*, (Haymarket, Chicago, 2005).

Sandra Ezquerra is a doctor in sociology as well as an anticapitalist and feminist activist. She currently conducts a research project on informal economic relations at Universitat de Barcelona and teaches social science methodology at Universitat de Vic. She is also an active member in the feminist and 15M social movements in Spain.

Catherine Samary teaches economics in Paris-Dauphine and is associated with the Institute of European Studies at the University Paris 8 St Denis. She is involved with editing the *Monde-Diplomatique Atlas*. She is a member of the scientific council of the French Attac, of the New Anticapitalist Party and of the Fourth International. She has written extensively on Eastern Europe and in particular, Yugoslavia.

Jean Sanuk is an economist, a specialist on Asia. He coordinated the recent IIRE economists' seminar.

Claudio Katz is an economist and researcher. He lectures at the University of Buenos Aires and is a Fellow at the International Institute for Research and Education. He is a member of the in the Argentine network 'Economistas de Izquierda' (Economists of the Left). You can consult his writings at www.lahaine.org/katz.

Preface

Özlem Onaran

This edited volume is a follow-up to our previous book 'Socialists and the Capitalist Recession' published in 2009. Four years after the onset of the crisis, our analysis of the systemic, multiple nature of the crisis combining economic, food, energy and ecological crises is even more pronounced. The policy reaction of the ruling elite, shaped by the existing pro-capital power structures, have been mere efforts to preserve the high profits via massive state intervention with an aim of going back to the 'business as usual' strategy of neoliberalism. The plans to rescue capitalism from itself have so far not only failed to address these multiple dimensions but also have been incapable of promoting the return to a stable economy as the rescue packages unleashed a so-called public debt crisis. The neoliberal policies as well as the power of the financial markets have remained unchanged.

We are also facing a multi-speed world economy with a stronger recovery in Latin America and Asia, especially China, while advanced capitalist countries are trapped in a weak recovery or even a deepening of the crisis, particularly in Europe with important repercussions for global capitalism. In particular China has been the main driver of growth since 2010 for the other developing countries and even for advanced capitalist countries like Germany; however this process has its limits. It is yet to be seen whether this will lead to a change in the international balance of power relations.

The book's main aim is to present a comparative analysis of the crisis in different regions and to contribute to the debates about alternatives with an emphasis on the multiple dimensions of the crisis.

In Chapter one, Michel Husson presents an outline of the reasons behind the crisis and the stages of the crisis. Chapter two by Andy Kilmister focuses on the particular intensity of the crisis in Britain and the deep rooted contradictions behind the crisis in the British economy. In Chapter three, Susan Pashkoff analyses the discourse and political economy of austerity with a focus on the latest evidence about distribution and unemployment in Britain. In Chapter four Sean Thompson brings in the multiple dimensions of the crisis, and aims at developing a broad ecosocialist industrial strategy with a focus on the case of Britain. Chapter five by John Rees discusses the relevance of Marx's political economy in understanding the crisis and developing strategies, and points at some controversies within the left in its interpretations.

In Chapter six Özlem Onaran analyses the consequences of the crisis for working people in Western Europe, and outlines transition demands for an alternative ecosocialist Europe. Eric Toussaint focuses more specifically on the debt crisis in Europe, and introduces alternative strategies in Chapter seven.

Sandra Ezquerra discusses an often neglected aspect of the crisis in the periphery of Europe: despite the vast literature on the crisis, there has not been much discussion about the specific consequences of the crisis and post-crisis management on women; Sandra Ezquerra engenders the analysis of the crisis with a focus on the Spanish State in Chapter eight.

Chapter nine by Catherine Samary reminds us of the forgotten fragilities in Eastern Europe, which is now facing yet another crisis after two decades of integration to global capitalism.

The following two chapters focus on the differences in the effects of the crisis and post-crisis management in Latin America and China, and improves our understanding of a swing in the centre of gravity of global capitalist accumulation. In Chapter ten Jean Sanuk discusses the growth regime in China, its relevance for global capitalism, and its intrinsic limits. Claudio Katz introduces the recent debates in Latin America in Chapter eleven, and points at the political aspects of crisis management, continuing fragilities, and the distributional consequences of the crisis management.

Finally, at the end of the book we are publishing an interview with Eric Toussaint, which discusses the new stages of the debt crisis in Europe since Summer 2011. This not only helps us to present an update on the latest events since the previous contributions were written, but also provides a very accessible yet informative piece, which can be used as part of activist work.

The depth of the present crisis has torn holes in the hegemony of neoliberalism and has led to serious political discontent. We hope that this global update three years after the crisis about the new stages of the crisis and the limits to recovery will help us to develop strategies to turn the popular discontent into a real challenge to the hegemony of capitalism.

WHERE IS THE CRISIS GOING?
Michel Husson

We have to pay for the sins of the past.
Klaus Schwab, 2008[1]

Three years after the outbreak of the crisis, one thing is certain: we're a long way from seeing its end. Capitalism has undergone a shock which calls into question its neoliberal form and, more profoundly its essential logic. To count on its self-reform is an illusion, because capitalism has no alternative other than to seek the recreation of its previous conditions of functioning, even when this is an impossible task. Nevertheless capitalism will seek to get out of this impasse by conducting a very violent antisocial offensive, which it has already started to do.

This is the theme of this chapter in which it is proposed to put this crisis in perspective. It goes back to the origins of financialisation in order to clarify the role of finance in the functioning of neoliberal capitalism. This presentation then allows us to better understand what is in crisis and to characterise the new phase into which we have entered, with the putting in place of austerity plans in Europe. We must then discuss the programmatic and strategic conditions for the emergence of an anticapitalist alternative.

The role of finance in the crisis

The outbreak of the crisis has generated an enormous amount of analysis that can be classified according to the answers they provide, or suggest, to two major questions about its nature: is it a financial or is it a systemic crisis? Is it a crisis of the neoliberal variant of

---

[1] Klaus Schwab is the founder and president of the World Economic Forum.

capitalism or of capitalism as a system? No-one denies that the crisis originated in a fairly narrow segment of global finance, the notorious subprime, which prompted some commentators to predict that it would be of limited scale. We now understand better the reasons which led this 'failure' to jeopardise the financial and banking system worldwide. There are plenty of accounts of this contamination revealing the dimensions of the truly insane excesses of finance. That said, can we separate the wheat from the chaff by contrasting good capitalism which invests and innovates, with speculative and predatory finance? It is important to understand that finance is not an excrescence: on the contrary it is an essential cog of capitalism in its neoliberal version.

Credit is necessary for the operation of capitalism. In the short term, it makes the link between businesses' purchases and sales. In the medium and long term, it helps to finance investment. Consumer credit facilitates access to household durables such as cars and housing. Without this lubricant, the economy has difficulty in running and the credit crunch, moreover, was one of the transmission belts of the financial crisis to the 'real economy'. The use of credit in itself is rational insofar as it enables the anticipation of future income. In the case of investment, the rule is simple: expected profits must cover interest payable. Outside periods of crisis, the interest rate must be lower than the rate of profit, the difference between the two serving as a 'lever' for capital accumulation. Throughout the period of the 'Golden Age', business investment was two-thirds self-financed, the rest being covered by credit. Capitalism worked without significant recourse to capital markets, i.e. shareholders.

The great neoliberal turn of the 1980s brought about a fundamental break. We can repeat here Michael Kalecki's[2] premonitory framework which distinguished three major actors: managers, rentiers and employees, and which considered two main configurations are possible: either an alliance of managers and employees leading to a form of 'an euthanasia of the rentier' (in the words of Keynes) or on the contrary an alliance of managers and rentiers at the expense of employees. And indeed it can be said that we have moved from one to the other.

The origins of financialisation are illuminating. It all began in 1979 when the U.S. Federal Reserve sharply and brutally increased its interest rates. This lever was deployed to change social and world power relationships as a response to the crisis of the mid-1970s. One of its immediate effects was to plunge many countries of the South into a deep and long-lasting debt crisis almost overnight. Interest

---

2   Michael Kalecki, 'Political Aspects of Full Employment', *Political Quarterly*, 1943, http://gesd.free.fr/kalecki43.pdf

rates leapt upwards, destabilising the balance of payments of these countries. It was a good example of the 'Shock Doctrine' discussed by Naomi Klein[3] but it is not just the South which was affected. This was ultimately about a lasting change in the triangular balance of power between entrepreneurs 'rentiers' and employees. While Fordist capitalism was not based on a gentlemen's agreement between workers and capitalists, and the balance of forces established after the war had a lot to do with it, finance was in any case reduced to a bare minimum, both in company and in household wealth investment.

After the recession of 1974-75 and the failure of classical stimulus policies, it was necessary to restore the rate of profit by smashing wage growth and restructuring the productive apparatus. It was in this period that we witnessed a shift of alliances: finance would henceforth be used as a means of pressure on wages, and its subsequent development cannot be understood without reference to these origins. Increases in interest rates promoted restructuring and forced companies to offset them at the expense of wages. So there was a very effective mixture of deliberate policies of governments and an offensive against wages.

These two aspects are closely intertwined, as evidenced by the timeline in the French case. In 1982 and 1983, the government abandoned any stimulus and moved to rigour and austerity. Under the pretext of fighting inflation, wages were decoupled from productivity gains so that the share of wages fell sharply throughout the 1980s. Corporate profitability recovered but remained burdened by interest rates: the beginning of the next decade was devoted to debt reduction, then, when this was achieved, a transfer of profits to dividends began. The declining share of wages was based on a general anti-union offensive marked by conflicts that served as symbolic political tests: the air traffic controllers' strike in the USA, the miners' strike in the United Kingdom, and the steelworkers' strike in France. As the director of the ultra-neoliberal Hayek Institute said, 'Thatcher and Reagan saved democracy from the reign of the street, without disproportionate violence. For this history will thank them.'[4]

The next step was to establish conditions conducive to the growth of finance: deregulation measures broke down barriers and financial markets were created from scratch. In France, it was a government initiative that built up Matif (the French futures market) from almost nothing from 1984 onwards. The programme was very clear: first, freeze wages, and then liberate finance. It was not the

---

3   Naomi Klein, The Shock Doctrine: The Rise of Disaster Capitalism, Metropolitan Books, 2007.
4   Drieu Godefridi, 'L'inéluctable moment Thatcher-Reagan des démocraties européennes', Les Echos, 5 Septembre 2005, http://gesd.free.fr/godfri.pdf

immanent laws of economics but of those of socio-economic imperatives. Capitalism can do without finance, but that goes hand in hand with a (relative) compromise with wage earners. The rise of finance was the product of political decisions, and the best evidence for this was the growing role of international institutions like the IMF and the WTO, one of whose main functions is to ensure the free movement of capital, which is also one of the fundamental principles of European neoliberal construction.

Several trends enable the definition of the financialisation process. The first, which will be discussed, is the increased share of value added which accrues to shareholders. The second, which is a sort of derivative phenomenon, is the growth in market capitalisation. The first phenomenon is real: dividends paid are non-invested profit. They correspond to a fraction of the annual surplus and are a counterpart of GDP. A shareholder who receives a dividend receives a real income which s/he may decide to consume or to reinvest. Financialisation is measured here by the share of dividends or profits in value added.

Market capitalisation is by contrast a stock whose valuation is virtual: it is 'fictitious capital' to quote Marx's expression. It is calculated as the sum of the value of all shares on the basis of their price at any given moment. Suppose I own 1,000 shares which constitute the capital of a company. If each share is priced at 1 euro, my credit is €1,000 and my business is valued at €1,000 of the total stock market capitalisation. Now suppose that the share price doubles: my shareholding goes up to €2,000. But this additional 'wealth' is a pure fiction. If the share price drops to one euro, everybody is back to square one and nothing has happened. The real test comes when a shareholder decides to recover his or her stake by selling all or part of his/her portfolio.

We must therefore distinguish between the rate of profit and the rate of financial return. The rate of profit is determined in the real economy while the financial rate of return is virtual in nature. Normally, there is a link between the two: the rate of return on shares anticipates changes in the rate of profit. But the major novelty of financialisation is that share prices soar and that all links are broken with businesses' actual profitability. This phenomenon is even more irrational in that the net contribution of financial markets in financing companies is marginal or even negative due to corporations' practice of buying back their own shares. The stock exchange is essentially a secondary market: shares that are exchanged are shares already issued and do not represent new money.

A return to the law of value (or simply to accounting logic) enables us to understand why the surge in stock returns is a pure fiction. The starting point is that new value is created through labour. This is then divided between wages, business profits, dividends, taxes, etc. The total amount of what is thus allocated cannot exceed the value of what has been produced. If there is any law in economics, it is this. Financial stocks should be considered a 'drawing right' on wealth produced. They have a 'face value' which is the price at which they traded in the financial market. They must be devalued if realisation of these drawing rights is sought and their sum exceeds available wealth. That's exactly what happened with the dot com boom in the early 2000s.

The important point is that finance does not create value but operates on its distribution. Retirement pensions provide a concrete example of this rule. One of the arguments in favour of pension funds was to say that the yield provided by capitalisation exceeded that provided by redistribution. Through redistribution, we can at best get the rate of GDP growth (2-3%) while capitalisation provides access to share returns which are two or three times higher. Admittedly, this argument has suffered from the financial crisis. But it was absurd even before this practical test: if an economy grows by 3% each year, total income cannot rise by 9% annually. While some funds may benefit from such a performance, it can only be at the expense of others.

But financialisation also bears down on corporate logic, and here an opposition between managers and shareholders is to be found. Managers set themselves a goal of maximum growth of the firm in the medium and long term (profit being only the means of accumulation) while shareholders seek the highest return possible in the short term. This results in a rebalancing at the expense of accumulation, in step with the growing power of shareholders. This updated theory of the firm is part of a post-Keynesian tradition and has opened a very fruitful path of analysis.[5] It shows that the relative weight of these two objectives leads to a different trajectory and in particular to a different investment behaviour. And it is clear from this point of view that contemporary capitalism is characterised by an increasing shareholder influence.

---

5   I would recommend the following works: Engelbert Stockhammer, 'Financialisation and the slowdown of accumulation', *Cambridge Journal of Economics*, vol.28,n°5, 2004, http://gesd.free.fr/stockh2004.pdf; Till van Treeck, 'Reconsidering the investment-profit nexus in finance-led economies', *Metroeconomica* 59:3, 2008, http://gesd.free.fr/treeck8.pdf; Özgür Orhangazi, 'Financialisation and capital accumulation in the non-financial corporate sector', *Cambridge Journal of Economics* vol.32, 2008, http://gesd.free.fr/orhangazi.pdf; Thomas Dallery, 'Post-Keynesian Theories of the Firm under Financialisation', *Review of Radical Political Economics*, vol.41, n°4, 2009, http://gesd.free.fr/dallery9.pdf

The risks of financialisation became clear with the current crisis undermining the dominant thesis. This argues that finance serves an irreplaceable economic activity by providing the resources needed, and by promoting high and responsive standards of economic efficiency. This *efficient markets hypothesis* has served as a justification for policies of systematic deregulation: that it is by freeing financial markets from any barriers that rationality can be maximised. Today, the same people who supported this position recognise the need for a minimum of regulation. But it's only lip service. Not only are the decisions taken in the field merely cosmetic, or indefinitely postponed, and, as noted by a group of dissenting French economists: 'The crisis is interpreted not as an inevitable result of the logic of deregulated markets, but as a result of the dishonesty and irresponsibility of certain financial actors poorly supervised by governments'.[6]

The main features of neoliberal capitalism

Contrary to the 'parasitical' view, we must instead stress the functionality of finance: it is part and parcel of neoliberal capitalism, which is the current phase of capitalism. Its growing influence is in itself an indication of the chronic disfunctionalities of capitalism as a system. In order to prove this and to go beyond the 'purely financial' explanation of the crisis, we will describe the main 'stylised facts' that characterise contemporary capitalism, namely: 1) a declining share of wages and an increase in the rate of profit, 2) a stagnation in the rate of accumulation, 3) an increase in the share of dividends.

Stylised fact No. 1: declining share of wages and rising rate of profit

The declining share of wages is a now almost universal phenomenon that has been identified by most international bodies such as the IMF, OECD and the European Commission.[7] This decrease is due to the non-distribution of productivity gains to wages. The sharing of the surplus between profits and wages is therefore modified to the detriment of the latter. In all cases, the chronology is similar: the share of wages was fairly stable until the crisis of the mid-1970s,

---

6   *Manifeste des économistes atterrés*, http://atterres.org/.
7   See Michel Husson, 'The upward trend in the rate of exploitation', *International Viewpoint* n°397, February 2008, http://hussonet.free.fr/parvaivp.pdf

which led to its increase. The reversal occurred during the first half of the 1980s: the share of wages began to decline, then tended to stabilise at a historically very low level.

With differences in the timing and profile of the development, this trend was almost universal, as highlighted by the International Labour Organisation: 'the wage (or labour) share of total Income has declined in nearly three quarters of the countries considered (...) The pattern of the decline has been similar in most countries: wage share has declined steadily over the past three decades, except in the late 1980s/early 1990s and again in the late 1990s. Secondly, the drop in wage share was particularly fast in the early 1980s and the early 2000s'.[8]

Chart 1: Wage share in value added USA + EU + Japan 1960-2008; Average weighted by GDP

Source: European Commission, Ameco Database

This decline in the wage share led to a restoration of profit rates in the major capitalist countries. The profit rate is calculated by relating the total profit to the value of capital employed. We can then break it down into two elements: in the numerator, we find the profit share i.e. the share of profits in the value added; the denominator includes the capital intensity, i.e. the volume of capital per unit of output.

---

8   Income Inequalities in the Age of Financial Globalization, World of Work Report 2008, ILO, http://tinyurl.com/WWR2008

The rate of profit therefore increases when the decline in the share of wages (thus increasing the profit share) and when production utilises capital more efficiently (capital intensity decreases). In a period where the share of wages declines, the rate of profit could only fall if a greater volume of capital were to more than offset the decline in the wage share. This is not what happened, and we can see that the rate of profit has tended to increase from the mid-1980s (Chart 2).

The evolution of the rate of profit enables us to see the periodisation already described.

From the high level reached during the 'Golden Age', the rate of profit began to decline, beginning from 1967 in the United States, and from the 1974-75 recession in other countries. This sharp decline wasn't slowed down by the Keynesian policies.

Chart 2: The profit rate in the major capitalist countries Germany + USA + France + United Kingdom 1960-2008; Average weighted by GDP

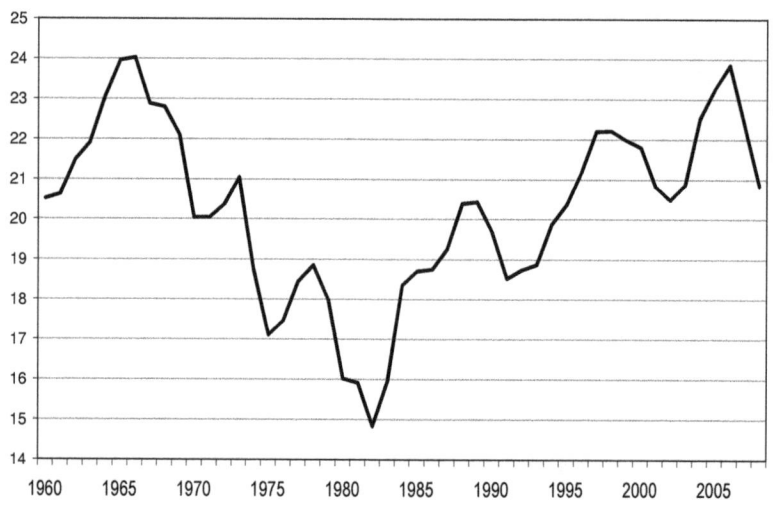

Sources: National accounts; Michel Husson, The rising tendency of the rate of profit, 2010

The turn to neoliberal policies in the early 1980s led to a sharp recovery in the rate of profit throughout the 1990s. Then, the upward movement continued, with wide fluctuations and with varied profiles depending on the country, until the recent crisis which has made it go sharply downwards.[9]

Stylised fact No. 2: the 'scissors' between profit and investment

The obverse of the decline in the share of wages was an increase in the share of profits, i.e. the share of value added which goes to profit: this is the primary distribution of income. The question that then arises is, on what has this extra profit been spent? In the early 1980s, wage restraint was justified by the 'Schmidt theorem' in the name of the then German chancellor, who had stated it thus: 'the profits of today are the investments of tomorrow and the jobs of the day after tomorrow.' Now the first part of this theorem didn't work, either in Europe or the U.S.: profit share increased but the rate of investment (relative to GDP) didn't follow. Beyond cyclical fluctuations, the investment rate stagnated and even moved downwards (Chart 3).

Chart 3: Profit and Investment USA + EU + Japan 1960-2008; Profit = profit share as % of value added; Investment rate as % of value added; Average weighted by GDP

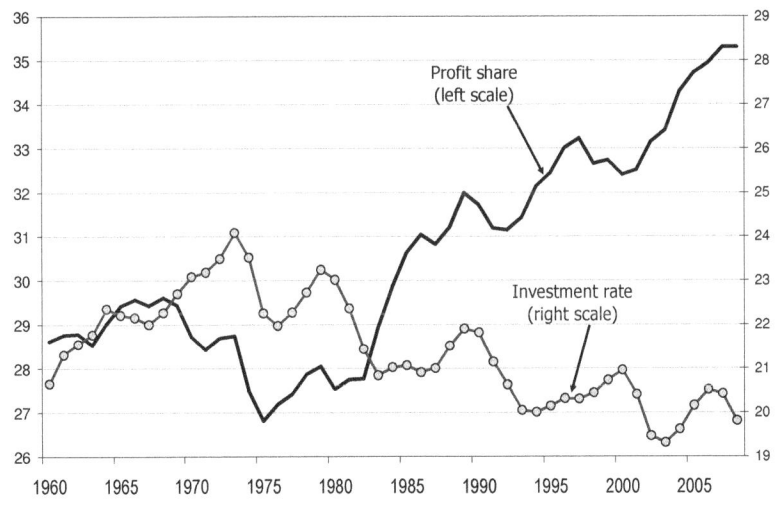

Source: European Commission, Ameco database

---

9   There is no consensus on this point. For the debate, see Michel Husson, 'The debate on the rate of profit', *International Viewpoint* n°426, July 2010, http://hussonet.free.fr/debaproe.pdf. The main contributions on this debate can be found at: http://hussonet.free.fr/tprof.htm

The decline in the share of wages combined with stagnant investment rates exhibits then a relatively unprecedented configuration in the history of capitalism, which challenges the main justifications for wage moderation as a way of restoring competitiveness. To the extent that the downward trend in the share of wages is a general trend among developed countries and where most of the international trade of these countries takes place between them, this moderation does not significantly alter their relative competitive positions. Between the EU and the USA, variations in exchange rates between the euro and the dollar have a far greater impact on their relative competitiveness than their wage costs. Within the EU, it's a zero sum game: what one country gains in market share, another loses.

In these circumstances, the observation of a decline in the wage share is enough to show that the effect of wage moderation on competitiveness has been hijacked. Suppose that a country lowers its wages and passes these reductions on in lowered prices to gain competitiveness: in this case, the share of wages should remain constant. The very fact that the share of wages has declined is a basis for asserting that wage moderation has not been used to restore competitiveness, but to restore company profitability.

The fact that this recovery in the share of profits has not attracted increased investment shows that it has been spent on something other than the expansion of productive capacity or improving non-cost based competitiveness, i.e. through innovation, improved product quality better tailored to demand. The fundamental question remains about what these extra margins were spent on.

Stylised fact 3: the rise of dividends

The arithmetic is simple: the share of wages is falling and that of investment stagnating. Something must be increasing.

The answer is obvious: the main counterpart of lower wages is a real explosion of dividends. Here we have to think about net dividends (i.e. deduct dividends paid by companies) to get an adequate measure of un-invested profit. It becomes apparent that today in France it amounts to nearly 13% of payroll as against 4% in early 1980. As shown in Chart 4 below, the development is the same in the United States and in the United Kingdom.

Chart 4: Dividends as % of net payroll, United States, France, United Kingdom, 1960-2008

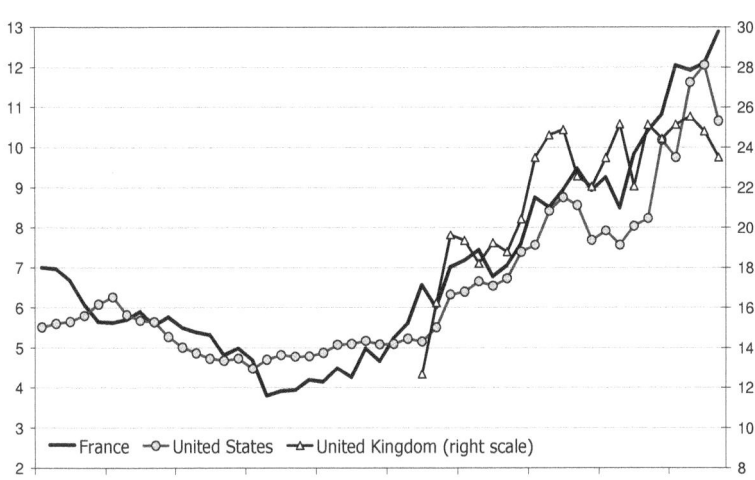

Sources: Bureau of Economic Analysis, INSEE, United Kingdom Economic Accounts (tables A22A and A12)

The structure of the crisis

All of those stylised facts lead to an overall schema for describing the operation of neoliberal capitalism and for reading the chain of events that led to the crisis. We must introduce here two contextual elements, i.e. changes in the environment of capitalism that does not result from its internal mechanisms. The first is the rising rate of unemployment, which tips the balance of power between capital and labour. This lever has led to the declining share of wages, the 'stylised fact' No. 1.

The second contextual element is what one might call the increased scarcity of profitable investment opportunities. The idea is the following: the same level of profitability is not associated with the satisfaction of various social needs. Moreover, if we think dynamically, the same profit opportunities are no longer the same as before, depending on the potential productivity gains associated with the sectors in which the investment takes place. However, social demand for manufactured goods is being replaced by demand for services, thus from high-productivity sectors towards sectors with lower productivity, all in a context of overall declining average productivity. These fundamental changes therefore lead to a narrowing of the field for profitable investment which explains the scissors between profit, which is being restored and investment which doesn't follow it: this is the 'stylised fact' No.2.

The declining share of wages and stagnant investment combine to lead to the third 'stylised fact', namely increased distribution of dividends to shareholders. This increase in distributed profit retroactively operates in two ways on the overall configuration. On the one hand it leads to a rise in the norms of profitability and demands a 'hyper-profitability' from businesses. Here we find the famous standard of a 15% return on equity, so often denounced. And rightly so, because an economy growing at best at 3% a year cannot sustainably provide such returns for shareholders. To try anyway to meet these requirements, companies have only one means at their disposal: the reduction in the share of the wage bill in their overall costs. In Figure 1, the two dotted arrows illustrate the feedback effects that reinforce the coherence of this model.

Figure 1: a general scheme of analysis

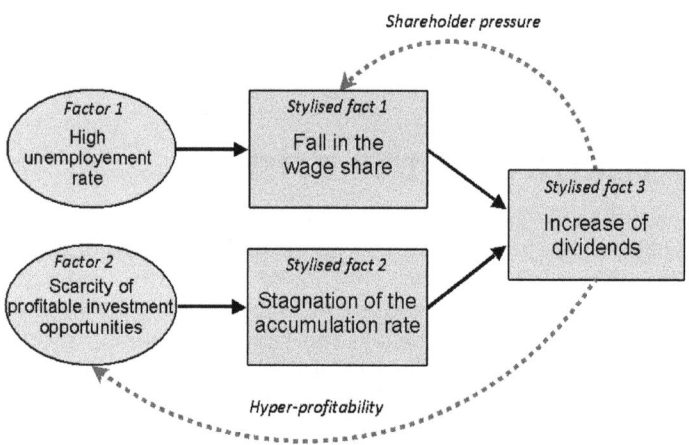

To escape its contradictions, capitalism should accept a lower return on capital, and finance should abandon its purely speculative activities. But this is completely impossible and that impossibility goes back to the essential features of the system. Capitalism is a system based on competition between capitals: any individual capitalist who refuses to fight the battle would eventually be condemned to bankruptcy, whatever his/her intentions. And this relentless logic is reinforced by globalisation.

Globalisation further hardens up all the schema's sinews. The placing of employees in competition worldwide, and the opportunities for shareholders to withdraw their bets almost instantly increases pressure on the employees. This organisation of the global economy was not born spontaneously: it was built deliberately and systematically by governments and their supranational emanations. The instruments of any possible regulation at the global level have been carefully removed, often by the very people who are now rediscovering their supposed benefits. The main consequence of this dismantlement is that there is no international body able to fix the rules of the game. This is the reason why the post-crisis period is characterised by increased rivalry among the major capitalist powers and at a European level, by a near total absence of cooperation that leads to an absolutely staggering generalised policy of austerity. All these trends are exacerbated by the great shift in the world: the most dynamic markets and the least expensive labour is to be found in emerging countries, and this 'attractiveness' results in a disconnect between exports and the domestic market of which Germany is a striking example.

Beyond universal deregulation and the total freedom of manoeuvre accorded to finance and capital, we have seen that the world economy has been structured around the China / USA duo, and that trade imbalances have increased. The capital flows necessary to finance these deficits come to provide liquidity and to seek hyper-profitability.

The image of the capitalist economy before the crisis was therefore that of an enormous mass of 'free capital' fuelled by the reduction in the share of wages and by global imbalances. Thanks to financial deregulation, capital moves freely in search of hyper-profitability that the concrete conditions of the production of surplus can only guarantee virtually. It is therefore logical that this forward flight has unravelled in the financial sphere, but this does not imply that it is a strictly financial crisis. Designating the financiers and the inventors of sophisticated and opaque 'derivatives' as the sole perpetrators of the crisis is to ignore its root causes.

The question of realisation: who's buying?

Neoliberal capitalism's arrangements favour the requirement of profitability, but pose *a priori* a problem of realisation: if the share of wages declines and investment is stagnating, who will buy the production? In other words what are, to use Marx's term, the reproduction schemas which are compatible with this new model?

The first answer is that household consumption did not follow the evolution of income redistribution at the expense of wages, and this could be our stylised fact No.4. In the United States, the share of wages has remained relatively constant, while household consumption has grown much faster than GDP. In Europe, the share of consumption in GDP has stayed roughly constant, despite a sharp decline in the share of wages (Chart 5). In both cases, the gap has grown between the share of wages and the share of consumption in order to compensate for the corresponding gap between profit and accumulation.

This gap between wages and consumption can be explained in two ways: either the savings rate has declined (households consuming a growing fraction of their income) or consumption resulting from non-wage income has increased more rapidly, offsetting the stagnation and even the decline in the consumption of wage earners.

Chart 5a: Wages and private consumption as % of GDP 1960-2008 (European Union)

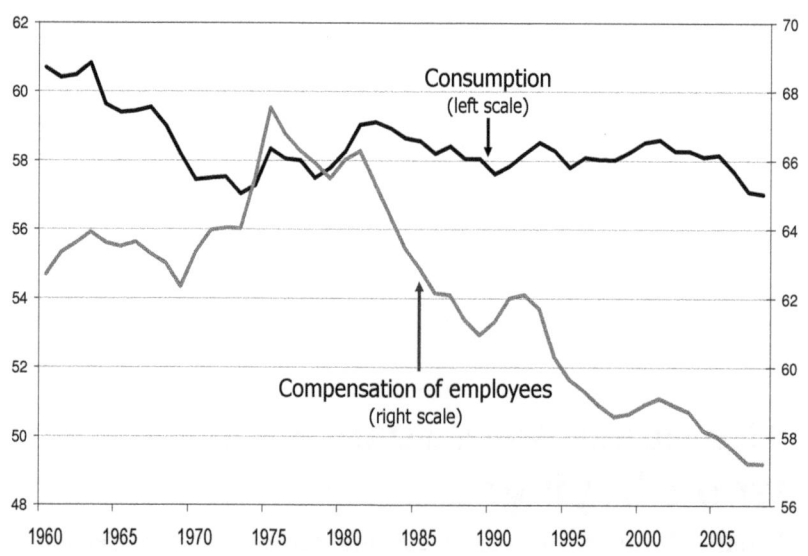

Chart 5b: Wages and private consumption as % of GDP 1960-2008 (United States)

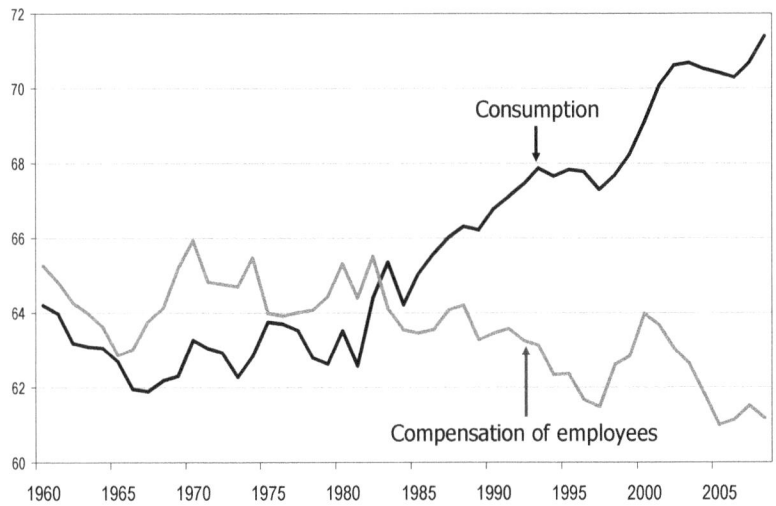

Sources: Bureau of Economic Analysis, Ameco.

All these mechanisms have played out differently depending on the countries involved, but finance capital is always the leading player. This is what fills the potential gap between wages and consumption, taking several routes. The first is the consumption of the 'rentiers': part of the surplus value accrued but not reinvested is distributed to holders of income from finance, who consume it. Finance introduces furthermore some blurring over between wages and unearned income: a growing proportion of income of some employees takes the form of financial compensation which can be analysed as a distribution of surplus value rather than as a real wage.

Reproduction is only possible if the rentiers' consumption buttresses that of employees in order to provide sufficient outlets. Rising inequality is therefore inherent in this model. In several countries finance has also allowed exponential growth in indebtedness of households whose consumption is increasing, not because of wage growth but due to a lower rate of savings. Finally, it enables the growth of U.S. credit by financing its trade deficit. Here we find the idea that finance is not a parasite on a healthy body but a means of 'filling the gap' in the reproduction of neoliberal capitalism. The crisis only reveals the contradictions of a capitalist configuration, specifically those that finance has so far helped to 'manage'.

The current crisis must be understood as the crisis of the neoliberal schema just described and which itself brought solutions to the previous crisis. This model was coherent in the sense that its elements made up a system but it was at the same time unequal, fragile and unbalanced. But it had, and still has the advantage of allowing the dominators to capture an increasing share of wealth produced. This model can no longer function, but the capitalists have no replacement. The period into which we are entering is entirely dominated by this contradiction: everything will be done to return to *business as usual,* while that is impossible.

The new phase of the crisis

We can distinguish several stages in the development of the crisis (see Table 1). After Phase 1 of its outbreak, came Phase 2 of the 'recovery', which is followed by a phase 3 today, so-called 'end of crisis'. Three conjunctural factors play in different ways in the course of these different phases: social stabilisers, raw material prices, and recovery plans. Social stabilisers, that is to say the means of securing income and employment (benefits, part-time working, etc...) actually helped to partially mitigate the magnitude of the recession. Then the stimulus helped to stimulate activity to an extent that it is difficult to assess due to our insufficient historical perspective. During Phase 2, the structural contradictions had less influence on the economy. The share of wages increased because the brake on real wages was less than the decline in productivity. The decline in activity and rising savings rates (particularly noticeable in the U.S.) reduced global imbalances. Finally, inasmuch as it was about injecting cash to save the banks, European institutions, including the European Central Bank (ECB), responded in a relatively coordinated manner.

Finally Phase 3 has opened faster than might have been expected, with the generalised turn toward austerity in Europe. It is characterised by a double reversal of the situation. The positive effects of conjunctural factors have been exhausted: budget cuts have followed recovery plans, companies are seeking to restore their margins by reducing wages and recruitment. Lastly, commodity prices have turned upward again. At the same time, structural contradictions are hardening: pressure is being exerted on wages once again, nothing is replacing the role of the deficit spending in the U.S. and several European countries, while the eurozone finds itself on the verge of breakdown under the blows of the 'financial markets'.

Table 1 - From mini-recovery to non-exit from crisis

	Phase 2 "Recovery"	Phase 3 "Exit" from crisis
Conjunctural factors • Stimulus packages • Social stabilizers • Raw material prices	Support for economic activity	*Exhaustion of positive effects* • Fiscal consolidation • Layoffs and wage austerity • Rising oil prices
Structural contradictions • Income redistribution • International imbalances • European fragmentation	Weak intensity	*Tightening of constraints* • Depressed demand • End of over-Indebtedness in the US • Increased intra-European competition
Growth	Small rebound	Stabilization/stagnation
Employment	Slight reduction	Abrupt adjustment

The medium-term prospects are therefore pretty bleak. In the third quarter of 2010, GDP in the EU was still 3.2% lower than its level before the crisis (Chart 6). And employment has not really got going again: it remains 3% below its pre-crisis level, corresponding to the destruction of 5.3 million jobs in the European Union (EU-15).

Chart 6: Growth, employment and unemployment, EU-15. 2001-2015

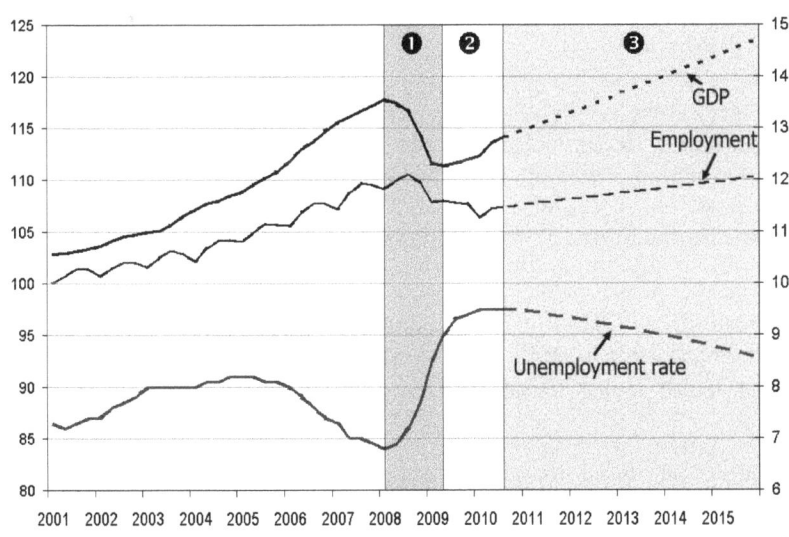

1: "trigger"; 2: "recovery"; 3: "end of crisis" Left scale: GDP and employment: 100 = 2001; Right scale: Unemployment rate in%

Source: Eurostat until 2010, then projection

Unemployment, which was already tending to decline over the two years preceding the crisis has taken a dramatic step upwards, since it has increased from 6.8% in first quarter of 2008 to 9.5% in the third quarter of 2010. The number of unemployed has grown over the same period from 13 to 18.4 million in the EU-15.

However, this rise in unemployment is underestimated if the withdrawal from the labour market of people who have given up looking for work and who have disappeared from the unemployment statistics are ignored. Without this withdrawal, we estimate that the unemployment rate would have been 1.5% higher at 11% instead of at 9.5%. If we extrapolate these trends assuming a GDP growth of 1.5% per annum, productivity growth of 0.5%, and growth of the labour force, we obtain the following main result: the unemployment rate will only fall very slowly in Europe. And it would stagnate if 'disheartened' people return to the labour market[10].

In the next few years, capitalism will be confronted with four major contradictions.

Four major contradictions

1 - Dilemma of redistribution: a return to profitability or to employment?

The crisis has abruptly halted the trend of profit to rise. This deterioration is explained largely by changes in labour productivity which have declined sharply since the number of employed has only been partially adjusted to the decline in production. But in the heat of competition, companies will seek to restore their profits, either by adjusting numbers employed, or by freezing or even lowering wages.

At the same time, devices such as short-time working and redundancy schemes gradually reach their limits,. One concern of international bodies is also to challenge the urgent measures taken in the crisis. Thus an IMF mission wrote in 2009 that: 'measures taken to support shorter working hours and raise social benefits - while important to shore up incomes and keep the labour force attached to the labour market - should have built-in reversibility'[11]. This adjustment of employment and wages will then trigger a new recessive loop, further reducing household income.

---

10 'Le poids de la crise sur l'emploi en Europe', note hussonet n°20, septembre 2010, http://hussonet.free.fr/empcrise.pdf
11 IMF, 'Concluding Statement of the IMF Mission on Euro-Area Policies', June 8, 2009, http://tinyurl.com/IMFeuro9

2 - Dilemma of Globalisation: resolving imbalances or global growth?

One of the main drivers of the global economy before the crisis was household overconsumption in the United States. It can scarcely be continued. The recent rise in the savings rate leads to a contradiction since a reduced consumption for a given income also means a less dynamic growth for the whole economy. The solution chosen by the Obama administration has been expressed by his economic adviser at the time, Lawrence Summers: 'The rebuilt American economy must be more export-oriented and less consumption-oriented, more environmentally-oriented'[12]. But this option assumes the improved competitiveness of U.S. exports, which can only be achieved through an additional devaluation of the dollar. More recently, another measure has been taken, consisting of a massive injection of money *(quantitative easing)*. This orientation can only widen imbalances in the global economy. If the dollar devaluation succeeds, it will certainly put pressure on an already faltering growth in Europe. Combined with money creation, it will then require emerging countries to revalue their currencies which will result in the further fragmentation of the global economy[13].

It comes back to the same fatal flaw: money creation is financing the budget deficit of the United States which itself funds U.S. household consumption. The greatest uncertainty now rests on the trajectory of the dollar and on the financing of the U.S. deficit by the rest of the world. Vice versa, a rebalancing of the Chinese economy would reduce its surplus but also its imports, much of which are drawn in by its exports. In summary, it is the entire configuration of the global economy that is challenged.

3 - Fiscal dilemma: reversal of deficits or social spending?

Crisis and recovery plans have led to the considerable swelling of deficits that European governments in particular have decided to get rid of, especially since they took no action to protect themselves from the onslaught of the financial markets. This was announced by the President of the ECB as early as 2009: 'the structural adjustment process should start in any case not later than the economic recovery.

---

12   Lawrence H. Summers, *Rescuing and Rebuilding the US Economy*, July 2009, http://tinyurl.com/lsexpor
13   Michael Hudson, *'US Quantitative Easing Is Fracturing the Global Economy'*, http://gesd.free.fr/hudsonqi.pdf

2011 consolidation efforts should be stepped up'[14]. This is to condemn Europe to low growth and social regression.

4 - European dilemma: everyone for themselves or coordination?

Europe is imploding as an economic entity. The fragmentation process had begun well before the crisis, but it has crossed a threshold to the extent that the EU countries have been unevenly affected by the crisis. A real economic coordination policy is therefore beyond reach, especially since the EU has voluntarily deprived itself of institutions that would enable it to conduct one: no budget, no exchange rate policy, and no tax coordination. The Europe of 'free and undistorted competition' is logically condemned to 'everyone for themselves' and we are witnessing a real debacle of the chosen construction method.

All these dilemmas draw a picture of 'regulatory chaos' which corresponds to capitalism navigating by sight between two impossibilities: the impossibility (and rejection) of a return to a relatively regulated post-war capitalism; the impossibility of restoring the operating conditions of the neoliberal model, because it was based on a now exhausted forward flight. The stalemate, once again, comes down to this: capitalism wants to return to its pre-crisis functioning, but it can't.

Elements of an alternative

We must first reject the idea that the debate on the interpretation of the crisis would have direct implications for programmatic proposals. Marx wrote that 'The ultimate reason for all real crises always remains the poverty and restricted consumption of the masses as opposed to the drive of capitalist production to develop the productive forces as though only the absolute consuming power of society constituted their outer limit'[15]. In spite of this clearly affirmed principle the dogmatic version of Marxism rests at bottom on a binary opposition between two analyses of the crisis: the first, centred on the concept of over-accumulation and a falling rate of profit is viewed as the only authentically Marxist one; the second, characterised as under-consumptionist is not viewed as Marxist but as Keynesian.

This not very dialectical interpretative framework shows a misunderstanding of an essential feature of capitalism: it is a mode of

---

14   Jean-Claude Trichet, press conference, Luxembourg, 2 July 2009, http://tinyurl.com/trichet9
15   Karl Marx, *Capital, Volume 3*, Chapter 30.

production that seeks to obtain the highest rate of profit possible but must also sell its commodities. This dual demand generates a permanent contradiction which manifests itself particularly vigorously during crises. We find here the mistake, pointed out by Mandel, which consists of 'arbitrarily splitting that which is organically linked, at the very heart of the capitalist mode of production (...). To wish to explain the phenomenon of crises exclusively by what happens in the sphere of production (the production of an insufficient quantity of surplus value to ensure to all capital an acceptable rate of profit), disregarding phenomena of realisation of surplus value, that is of circulation, thus of the market, is in reality to disregard a fundamental aspect of capitalist production, that of a generalised commodity production'[16].

Most of the time, the accusation of 'under-consumptionism' rests on other quotations from Marx, criticising theories which make insufficient consumption the mainspring of crises. But this respect for orthodoxy forgets one of the essential contributions of Marx, namely his study of the conditions of reproduction of capital. It is however a key question that can be summarised thus: who buys what is produced by the exploited employees? It is all very well (for an employer) to exploit their workers but the profit drawn from it remains virtual so long as it is not realised by the sale of commodities. This question is posed during the cycle, but it is posed in a structural manner over the long term. The upwards tendency of the rate of exploitation observed since the early 1980s poses a problem from the viewpoint of realisation. If the share of the consumption of employees falls in relation to the new wealth produced, the question is who will buy the rest?

To say that capitalism in its neoliberal phase faces a chronic realisation problem does not amount to support for the so-called under-consumptionist theses. The theorists of under-consumption, from Sismondi to Baran and Sweezy via Rosa Luxemburg, argued that capitalism was structurally incapable of realising profit and that it had need of external outlets. Nobody supports this thesis to this degree of generality, but the fall in the share of wages highlights a manifest problem of realisation that is met by actually existing capitalism and that it resolves through the consumption of the rich and through indebtedness.

To sweep aside this question by saying that only over-accumulation and overproduction are the causes of the crises, through the fall in the rate of profit, amounts to forgetting that over-accumulation and under-consumption are both aspects of the same

---

16 Ernest Mandel, *L'explication des crises capitalistes*, 1982, http://gesd.free.fr/mandel82.pdf

reality, as formulated very well by Chesnais: 'Over-accumulation has automatically an 'opposite', so to say, under-consumption'.[17] And vice versa. Marx himself repeatedly emphasized the crisis of realization, for instance in this passage which is very relevant to the present-day where he presents this crisis as the result of the power of capital: 'What then does *overproduction of capital* mean? (...) Defined more closely, this means nothing more than that too much has been produced for the purpose of *enrichment*, or that too great a part of the product is intended not for consumption as revenue, but *for making more money* (for accumulation): not to satisfy the personal needs of its owner, but to give him money, abstract social riches and capital, more power over the labour of others, i.e. to increase this power'.[18]

The viewpoint adopted as to the evolution of the rate of profit says nothing on the political implications although there is a great temptation to establish facile connections. For example, those who hold that the fall of the share of wages is a fundamental cause of the crisis, see themselves accused of Keynesianism or 'underconsumptionism'. If they say that wages are too low, they are arguing for a wage-led recovery which would save capitalism. After all, this form of rhetoric is reversible: those who think that the main cause of the crisis is the fall in the rate of profit could be accused of being in an underhand way in favour of a lowering of wages so as to re-establish profits.

Another line of demarcation separates those who analyse this crisis as a financial crisis and those who consider it as a crisis of the system itself. And that leads effectively to different orientations: regulationist-reformist in the first case, anti-capitalist in the second. Again we could discuss this opposition: after all, one could very easily hold that this crisis is financial and be at the same time anti-capitalist, even if this position does not exist in practice. More generally, anti-capitalism is not indexed on the rate of profit. The reasons that we have all criticised this system are not located in the evolution — upwards or downwards — of the rate of profit.

We should carefully distinguish theoretical debates from programmatic ones, and avoid thinking that theoretical analysis of the conjuncture supplies us mechanically with the key to the strategic issues. That capitalism as a system is the target is a point of agreement, which should not be spoiled by polemics which play on words. To take an example, the idea according to which capitalism would be increasingly less capable of satisfying social needs was

---

17 François Chesnais, 'Crise de suraccumulation mondiale ouvrant une crise de civilisation', *Inprecor* n°556/557, 2010, http://gesd.free.fr/fc101.pdf
18 Karl Marx, *Theories of Surplus Value*, Chapter XVII, http://tinyurl.com/TPVCH17

mocked by Gill[19] as an absurdity, since this is not the objective of capitalism. However the latter must sell its commodities and it could not do it if they were deprived of use value, in other words did not respond to any social need. To fulfil this necessary condition, it shapes needs and the allocation of incomes. But one of the characteristics of contemporary capitalism is that this is increasingly difficult: the gap is growing between profitable supply and social demand, and capitalism tends increasingly to reject the satisfaction of elementary needs in the name of its criterion of profitability. There is here a critical line which touches the very bases of the system — that which I call the mode of capitalist satisfaction of social needs — and goes much further than the study of the rate of profit. Capitalism has its own logic, but it is increasingly irrational from the viewpoint of humanity (and of the planet). And that allows once again criticism of the system on other bases than its chronic instability.

The debate is strategic. As always it concerns the articulation of immediate slogans and the socialist perspective. The crisis is exacerbating the tension between these two political levels. On the one hand, its immediate effects are equivalent to a growing social regression and, on the other hand, its breadth demonstrates the fragility and growing illegitimacy of the system. The construction of a transitional approach is then all the more necessary, but in a more difficult sense. It is necessary both to fight tooth and nail against the measures for 'exit from crisis' and open a radical, hence anti-capitalist alternative perspective. It seems to me that the question of the division of incomes is a good point to hang around the principle 'we won't pay for their crisis'. That has nothing to do with a 'wage led recovery' but with a defence of wages, jobs and social rights on which there should not be any dispute. Then comes the idea of control over what they do with their profits (pay dividends or create jobs) and our taxes (subsidising the banks or financing public services). The issue is to pass from defence to control and it is on the basis of this switch that the challenge to private property (the real anti-capitalism) can acquire a mass audience.

This approach can be discussed and should be worked on, but it is counterproductive to rule it out as reformist, or regulatory, opposing to it the single revolutionary posture of calling for the overthrow of the system without having a precise idea of what roads mobilisations can take and the concrete targets they should seek. On a more tactical level, the 'razor sharp' delimitations seeking to separate the good anti-capitalist wheat from the anti-neoliberal chaff represent very often a useless expenditure of energy. In the current conjuncture

---

19   Louis Gill, 'Les faux pas d'Alain Bihr, les dérives de Michel Husson', *Carré Rouge* n°43, mars 2010, http://gesd.free.fr/derives.pdf

it is enough to fight to the end for a just and clearly defined demand, to come directly up against the lines of defence of the system.

A European strategy for the left[20]

The global effects of the crisis have been made even worse by what is happening in Europe. For thirty years the contradictions of capitalism have been overcome with the help of an enormous accumulation of phantom rights to surplus value. The crisis has threatened to destroy them. The bourgeois governments have decided to preserve them claiming that we have to save the banks. They have taken on the banks' debts and asked for virtually nothing in return. Yet it would have been possible to make this rescue conditional on some assurances. They could have banned speculative financial instruments and closed the tax loopholes. They could even have insisted that they take responsibility for some of the public debt that this rescue increased so dramatically.

We are now in the second phase. Having shifted the debt from the private sector to the public the working class has to be made to pay. This shock therapy is delivered through austerity plans which are all broadly similar – a cut in socially useful spending and hiking up the most unfair taxes. There is no alternative to this form of social violence other than making the shareholders and creditors pay. That is clear and everyone understands it.

The collapse of a ruling class plan

But the European working class is also being asked to pay for the collapse of the ruling class project for Europe. The ruling class thought that it had found a good system with the single currency, the budgetary stability pact ('Stability and Growth Pact'), and the total deregulation of finance and the movement of capital. By creating a competition between social models and wage earners squeezing wages became the only means of regulating inter-capitalist competition and intensifying the inequalities that benefitted only a very narrow stratum of people in society.

However this model put the cart before the horse and wasn't viable. It presupposed that the European economies were more homogeneous than they actually are. Differences between countries increased due to their place in the global market and their sensitivity to the euro exchange rate. Inflation rates didn't converge and interest

---

20   This section is taken from *Socialist Resistance*, December 29th, 2010, http://tinyurl.com/SRMH10

rates favoured property bubbles and so on. All the contradictions of a curtailed programme of European integration which the euro liberals are discovering today existed before the crisis. But these are blowing apart under speculative attacks against the sovereign debts of the most exposed countries.

Underneath the abstract concept of 'financial markets' there are mainly European financial institutions which speculate using capital which states lend to them at very low interest rates. This speculation is only possible due to the states' policy of non-intervention and we should understand it as a pressure applied to consenting governments to stabilise budgets on the back of the people of Europe and to defend the banks' interests.

Two immediate tasks

From the point of view of the working class it's obvious what has to be done: we have to resist the austerity offensive and refuse to pay the debt which is nothing but the debt from the banking crisis. The alternative plan on which this resistance must be based demands another way of sharing society's wealth. This is a coherent demand. It is in fact against the squeezing of wages, in other words the appropriation of an increasing portion of surplus value by capital.

The alternative requires a real fiscal reform which takes back the gifts which for years have been given to businesses and the rich. It also implies the cancellation of the debt. The debt and the interests of the majority of the population are completely incompatible. There can be no progressive outcome to the crisis which does not put the debt in question, either by defaulting on it or restructuring it. In any case some countries will probably default and it's therefore important to anticipate this situation and say how it should be managed.

Leaving the euro?

The offensive the peoples of Europe are facing is undeniably made worse by the European straightjacket. For example the European Central Bank, unlike the Federal Reserve in the United States, cannot monetise public debt by buying treasury bonds. Would leaving the euro allow the straightjacket to be loosened? That is what some on the left like Costas Lapavitsas and his colleagues are suggesting for Greece as an immediate step. He proposes that it is done immediately without waiting for the left to unite to change the eurozone, something he thinks is impossible.

This idea is put forward elsewhere in Europe and is met with an immediate objection that even though Britain is not part of the eurozone it has not been protected from the climate of austerity. It is also easy to understand why the far right, such as the Front National in France, want to leave the euro. By contrast it is hard to see what could be the merits of such a slogan for the radical left. If a liberal government were forced to take such a measure by the pressure of events it is clear that it would be the pretext for an even more severe austerity than the one we have experienced up to now. Moreover it would not allow us to establish a new balance of forces more favourable to the working class. That is the lesson that one can draw for all the past experiences.

For a left government leaving the euro would be a major strategic error. The new currency would be devalued as that is, after all, the desired objective. But that would immediately open up a space, which the financial markets would immediately use to begin a speculative offensive. It would trigger a cycle of devaluation, inflation and austerity. On top of that, the debt, which until that point had been denominated in euros or in dollars, would suddenly increase as a result of this devaluation. Every left government which decided to take measures in favour of the working class would certainly be put under enormous pressure by international capitalism. But from a tactical point of view it would be better in this test of strength to use membership in the euro zone as a source of conflict.

It is basically true that the European project based on the single currency is not coherent and is incomplete. It removes a variable of adjustment, the exchange rate, from the set of different prices and salaries inside the euro zone. The countries in the periphery thus have the choice between the German path of freezing wages or suffering a reduction in competitiveness and loss of markets. This situation leads to a sort of impasse and there are no solutions that can be applied straight away: going backwards would throw Europe in a crisis which would hit the most fragile countries hardest, and beginning a new European project seems out of reach at the moment.

If the euro zone explodes the most fragile economies would be destabilised by speculative attacks. Not even Germany would have anything to gain because its currency would appreciate in value uncontrollably and the country would undergo what the Unites States is today trying to impose on several countries with its monetary policy.

Other solutions exist which need a complete recasting of the European Union: a budget which is financed by a common tax on capital and which finances harmonisation funds and investments which are both socially and ecologically useful and richer countries help poorer ones with their public debt. But again this outcome is not possible in the short term, not through lack of alternative plans but because implementing them requires a radical change in the balance of forces at the European level.

What should we do at a very difficult moment like this? The struggle against the austerity plans and refusing to pay the debt are the launch pad for a counter offensive. We then have to make sure that the resistance is strengthened by arguing for an alternative project and work out a programme which offers both 'practical' answers as well as a general explanation of the class content of the crisis.[21]

The specific task of the radical, internationalist left is to link the social struggles happening in each country with arguing for a different kind of Europe. What are the ruling classes doing? They are facing up to the policies they have to follow because they are defending interests which are still largely nationally based and contradictory. Yet as soon as they have to impose austerity measures on their own working class they present a solid united front. There are better things to do than emphasise the very real differences that exist between the countries. What's at stake is having an internationalist point of view on the crisis in Europe. The only way of really opposing the rise of the far right is by suggesting other targets than the usual scapegoats. We can affirm a real international solidarity with the people who are suffering most due to the crisis by demanding that the debts are shared equally across Europe. Thus we have to oppose an alternative project for Europe to that of the European bourgeoisie which is dragging every country backwards socially. How is it possible not to understand that our mobilisations, which are faced with coordination of the ruling class at a European level, need to be based on a coordinated project of our own? While it is true that struggles happen in a national framework they would be strengthened by a perspective like this instead of being weakened or led down nationalist dead ends.

For a European Strategy

The task is as difficult as the period which the crisis has opened. However the radical left must not get locked into the impossible choice between the risky adventure of leaving the euro and a utopian idea of currency harmonisation. We could easily work on some intermediate targets which challenge the European institutions. For example:

---

21   See Özlem Onaran, 'Fiscal crisis or a crisis of distribution?', *International Viewpoint* n°424, May 2010, http://tinyurl.com/IVP1856; Bloco de Esquerda (Left Bloc) Portugal: 'On the crisis and how to overcome it', May 23rd 2010.

- The states of the European Union should borrow directly from the ECB at very low rates of interest and private sector banks should be obliged to take over a certain proportion of the public debt.

- A default mechanism should be put in place, which allows public sector debt to be written off in proportion to tax breaks for the rich and money spent on bank bailouts.

- Budgetary stabilisation has to be reformed by a fiscal reform which taxes movements of capital, financial transactions, dividends, large fortunes, high salaries and incomes from capital at a standard rate across Europe.

We have to understand that these objectives are neither further, nor closer away than an 'exit from the euro' which would be beneficial to working people. It would definitely be absurd to wait for a simultaneous and co-ordinated exit by every European country. The only strategic hypothesis that one can then conceive of must take as its starting point the experience of a social transformation which starts in one country. The government of the country in question takes measures, for example imposing a tax on capital. If it is thinking clearly it will anticipate the retaliation for which it will be the target and will impose controls on capital. By taking this fiscal reform measure it is openly in conflict with the rules of the European game. It has no interest in unilaterally leaving the euro. This would be an enormous strategic mistake since the new currency would immediately come under attack with the aim of pulling down the economy of the 'rebel' country.

We have to give up on the idea that there are 'technical' shortcuts, assume that conflict is inevitable and build a favourable balance of forces of which the European dimension is a part. One point of support for that is the ability to damage capitalist interests. The country, which starts, could restructure the debt, nationalise foreign capital etc, or threaten to do it. The 'left' governments of Papandreou in Greece or Zapatero in Spain have not even dreamed of doing this.

The main point of support comes from taking the measures cooperatively. This is completely different from classic protectionism, which basically always tries to gain ground by nibbling at parts of the global market. Every progressive measure on the other hand is effective to the extent that it is shared across a number of countries. We should therefore be talking about a strategy, which is based on the following idea: we are willing to tax capital and we will take the necessary steps to protect ourselves. But we are also hoping for these measures, which we propose, to be implemented across Europe. We can sum up by saying that rather than seeing them in opposition to each other we have to think hard about the link between breaking the neo-liberal European project and our project of creating a new Europe.

Translated by Peter Cooper

THE CRISIS IN BRITAIN

Andy Kilmister

Introduction

The impact of the global economic crisis on Britain results from the interaction between the general nature of that crisis and the specific characteristics of British capitalism. While many aspects of the crisis in the UK are replicated elsewhere it has a particular intensity in the British case and poses especially acute problems for capital. These problems arise from deep rooted contradictions in the British economy and from the attempts made by various governments and their allies to solve these in the past; attempts which in many ways have laid the foundation for the difficulties they now face in resolving the crisis.

The crisis arises out of a fundamental problem for capitalism; the conflict between generating profits in the process of production and realising those profits through the exchange of goods and services. The first objective requires continual attempts to limit the purchasing power of workers and this in turn subverts the second objective, restricting the growth of the market and threatening the stability of capitalist growth. There are a number of ways in which this contradiction can temporarily be resolved but all of them lead to renewed difficulties.

There are four main ways in which demand for goods can be maintained in the face of cutbacks in wages. Spending can come from investment but by building up capital at the expense of living labour, which alone can generate profits, this tends to lower the profit rate over time. Export demand provides a possible outlet for particular national capitals but only displaces the problem onto an international level since not all countries can run trade surpluses. Government spending can provide a source of demand but in order for profitability to be maintained such spending must be financed by taxes on workers and this in turn lowers their spending even more. Finally, luxury consumption by capitalists can allow profits to be realised but in turn raises a number of further problems. Such consumption is unlikely to provide a broad and stable enough base to ensure continued profitability, especially as it has become more global over time. When carried out in a context of international competition it diverts production into areas which lower national competitiveness. There are also serious political consequences arising from obvious reliance on consumption by the wealthy as a key economic strategy.[1]

The contours of British capitalism

The general difficulty of reconciling the generation and realisation of profits has assumed a particularly sharp form in Britain owing to the nature of capital in this country. A central characteristic of British capitalism is its extremely international character. The fact that Britain was the first country to industrialise with the resulting commitment to free trade and open markets coupled with the legacy of imperialism and the role of the City of London in both the import and export of capital and commercial and trading activities has meant that there is a greater disjunction between British capital and capital located in the geographical territory of Britain than for any other major industrialised country. This in turn has meant that domestic investment and exports have been historically weak and capitalist strategies have to a considerable extent focused on production abroad and the recirculation of profits through the financial sector at home rather than on building up a domestic base.

The problems caused by this were masked to some degree in the 1950s and early 1960s by post-war Keynesian expansion but became increasingly apparent as the 'long boom' began to break up in the late 1960s and led to a serious challenge to aspects of capitalist rule in the early 1970s. The initial contradictions arose as the relative strength of British trade unions at the point of production prevented employers from pushing wages down in order to generate more profits. Consequently those employers tried to recoup their funds by raising prices and this led to growing inflationary pressures. The

---

[1] A particular aspect of this kind of approach which has been much debated is the role of military production as a possible source of demand combining the third and fourth elements discussed above. This raises a number of complex issues; see for example M Kidron (1970) *Western Capitalism since the War*, Penguin, chapter 3 and E Mandel (1975) *Late Capitalism*, Verso, chapter 9

result of this was an inability to compete internationally (made worse by the need to keep the value of the pound fixed in order to satisfy the City) and worsening trade deficits. The result was continued instability. The attempt to provide a basis for the realisation of profits constantly ran up against the barrier presented by foreign trade as the Bank of England was forced to slow the economy down (normally by raising interest rates) in order to improve the balance of payments. The problem was that as soon as soon as the Bank lowered interest rates in order to expand the economy imports rose in line with increased incomes pushing the trade balance into deficit. The only way in which demand for imports could be kept low enough to stop such a deficit was to slow the economy down to such a degree that profits could not be realised because of the lack of growth. The attempts to generate profits in production led to rising prices and the threat of trade deficits which in turn led to central bank policies which undercut the possibility of realising those profits in the international arena. An important underlying cause of this situation was the inability of capital located in Britain to export successfully, largely as a result of the international orientation of British capitalism outlined above.

The response to this situation by the Labour government under Harold Wilson in the 1960s was twofold. Firstly, the pound was devalued providing the basis for a generalised cut in real wages and restoration of international competitiveness. Devaluation of the currency lowers export prices in the world market and in this way can lay the basis for realising profits. But at the same time devaluation raises import prices and so cuts the living standards of workers. The generation of profits is dependent on workers not responding to this cut by demanding higher wages which would erode the new found competitiveness. As a result the restoration of profits was dependent on workers failing to restore their incomes through successful wage bargaining or industrial action. Wilson thus tried to combine the devaluation with legislation limiting trade union rights. However, he was unable to get the Labour Party to agree to this and was forced to abandon the strategy.

The Conservative government under Heath in many ways adopted a similar approach to that of Wilson but were initially somewhat more determined. The pound was not simply devalued but was allowed to float freely downwards and anti-trade union legislation was passed. But the attempt to raise profits in this way quickly led to severe problems in realising those profits and the economy slowed sharply with unemployment rising to more than 1 million. Heath and his chancellor, Anthony Barber, reversed track and expanded credit, fuelling an inflationary boom. This boom was halted by the international crisis of 1974-75 and the government fell in the wake of the failure of its attempt to attack working class resistance to cuts in living standards.

The following Labour government tried a different means of reconciling the generation and realisation of profits. The trade union leadership were to be bought off allowing for cuts in real wages and this was to be justified by a commitment to maintaining Keynesian expansion of the economy, coupled with some tax-based redistributive measures and limitation of the prerogatives of capital, for example equal pay legislation. The combined arrangement was known as the 'social contract'. The left of the party, led by Tony Benn argued for more far-reaching measures to ensure growth; such as import controls, nationalisation and planning agreements. This agenda was not adopted but even the modest taxes on capital and monetary stimulus between 1974 and 1976 proved too much for international capital and the City and the sterling crisis of the autumn of 1976 led to an IMF inspired package of public spending cuts and the abandonment of Keynesianism by the Callaghan-Healey team. This in turn coupled with the continual cuts in real wages resulting from the social contract led to a partial breakdown in the relationship between the government and the union leaders and the loss of the following election in May 1979.[2]

The Thatcher government which followed initially based its economic policy on a combination of monetary targets and cuts in public spending. Strict control of the money supply was to force workers into accepting lower wages with unemployment as the only alternative since wage rises would not be financed by credit expansion. At the same time an environment of low taxes and free markets would ensure that profits could be realised in an expanding economy. Predictably while this strategy had some success in allowing profits to be generated in production (though ironically it was less effective than the social contract in restraining wages and no more so in increasing productivity) it was disastrous even for capital in providing an environment where those profits could be realised in exchange. This was partly because of the neglect by the Tories of the historic weaknesses of British capitalism detailed above and their naive belief that free markets and low taxes would be sufficient to boost domestic investment and exports. In addition though the monetarists paradoxically failed to analyse the characteristics of modern financial capital and the role of the City, in particular the internationalisation of this role since the sterling devaluation of 1967 – an internationalisation which they themselves did much to promote

---

2   A good account of this period is provided in D Coates (1980) *Labour in Power? A Study of the 1974-79 Labour Government*, Longman.

with what was probably their most far-reaching initial act, the suspension (and effective abolition) of exchange controls in 1979.[3]

The result was that the monetary targets adopted by the Bank of England were continually overshot and that every attempt to control a particular measure of the money supply led to a change in the form of money and the growth of some other variety of credit. At the same time the high interest rates which formed part of this strategy led to a dramatic inflow of funds from abroad which both contributed to the failure to restrain monetary growth and also pushed up the value of sterling. The uncompetitive currency and the abandonment of any government attempts to expand the economy to allow profits to be realised resulted in a serious recession with unemployment rising to over 3 million. While Thatcher remained in power as a result of various political factors, notably the failure of the Labour Party and trade union leadership to mount an effective challenge to Tory rule or to support those who were challenging it, especially the miners, from the mid-1980s onwards the economic strategy adopted by the government changed decisively.

Neo-liberalism and British capital

In the wake of the failure of the original monetarist approach to solve the problems of British capitalism a set of arrangements arose which can usefully be described as 'neo-liberalism'. It can be seen that these arrangements followed two decades of unsuccessful attempts by various governments and their allies to create a framework which could combine the generation and realisation of profits given the specific weaknesses of capital in the UK. What emerged in the 1980s was largely not consciously created through planned strategic initiatives. It can better be seen as a mutually reinforcing set of arrangements which allowed for the temporary resolution of the contradictions between production and exchange in the specifically British context. In that sense it has affinities with the idea of a 'mode of regulation' coupled with a 'regime of accumulation' developed by regulation theorists in their analyses of the long boom of the 1950s and 1960s[4]. However, as has been extensively discussed there is a danger within regulation theory of neglecting the instability of capitalist accumulation resulting from the pressure of class struggle and collapsing into a functionalist viewpoint in which change

---

3   The transformation of the role of the City in this period is well described in J Coakley and L Harris (1983) *The City of Capital*, Blackwell
4   These ideas were first developed in M Aglietta (1979) *A Theory of Capitalist Regulation: The US Experience*, NLB

becomes inconceivable[5]. In the British case neo-liberalism should rather be seen as a tentative and contradictory framework which, while it had sufficient durability to last for two decades, was always under threat and eventually provided the basis for the crisis which erupted in 2007.[6]

Neo-liberalism in Britain had three main elements, which reoccur in other contexts but assumed a particularly significant form in the British context. The first of these was a reliance on debt as the basis for continued growth. Borrowing came to represent the way in which the contradiction between generating and realising profits could temporarily be resolved. Neo-liberalism involved an employer's offensive which not only limited wage rises but also intensified work pressures through a variety of measures designed to increase productivity.[7] At the same time the assault on trade unions and the changes in industrial structure, notably the rise of financial and commercial services, the decline in manufacturing and the growth in low-wage employment in areas such as retailing, tourism and sweatshop manufacturing led to soaring income inequality.

The combination of restricted wages, increased output through higher productivity and inequality could be expected to lead to problems in providing a stable consumption base to allow the sale of output and the realisation of profits. Such problems were mitigated by the growth of debt which allowed consumption to continue to grow[8]. Supporters of neo-liberalism argued that this was not a problem because consumption was growing roughly in step with output and because the acquisition of household assets also paralleled the growth of debt. Both these arguments miss the point. The rise of borrowing did not allow consumption to outstrip output so much as to allow consumption to rise at a time when downward pressure on wages would otherwise have limited spending growth. It was the combination of relatively stable consumption and the resurgence of

---

5   See for example S Clarke 'Overaccumulation, Class Struggle and the Regulation Approach' (*Capital and Class* no.36 Winter 1988)
6   It should also be emphasised that to define the period since the mid-1980s in this way is not to endorse any view that the critique of capitalism can be in some way supplanted by the struggle against neo-liberalism. Neo-liberalism here is simply the particular form which capitalism took in Britain during this time period. For further discussion of the use of the concept of neo-liberalism see A Kilmister `Understanding Neo-Liberalism' (*Socialist Outlook* no.3 Spring 2004)
7   For an overview see T Richardson and A Kilmister 'New Management Techniques: The British Experience' (*International Marxist Review* no.15 Spring 1994)
8   The link between increased inequality and the growth of borrowing in the US context is highlighted by R Rajan (2010) *Fault Lines: How Hidden Fractures still Threaten the World Economy*, Princeton University Press. Rajan is a former chief economist at the IMF. For an account of the British context see G Turner (2008) *The Credit Crunch: Housing Bubbles, Globalisation and the World Economic Crisis*, Pluto.

profits generated in production that was crucial here. While household assets and liabilities rose simultaneously they were not held by the same people. Increased inequality drove a wedge between those households able to accumulate growing wealth, at least on paper, through rising stock and housing markets and those taking on ever more debt.

The second pillar of neo-liberalism in Britain was two decades of low commodity, raw material and energy prices. The significance of this was two-fold. Firstly, it provided the basis for the relatively low interest rates which in turn allowed for the upturn in credit. From the early 1990s, when the UK left the European Exchange Rate Mechanism (ERM), the Bank of England was given first informal and then formal independence in setting short-term rates to control inflation. It was able to keep rates low primarily because of the lack of inflationary pressure from abroad[9]. This was reinforced from the mid-1990s onwards by the growth of low-cost manufacturing imports from a range of sources, especially China. Secondly, cheap imports helped to moderate wage claims and allow both for increased profitability in production and for extra demand for British produced goods as households were able to switch some spending owing to lower prices for necessities.

The third central requirement for this neo-liberal framework was a continued inflow of foreign capital. This was necessary for a number of reasons. Firstly, with domestic investment remaining weak British exports continued to find it hard to compete internationally and there was an ongoing trade deficit. In order to avoid further declines in the value of sterling this had to be covered by international borrowing. Secondly, it was global capital that provided much of the basis for the explosive growth in the financial sector during this period. Thirdly, inflows of productive investment from abroad became significant both in providing jobs in what remained of British manufacturing industry and in testing out many of the 'new management techniques' underlying the employer's offensive described above[10]. Fourthly, it was foreign capital that provided a large component of the increase in credit during this period. At the same time a considerable amount of the trade deficit was also covered by the difference between the earnings on UK investment abroad and

---

9   For an analysis which discusses this and assesses the extent to which government and central bank claims to have tamed inflation through superior economic policies actually rested on international factors of this kind see S G B Henry 'Monetary Policy, Beliefs, Unemployment and Inflation: Evidence from the UK' (National Institute of Economic and Social Research Discussion Paper 305, 2008, available at http://www.niesr.ac.uk/pdf/250208_131233.pdf)

10   For an early account of this in the motor industry see P Garrahan and P Stewart (1992) *The Nissan Enigma: Flexibility at work in a Local Economy*, Mansell.

that paid out to foreign investors within Britain with the former being consistently higher than the latter. This in turn emphasises the continuing divergence between the interests of British capital in general and that portion of British capital located in the territory of the UK outlined above. Consequently, neo-liberalism depended on open capital flows and relatively stable exchange rates and these were provided by the international monetary arrangements that began to take shape in the 1980s and increasingly prevailed after the late 1990s partly in response to the Asian crisis of 1997-98.[11]

The three elements of neo-liberalism set out here supported one another to provide a framework which allowed for relatively sustained growth from the mid-1980s to 2007. This did not happen immediately; the abandonment of monetary targets by the Thatcher government was initially followed by a credit-based boom coupled with a housing market bubble under Chancellor Nigel Lawson which the government then tried to rein in through joining the ERM with the Bank of England supporting this through higher interest rates. However, following the exit from the ERM in 1992 macroeconomic performance was steady enough compared to previous experience to be described by observers as the 'great moderation'. This was undermined, however, both by problems within the neo-liberal framework itself and by the impact of this framework on the British economy.

The contradictions of neo-liberalism

The three pillars of neo-liberalism appeared at first sight mutually to reinforce each other in order to provide a solution to the endemic problems of capitalist instability. In this way they underlay Gordon Brown's infamous pledge that there would be 'no return to boom and bust'. High levels of debt allowed profits both to be generated and realised while inflows of capital provided the funds to support lending and low inflation arising from cheap imports allowed for low interest

---

[11] These arrangements have occasioned a great deal of discussion, which focuses in particular on the idea that they constituted a stable system analogous to the Bretton Woods system of fixed exchange rates in the 1950s and 1960s which could as a result be designated as 'Bretton Woods 2'. The difference between the two systems was seen as lying in the location of those countries providing capital and running trade surpluses with China and other East Asian countries taking the place of Japan and (West) Germany. While suggestive in many respects the Bretton Woods 2 hypothesis encounters many of the same problems with regard to assuming excessive stability given the crisis-ridden nature of capitalism as do the regulation school analyses discussed earlier. For further detail see M Dooley, D Folkerts-Landau and P Garber 'The Revived Bretton Woods System' (*International Journal of Finance and Economics* 9, 2004 available at http://web.ku.edu/~intecon/Read/Dooley04.pdf).

rates which could encourage borrowing. In turn the growth provided by the framework attracted further capital from abroad. Yet each of the pillars itself rested on contradictory and unstable foundations.

Clearly any attempt to base growth on continually increasing borrowing will eventually run up against the inability of debtors to meet their obligations. While this was pointed out on numerous occasions during the 1990s and 2000s[12] apologists for neo-liberalism pointed to the corresponding growth in asset values during this period. Yet, as discussed above, in the first place these assets were often not held by those accumulating growing debts and in the second place this meant that the sustainability of borrowing required continual increases in asset prices, often supported by spending generated by the borrowing itself. This 'Ponzi scheme' was inherently unstable and broke down in 2007 as the housing market slumped and as households recoiled from taking on increasing levels of debt.

The limits to low import prices are largely ecological in nature. Since around the year 2000, prices of food, energy and a number of key minerals have begun to rise as a result both of ecological constraints and precisely that growth in new centres of manufacturing production such as China which is necessary for the neo-liberal framework. In 2008 these price rises became acute, especially in the case of food and fuel, sparking off food price riots in a number of countries and the relative recovery of sections of the global economy in 2011 has had the same effect. Attempts to reverse this trend through new technologies such as shale gas production threaten horrendous ecological consequences[13]. For Britain which has shifted in recent years to a reliance on imported energy and which has a longstanding reliance on cheap food imports allowing for low wages (dating back in various forms to the Corn Laws controversy of the 1840s) the consequences of such developments are very serious. It is also unclear, given recent industrial unrest and growing reports of labour shortages (partly resulting from demographic changes) in China, to what extent the low prices of manufactured imports that have typified the last two decades will be maintained.

It is also increasingly unclear that the exchange rate stability of the last two decades will persist indefinitely. Internationally, surplus countries have continued to declare a commitment to export production as a central element in their growth strategies. However, the danger of continued global imbalances is becoming more

---

12   One of the most consistent critics was the economist Wynne Godley in numerous articles published by the Levy Institute in the US: see for example W Godley, A Izurieta and G Zezza 'Prospects and Policies for the US Economy: Why Net Exports must now be the Motor for US Growth' (Levy Institute Strategic Analysis, August 2004, available at http://www.levyinstitute.org/pubs/stratan-jul-04.pdf).
13   See the recent controversy over the documentary film Gasland.

apparent both for surplus and deficit economies. For the deficit countries the inflows of funds are now seen as potential sources of speculative finance which can have a destabilising effect. In the surplus countries there is both dissatisfaction over the low returns being earned from foreign investment and, more importantly, worry over the security of returns from such investment given the instability within the receivers of funds. So far these contradictions have expressed themselves primarily not in relations between the major global currencies but in developments within the euro-zone, in particular through the crises faced by debtor nations such as Greece, Ireland and Portugal and the response of the central creditor within the zone, Germany. However, the historical weakness of Britain's trade position referred to above has contributed to similar problems in the wake of the current crisis with a resulting sharp decline in the value of sterling. The likelihood is that exchange rate instability will increase internationally in the future and that the UK will not be immune from this.

In addition to these general limits to the neo-liberal strategy the illusion of stability provided by the great moderation in Britain covered a number of significant tensions and imbalances which emerged into the open after 2007 as a result of the crisis. Three of these have been particularly significant.

Firstly, growing regional inequalities in the UK coupled with the deregulation of housing markets and deep declines in social housing have led to a massive growth of speculation and instability in the property market. This has expressed itself in periodic booms coupled with shorter but significant slumps. In turn speculation of this kind encouraged the growth of borrowing both in order to buy property and through the use of housing wealth as collateral to support borrowing for other purposes. The rise in house prices has been a central element in growing inequalities in wealth both within and to some extent between generations.

Secondly, British capitalism has based pension provision to a very high degree on the performance of financial assets as shown in the returns of pension funds, with only a residual state pension funded through taxation. This has both supported the growth of the City and the financial sector and has meant that pensions in turn have become dependent on the performance of that sector. During the heyday of neo-liberalism when pension funds were running surpluses many of them took 'holidays' from making provisions for future payments which further increased their vulnerability to any changes in underlying financial conditions.[14]

---

14   There has been much discussion about the alleged cost of public sector pensions in the UK. However, the really significant future pension liability in Britain

Thirdly, the long-term weakness of British capital coupled with its international orientation and the consequent low-tax strategy pursued by governments over a lengthy time period has led to a weakness in infrastructure which in turn potentially threatens the future profitability of domestic industry. This applies both to physical infrastructure such as the transport system and to spending in areas such as education, health and social services. This situation was made worse by the reliance of the Thatcher and Major governments on cutbacks in public spending. After initially following the same approach as Major with regard to government expenditure the New Labour governments after 2002 shifted towards raising spending, both as an attempt to rectify the weaknesses in infrastructure and also in order to support demand for goods in the wake of the slowdown of the early 2000s following the 'dot-com' crash. This however meant that in 2007 the government entered the crisis running a deficit, although with a relatively low level of outstanding debt as a result of the previous expenditure constraints.

These tensions and imbalances accentuated one another. Regional inequality both fed into and was worsened by both speculation in property and weaknesses in infrastructure while in turn weaknesses in pension provision led to further housing investment as higher income workers with inadequate retirement support tried to recoup the situation by buying rental property. This combination of factors created a number of underlying vulnerabilities in the British economy which magnified the deeper effects of the fracturing of the neo-liberal framework after 2007.

The impact of the crisis

The immediate impact of the crisis in Britain was a dramatic weakening of the first of the three pillars of the neo-liberal framework outlined above, the reliance on debt. Bank lending seized up as a result of the bad loans in the system and this in turn led to a loss of confidence in particular institutions either by depositors or by shareholders or both. A number of banks had to be either partially or completely nationalised to avert either bankruptcy or a collapse in their capital as share prices plummeted. This 'credit crunch'

---

arises from the large number of private sector workers with little or no future provision who will eventually have either to be supported by the state or live in poverty. This was acknowledged in a partial way even by the Hutton report on public sector pensions which drew back from recommending reduction of such pensions to the level prevailing in the private sector – much to the disgust of employers' organisations such as the CBI who see this as hindering private bids for public sector contracts.

developed during late 2008 and early 2009 into the most serious recession in the UK since the 1930s.

It is important to recognise that this did not primarily arise from the direct support given to banks. This support took three forms; bail-outs to cover the loss of value involved in failed loans, loans to replace the credit which had become unavailable owing to lack of confidence and guarantees attached by lending undertaken by private banks. Of these only the first involves a direct cost to capital while the second and third will only result in losses to the central bank if the banks default on their loans (something which has not happened so far and is unlikely to in the future). It is the first form of support which represents the devalorisation of existing capital.

It is hard to estimate the precise amount lost by the banks and other investors during the crisis through the build-up of bad debt since the proportion of payments which will eventually be recoverable is still unknown. But while the losses are significant they are not enough on their own to have caused a crisis of the depth seen in Britain since 2007. Rather, the crisis has arisen because of the removal, at least temporarily, of high levels of private borrowing as a key engine of growth.

This has happened for reasons connected with both the supply and demand for debt. On the one hand both households and companies have increasingly become unwilling to borrow while on the other hand banks and other lenders are more cautious in extending credit. In addition, regulatory initiatives such as larger capital requirements for banks have cut back the supply of loans. The result has been that the ability of the financial system to resolve the contradiction between generation and realisation of profits has been severely curtailed. The level and rate of profits generated in production remains high and this differentiates this crisis from previous crises such as that of the 1970s. But firms are increasingly unable to realise these profits in exchange owing to the collapse of that portion of demand based on debt – both debt-fuelled consumption and the investment that previously took place in areas like retailing which depended on such consumption.

The gap between the generation and realisation of profits has been worsened by developments with regard to the other two key elements of the neo-liberal framework. A slowdown in capital flows into the UK combined with a decline in profits generated abroad has led to a fall in the value of the pound. At the same time, as noted above, food and fuel prices are also rising steeply once again after a brief hiatus during the worst of the slump. The effect of both of these developments has been the biggest decline in real wages since the 1970s which has further depressed both consumption demand and investment in consumer goods and services. These developments have been strengthened considerably by the crises in both the housing market and in pensions outlined above. Household spending has fallen as house prices have slumped while uncertainty over future pensions has also encouraged savings. In addition many current pensioners have seen their income from past savings fall as interest rates have been cut in the wake of the crisis. These interlocking factors have combined to lower the rate of growth significantly.

The most obvious consequence of this slowdown in growth has been a large rise in government borrowing with the resulting budget deficit becoming the central issue in British politics. The previous analysis shows not just that this deficit is an effect rather than a cause of the crisis but also that it has arisen as a result of the structural weakness of British capitalism; something that was temporarily obscured by the neo-liberal framework of the previous two decades but which has now once more become apparent. The deficit has grown for two reasons. Firstly, the Brown government took various measures to substitute public demand for collapsing private spending in order to mitigate the worst effects of the recession. This was the so-called 'fiscal stimulus'. However, the impact of this was relatively modest compared to the growth in the overall deficit[15]. The main reason for the rise in government debt was the collapse in tax revenues and growth in benefits spending caused by the economic slowdown.

The response of all three political parties and the Bank of England to the crisis has been remarkably similar and despite protestations remains within the neo-liberal consensus which prevailed before the crisis. The central policy adopted has been the reduction of interest rates to try and stimulate demand, including precisely that consumer and corporate borrowing which underlay the crisis in the first place. However, this has proved difficult given the factors outlined above and so has necessitated extraordinary measures, in particular the injection of £200 billion into the banking system by the central bank through its programme of 'quantitative easing', namely the purchase of long-term government bonds from the financial sector. Even this has largely failed in its objective as most of the extra funds have been used by the banks to build up their reserves in the face of financial weakness and new regulatory initiatives. Much of the rest has either been used to purchase financial

---

15   Researchers from the National Institute for Economic and Social Research estimate the cumulative impact of the fiscal stimulus as being of the order of 0.62 percent of GDP across 2008, 2009 and 2010. See Table 2 in R Barrell, T Fic and D Holland 'Evaluating Policy Reactions to the Financial Crisis' (*National Institute Economic Review* no.207 January 2009)

assets rather than providing money for productive investment or has flowed overseas. The money supply and bank lending to industry have only grown sluggishly.

A further dose of quantitative easing was being actively planned in the wake of the 2010 election to cushion the impact of the expenditure cuts imposed by the new coalition government. But this has had to be put on hold as a result of increased inflation caused by global price rises. Despite the close collaboration between the government and the Bank of England during the crisis the neo-liberal emphasis on central bank independence was quickly reasserted thereafter. This emphasis and the associated requirement for the Bank of England to focus purely on anti-inflationary goals acts as a significant constraint both on attempts to stimulate demand through monetary growth as well as on any possibility of using the erosion of the debt burden through inflation as a way of partially resolving the crisis[16].

Both Labour and the Tories acknowledge that monetary growth cannot entirely resolve the problems highlighted by the crisis for the reasons given above. As a result they concur in supporting a 'rebalancing' of the economy away from consumption towards investment and exports. This would be combined with some regulation of the financial sector to ensure that increases in credit are directed to productive activity rather than creating booms in asset prices. The aim is to overcome the contradictions of British capitalism by providing a stable environment for the realisation of profits based on production for the global market and investment to support such production.

The problem here is that such strategies depend on a leap of faith in order to believe that such rebalancing can overcome the historic weaknesses of UK capital with regard to both investment and exports. In part such a belief is based on the fall in the value of sterling that has occurred since the onset of the crisis. But such falls have happened before. The belief in the possibility of rebalancing is also founded on two further developments. Firstly, it is thought that after two decades of neo-liberalism the potential for workers to resist the cut in real wages associated with devaluation has been decisively weakened. Secondly, the rise of economies such as the 'BRIC' countries is believed to provide a potential source of demand for British exports which can lay the basis for economic recovery. The

---

16   Ironically, the IMF chief economist Olivier Blanchard has suggested raising inflation targets from 2% to 4% as a way of reducing the real impact of debt repayments but this has not met with any approval by OECD central banks or governments. See O Blanchard, G Dell'Ariccia and P Mauro 'Rethinking Macroeconomic Policy' (IMF Staff Position Note SPN/10/03 February 2010 available at http://www.imf.org/external/pubs/ft/spn/2010/spn1003.pdf)

approach which has emerged as a consensus then is based on a sharp attack on working-class living standards coupled with cheap money flowing to export and investment sectors while domestic consumption remains restrained.

The main difference between Labour and Conservatives within the boundaries of this general framework is over the speed with which export and investment demand can grow sufficiently to replace government spending in maintaining growth. The Brown government placed a greater emphasis on the need to maintain spending in order to stop a further slowdown while the coalition has embarked on a more rapid programme of deficit reduction. This has been justified partly in terms of the danger of a loss of confidence in the UK by the international bond markets which would raise interest rates and partly in terms of the burden placed on future generations by rising government debt levels.

Neither of these arguments are convincing at least in the short-term. At a time of surplus global savings and a dearth of profitable investment opportunities there is little likelihood of the British government being unable to fund the deficit in the immediate future[17]. Any future interest payments on government debt would represent a transfer within future generations not an inter-generational transfer and the impact of government borrowing on future generations will depend upon what that borrowing is spent on and the consequent benefits that it might bring in later years. The speed with which deficit reduction policies are being adopted relies not so much on economic arguments even within the bounds of capitalist rationality as on a political desire to use the crisis to push through far reaching social changes according to the model of the 'shock doctrine' analysed by Naomi Klein[18] Longer-term questions of the sustainability of the government's financial position depend on a range of assumptions about demographic changes, growth rates, interest rates, inflation and the like. However, what is significant in this context is not so much the disagreement over the deficit in the short-term but the remarkable degree of political consensus both about the need to reduce spending in the long-term and about the kind of economic strategy which might resolve the crisis faced by the British economy. Rebalancing towards exports and investment

---

17   See for example R Barrell and S Kirby 'Fiscal Policy and Government Spending' (*National Institute Economic Review* no.214 October 2010). Barrell and Kirby conclude that 'there appears to be no reason to think that the burden of interest payments is currently expected to be excessive, and real borrowing costs facing the government are very low. In addition, there is little evidence to suggest that market perceptions of the risk of a government default have been worryingly high' (p.F63)

18   N Klein (2007) The Shock Doctrine: The Rise of Disaster Capitalism, Allen Lane

combined with low interest rates has become the 'common sense' of UK capitalism.

Strategies for the future

While this strategy is extremely seductive for British capital it will have to overcome huge problems if it is to succeed in resolving the contradictions outlined above. Firstly, the regulation proposed for the financial sector is currently far too weak to ensure the kind of rebalancing proposed. If credit is kept cheap then there is a strong likelihood that it will continue to flow into consumption spending or asset price booms as has happened over the last two decades rather than into the export sector. Secondly, the strategy is premised both on a willingness to take in greatly increased exports by countries such as China (which in turn would require currency revaluations) and on success for Britain in obtaining large shares of those new export markets. Both of these are improbable. Consumption demand in such economies is likely to increase in the future and this is also likely to be combined with a rise in the value of their currencies. But the most probable outcome of these developments will be an increasing turn towards the home market by domestic companies, perhaps in combination with foreign investors, rather than a rapid rise in imports. If such a rise does occur then there is no clear reason to suppose that British capital is in an especially advantageous position to take advantage of it despite the temporary boost given by a sterling devaluation. Thirdly, the strategy is premised on low interest rates and the easy availability of funds for the investment required in building up export production. But the end of the era of cheap commodities, energy and manufactures is likely to open up a contradiction between this goal and the aim of low inflation. Any upsurge in UK inflation will in turn wipe out the advantages provided for exports by low currency values. Only a continuing squeeze on the income of workers in order to maintain low export prices while imported inputs rise in value could provide the basis for such an approach. Such an outcome cannot be ruled out. But the struggles which would ensue if this framework were to be adopted underline the inherent riskiness and instability associated with this strategy.

Other chapters in this volume set forward precise demands for socialists to raise in the wake of the crisis. But the above analysis indicates some general points which are relevant for the specific case of Britain. Three conclusions can be drawn. Firstly, the crisis in Britain is not simply the result of the last two decades of deregulation and debt. Rather, the policies followed in those decades represented a partial and temporary resolution of much deeper contradictions within British capital. This resolution has now been shattered and those contradictions have emerged in a sharper and more acute form than previously. Secondly, any socialist response to the crisis has to recognise the interlocking nature of the various elements of the neo-liberal framework which led to that crisis, in particular the relationship between debt and international flows of capital, commodities and manufactures. Thirdly, critiques of the approaches being adopted by British capital to the crisis need to go beyond the defence of public spending against coalition cuts, important though this is, to take in the emergent strategy of a rebalancing of the economy towards investment and exports. Given the nature of international capitalist competition such a rebalancing must inevitably be based on shifting resources from wages to profits and making workers pay for overcoming the crisis. An analysis based on these conclusions can provide the basis for outlining an alternative reconciliation between production and exchange than those on which the strategies of British capital have been based. Such reconciliation would move beyond immediate responses to the crisis to examine the potential for a different kind of economy which could resolve the contradictions of the British economy in the interests of working people.

AUSTERITY AND THE LIES THAT IMPOVERISH

Susan Pashkoff

For anti-capitalists, the impact of the introduction of austerity measures was obvious. As expected, these measures have led to increased unemployment, impoverishment of the poor and working class and the destruction of public services. Rather than leading to increased economic growth driven by the impoverishment of the poor and the working class, the UK is falling deeper into recession; growth rates are being constantly downgraded and now are projected by the Bank of England to be 1% for 2011-12.

It has been revealed that 111,000 public sector workers have lost their jobs since March.[1] General unemployment has risen to 8.3% (2.62m people) up by 129,000 August, jobseeker allowance claimants have risen by 5,300 (in the UK at 1.56m people, up by 135,600 on the year)[2], youth (ages 16-24) unemployment has reached 1.02 m (21.9% of economically active population)[3]. The Institute for Fiscal Studies

---

1   See the November 2011, labour market statistics from the Office for National Statistics (ONS): http://www.ons.gov.uk/ons/rel/lms/labour-market-statistics/november-2011/statistical-bulletin.html; http://www.bbc.co.uk/news/business-15234228.
2   See the report by *The Guardian* (http://www.guardian.co.uk/news/datablog/2010/nov/17/unemployment-and-employment-statistics-economics). For more detail see, the ONS: http://www.ons.gov.uk/ons/rel/lms/labour-market-statistics/november-2011/statistical-bulletin.html.
3   See, the reports from the BBC (http://www.bbc.co.uk/news/business-15747103, and http://www.bbc.co.uk/news/business-15271800) and the ONS

(IFS) has projected that government policies would increase the number of children living in poverty by 600,000 in the next four years up to 1 in 4 (from 1 in 5 from the last government), median household income has fallen and is expected to continue to fall and would increase both absolute and relative poverty in the UK. We are experiencing falling money wages brought about by attacks on benefits and pensions and real wages (what wages can purchase) caused by rising food and energy prices, rising rents, increased VAT and other potentially inflationary policies (*e.g.*, quantitative easing).

It is not as though it was not obvious what the impact of these austerity measures would be; clearly if you cut money to the state sector and prohibit local councils from increasing council tax (they have renewed this prohibition again this year), services and jobs will be cut. It was also clear that when they pegged benefits to the Consumer Price Index (CPI) rather than the Retail Price Index (RPI), that benefits would be cut (that was the aim of the policy after all).[4] Cutting child-tax credits clearly only affects those paying taxes, so that would affect the working and middle class; but cutbacks to child benefit, education spending, and provision of local services affects the poor, working and middle classes. Perhaps it was not obvious that making people poorer would actually impoverish them; while many of us thought it was definitional, it seems that some government ministers never bothered to check their dictionaries or believe that impoverishment is a necessary precondition to ensuring economic growth.

The point is that the situation is far worse than expected. One wonders what projections they were using as this was obvious to all those that were not deluded by the fantasies of neoliberals (or those that are blinded by their greed and immorality) when they heard the government's policies.

(http://www.ons.gov.uk/ons/rel/lms/labour-market-statistics/november-2011/statistical-bulletin.html).

4   The main difference between the two indexes of inflation is that the RPI contains housing costs, council taxes and mortgage interest payments, see for further differentiation between these two indices of inflation: http://www.google.co.uk/url?sa=t&rct=j&q=differences%2Bbetween%2BRPI%2Band%2BCPI&source=web&cd=7&ved=0CFAQFjAG&url=http%3A%2F%2Fwww.ons.gov.uk%2Fons%2Fguide-method%2Fuser-guidance%2Fprices%2Fcpi-and-rpi%2Fdifferences-between-the-rpi-and-cpi-measures-of-inflation.pdf&ei=6dvCTrHjBYGZ8QO8lcGECw&usg=AFQjCNHOty98RHNnmpkM9gUorfLY_BKSVA&cad=rja).

Public sector workers job losses

Numbers of public sector workers that have been laid off so far (111,000) since March alone indicate that earlier estimates of 610,000 job losses were more accurate than the revised estimate of 4100000.[5] In the university sector and further education sectors alone they are saying that over 40,000 jobs are at risk.[6] Needless to say, the Office of Budget Responsibility (OBR) either underplayed or miscalculated public sector job losses in their second estimate.

In June 2010, the OBR forecast that the government's spending cuts, designed to reduce its budget deficit, would lead to 610,000 public sector job losses between 2010/11 and 2015/16. However, in November last year it reduced this projection to 410,000.

The CIPD (Chartered Institute of Personnel and Development) said that, based on the current rate of job cuts, the actual number of jobs lost in the public sector was likely to be 610,000 - "exactly the same as the initial OBR projection".[7]

According to the Office of National Statistics:

> The number of people in public sector employment was 6.04 million in June 2011, down 111,000 from March 2011. The estimate for March 2011 includes 15,000 people employed on a temporary basis in connection with the 2011 Census, but there were only 1,000 people employed in these temporary jobs in June 2011. Excluding people employed in temporary Census posts, the fall in public sector employment between March and June 2011 was 97,000. The number of people in private sector employment in June 2011 was 23.13 million, up 41,000 from March 2011 (ONS, November 2011, labour market statistics, *Statistical Bulletin*).[8]

While the initial effect of the economic crisis certainly hit men harder as it impacted upon sectors in which male employment is dominant in the advanced capitalist world (*e.g.*, manufacturing, finance sector and construction), austerity measures are hitting women harder as they

---

5 See this report by the BBC: http://www.bbc.co.uk/news/business-15234228.
6 See the following reports from University and College Union: http://www.ucu.org.uk/index.cfm?articleid=5225 and
  http://www.ucu.org.uk/index.cfm?articleid=4748.
For the impact of cuts on universities in Europe, see
http://www.google.co.uk/url?sa=t&source=web&cd=7&ved=0CEcQFjAG&url=http%3A%2F%2Fwww.eua.be%2FLibraries%;
for adult education in the UK see these pieces from UCU:
http://www.ucu.org.uk/index.cfm?articleid=4508,
http://www.ucu.org.uk/index.cfm?articleid=4083.
7 http://www.bbc.co.uk/news/business-15234228
8 See, http://www.ons.gov.uk/ons/rel/lms/labour-market-statistics/november-2011/statistical-bulletin.html

work in sectors that are under attack (*e.g.*, state and public sectors: education, health-care, carers, and civil sector workers). While women still predominately work in traditional sectors, many of which are in the public sector, ironically, it is probably due to legislation preventing gender discrimination in public sector hiring that has also led to large numbers of women employed in the sector; as such, they are more vulnerable to cuts in the sector. Cuts in the public sector (both in terms of employment and wage and pension benefits) are affecting women that are more concentrated in the sector at all levels.

> What seems to have happened is that the initial impact of the crisis hit the manufacturing, financial and construction sectors hard, the domain of predominantly male workers in developed countries. It was men in manufacturing that were among the first to experience job cuts. But the impact of the crisis and associated job losses have since expanded to other sectors, including service sectors where women are mainly employed (Sara Elder, 2010, p. 49).[9]

The difference between the two is that while the initial impact on male employment was a direct result of the economic crisis. What we are now seeing is a direct attack on the public sector in which women workers are more concentrated. This attack is being conducted by various State governments, the EU, IMF and the ECB (European Central Bank); the latter three known collectively as the *Troika*. In the UK, this attack has been done by the government independently of pressure by the *Troika*. So, the working class is now facing attacks for a situation which not only has it not created, but which has been deliberately provoked by bailing out the banking sector that was actually responsible for causing the crisis. As workers' incomes have fallen throughout the advanced capitalist world since neoliberalism has taken hold, women's incomes are an essential part of household income. The idea that women have the choice to stay home and tend to their children is becoming rather quaint as the middle class has now joined the working class and poor in facing the misery imposed by our governments and the Troika. With unemployment rising due to the economic crisis, women's incomes are essential for survival. Yet, we are watching an attack on women's employment and incomes as part of government austerity measures.

> The number of women out of work is at a 23-year high, with cutbacks in the public sector hitting women particularly hard: two-

---

9   Sara Elder, *"Women in Labour Markets: Measuring Progress and Identifying Challenges,"* ILO publications, Geneva, March 2010, http://www.ilo.org/wcmsp5/groups/public/@ed_emp/@emp_elm/@trends/docume nts/publication/wcms_123835.pdf.

thirds of the 130,000 jobs lost in local authorities since the first quarter of 2010 were held by women.[10]

While there have been some increases in private sector employment; those jobs lost in the public sector are not necessarily replaced by the private sector. Replacement of public jobs lost in education, health care services, clerical work are not being met by private sector hiring. What is important to note is that even if public sector workers are hired in their fields, these jobs are not union jobs; wages will necessarily be lower, and hard earned tenure and seniority will be lost (average weekly wages in the private sector are £460 as compared to £477 in the public sector).[11] To add insult to injury, these workers are not only losing their steady income and in some cases their careers, but are now facing the prospect of lower benefits due to government policy.

Rising general unemployment

Unemployment levels have not been this bad since 1994; this is a 17 year high. Unemployment had risen by 114,000 from June-August, this trend is continuing. Keep in mind that these are the official unemployment statistics:

According to the Office of National Statistics (ONS), for July to September 2011:

- The employment rate for those aged from 16 to 64 was 70.2 per cent, down 0.4 on the quarter. There were 29.07 million people in employment aged 16 and over, down 197,000 on the quarter.
- The unemployment rate was 8.3 per cent of the economically active population, up 0.4 on the quarter. There were 2.62 million unemployed people, up 129,000 on the quarter. The unemployment rate is the highest since 1996 and the number of unemployed people is the highest since 1994.
- The inactivity rate for those aged from 16 to 64 was 23.3 per cent, up 0.1 on the quarter. There were 9.36 million economically inactive people aged from 16 to 64, up 64,000 on the quarter.

---

10   See, from *The Guardian* discussing the report from the Fawcett Society: http://www.guardian.co.uk/society/2011/nov/04/women-equality-clock-back-fawcett.
11   See ONS: http://www.ons.gov.uk/ons/rel/lms/labour-market-statistics/november-2011/statistical-bulletin.html

- Total pay (including bonuses) rose by 2.3 per cent on a year earlier, down 0.4 on the three months to August 2011 (with both the private and public sectors showing lower pay growth).
- Regular pay (excluding bonuses) rose by 1.7 per cent on a year earlier, down 0.1 on the three months to August 2011 (ONS, 16 November 2011, Statistical Bulletin).[12]

The British Government is still claiming that these figures are the result of the impact of the financial crisis and problems in the eurozone rather than placing the blame on their austerity measures; in response, the government is offering job training for 50,000 workers. As an understatement, this is insufficient and it will not even make a dent in the unemployment statistics. It is becoming quite obvious that cutbacks in the public sector are not being met by private sector investment and increasing employment.

In fact, following a quarterly survey of 1000 employers, the CIPD has concluded that many firms are essentially not recruiting people; unsurprisingly given the lack of growth in both the UK and the EU, hiring people does not make any sense as demand for goods is falling along with expected effective demand which conditions employment and investment decisions.[13] They see no positive signs of improvement in the UK jobs market in either the short or medium term. What is interesting that most of the reporting in the media has the causality reversed; it is lack of growth that is inhibiting hiring, rather than insufficient hiring inhibiting economic growth. The revival of Say's Law argumentation ignores the demonstrable fallacy in the notion of causality in which supply supposedly creates demand (or savings determine investment). Government policies leading to rising unemployment, wage, pension and benefit cuts mean that employers are not convinced that they can actually sell their goods and services, as such, they will not increase investment, employment and the size of productive units. Somehow we are supposed to be grateful that private sector employers are neither planning on increasing redundancies, cutting back on off-shoring jobs nor hiring less migrant labour; but if that is good news, the UK labour force is in deep trouble.

---

12   See, ONS, 16/11/2011, Statistical Bulletin, Labour Market Statistics: http://www.ons.gov.uk/ons/rel/lms/labour-market-statistics/november-2011/statistical-bulletin.html.
13   See http://www.managementtoday.co.uk/go/news/article/1103811/hiring-freeze-killing-growth-claims-cipd/.

The survey of more than 1,000 employers, found employers seem to be hedging their bets on all employment-related decisions in response to the current economic uncertainty. Hiring intentions - as well as redundancy intentions - have fallen across all sectors compared with recent previous reports.

The proportion of firms intending to hire migrant workers, which has risen steadily in recent consecutive quarters, has also fallen to 19% from 25% during the past three months. Meanwhile, the proportion of firms planning to offshore jobs to other parts of the world has also decreased to 6% from 10% in the past year. India remains the most popular destination for offshoring, with half of employers surveyed planning to locate some or all of their operations in India. The functions most likely to be offshored are finance and accounts and IT support.[14]

Nor will the £75billion of Quantitative Easing (QE) lead to increased investment by the private sector due to the lack of profitability of investment in productive industries (see realisation crisis below).[15] What quantitative easing will do is socialise private debt (that is what is being exchanged for government bonds) in anticipation of further bank crashes expected due to Greek default. The Belgian Bank, Dexia was bailed out on October 10th; it will be the first of many and it was heavily "invested" in Greece.[16] More importantly, QE will increase inflation and lower real wages (especially hard for those on fixed benefits and pensions), and lead to further hoarding by banks and the wealthy or investment in short-term speculative investments (exacerbating an already unstable financial market).

Falling incomes and increasing poverty

Another piece of evidence that we are clearly **not** "all in this together" is that contrary to the government's claim that austerity measures

---

14   See the following from *HR magazine* discussing the report from the CIPD on private sector lack of hiring: http://www.hrmagazine.co.uk/hro/news/1020428/employers-freeze-plans-hire-redundancies-light-continuing-economic-uncertainty-cipd-reports. See CIPD, *Labour Market Outlook*, autumn 2011, http://www.cipd.co.uk/binaries/LMO%20Autumn%202011.pdf, see pps. 6-10.
15   See BBC report on quantitative easing introduced by the Director of the Bank of England: http://www.bbc.co.uk/news/business-15210112.
16   See, BBC on the bailout of Dexia, 10, October 2011: http://www.bbc.co.uk/news/business-15235915.

were not responsible for current UK economic problem, there is no doubt that they are clearly implicated in the fall in income, rising poverty and the evidence that it was not only that the poor are getting poorer, but the middle class is getting poorer as well.[17]

According to the Institute for Fiscal Studies (IFS), this is the biggest fall in median household incomes since the 1970s, a £2,000 drop in income for median households. Rising costs due to increased petrol prices, rising energy bills, and rising food prices are undercutting household income; part of this is due to increased VAT introduced by the government and part of it is due to increased prices due to inflation.

According to the IFS:

> The period between 2009–10 (the latest household income data available) and 2012–13 is likely to be dominated by a large decline in real incomes across the income distribution. Absolute poverty is forecast to rise by about 600,000 children and 800,000 working-age adults. Median income is expected to fall by around 7% in real terms, which would be the largest three-year fall for 35 years.

In the longer term, the planned introduction of Universal Credit will act to reduce both absolute and relative poverty. The long term effect of Universal Credit is to reduce relative poverty by about 450,000 children and 600,000 working-age adults in 2020–21. However, the net direct effect of the coalition government's tax and benefit changes is to increase both absolute and relative poverty. This is because other changes, such as the switch from RPI- to CPI-indexation of means-tested benefits, more than offset the impact on poverty of Universal Credit.

Absolute and relative child poverty are forecast to be 23% and 24% in 2020–21 respectively. These compare to the targets of 5% and 10%, set out in the Child Poverty Act (2010) and passed with cross-party support. This would be the highest rate of absolute child poverty since 2001–02 and the highest rate of relative child poverty since 1999–2000. Modelling of scenarios in which employment rises by more than expected or take-up of benefits increases (perhaps as a consequence of Universal Credit strengthening work incentives or being easier to understand for benefit claimants) suggests that such

---

17 See Institute for Fiscal Studies report, press release 11 October 2011: http://www.ifs.org.uk/publications/5710; and full press release by Mike Brewer, James Browne and Robert Joyce: http://www.ifs.org.uk/pr/poverty_pr_1011.pdf, see also: http://www.bbc.co.uk/news/education-15242103

factors cannot be relied upon to make a large difference to poverty rates (Brewer, Browne, and Joyce, 2010, p.1).[18]

Having an income below 60% of the average is defined as poverty; both absolute (in the sense of the poverty level) and relative poverty (in the sense of comparison to median household income in a specific year) are set to rise. From the IFS, we have the following projections:[19]

> The tables below shows the central poverty forecasts from the report. An individual is considered to be in relative poverty if it lives in a household whose income is below 60% of the median in that year, and in absolute poverty if it lives in a household whose real-terms income is below 60% of the 2010–11 median. The relative poverty line therefore moves each year with the income of the median household, but the absolute poverty line is fixed in real terms.

Relative poverty

	Children		Working-age parents		Working-age adults without children	
	Millions	%	Millions	%	Millions	%
2009 (actual)	2.6	19.7	2.3	17.1	3.4	15
2010	2.5	19.3	2.1	16.6	3.5	15
2011	2.5	19.2	2.2	16.7	3.6	15.1
2012	2.6	19.6	2.2	17	3.7	15.1
2013	2.8	21.6	2.4	18.3	3.8	15.5
2014	2.9	22	2.4	18.5	3.8	15.3
2015	2.9	22.2	2.4	18.5	4	15.9
2020	3.3	24.4	2.6	20	4.9	17.5

Absolute poverty

	Children		Working-age parents		Working-age adults without children	
	Millions	%	Millions	%	Millions	%
2009 (actual)	2.2	17	2	14.9	3.1	13.6
2010	2.5	19.3	2.1	16.6	3.5	15
2011	2.8	21.1	2.4	18.1	3.7	15.7
2012	2.8	21.8	2.4	18.7	3.9	16
2013	3.1	23.2	2.5	19.5	4	16.3
2014	3	22.9	2.5	19.2	4	16
2015	3	22.8	2.5	19	4.1	16
2020	3.1	23.1	2.5	19	4.7	16.8

Source: Brewer, Browne and Joyce, (2011, p. 3).[20]

---

18   Brewer, Browne, and Joyce (2010), "Universal Credit Not Enough to Prevent a Decade of Rising Poverty," Press release, October, Institute for Fiscal Studies, in http://www.ifs.org.uk/pr/poverty_pr_1011.pdf.
19   http://www.ifs.org.uk/pr/poverty_pr_1011.pdf
20   http://www.ifs.org.uk/pr/poverty_pr_1011.pdf

68 Capitalism – crises and alternatives

What is the government response to these projections? "The stats are not taking into account that people are being forced back to work due to cuts in benefits" say Iain Duncan Smith, secretary of works and pensions. What the government and its ministers are not understanding (or they are simply lying) is that there are no jobs for these so-called slackers to get. To make the situation even harder, increased unemployment of public sector workers means that the long-term unemployed need to compete with those recently unemployed for low-wage, low skilled jobs that are simply not coming into existence as much as the Tories are cutting corporate taxes, babbling about flexible labour markets or waving their magic wands.

Rising numbers of people are using food-banks to cover fallen income due to benefit cuts and cuts in work hours for those already on low wages.[21] This is especially the case for young people that are experiencing high rates of unemployment:

> The Trussell Trust said the numbers of people using its food banks had increased from 41,000 last year to almost 61,500 in the past 12 months. In some areas such as Exeter, Cardigan and the Isle of Wight, the number of young people was as high as 70 to 80%.[22]

To contribute to impoverishment, rents are rising spectacularly:

> Shelter say that private rents are unaffordable in 55% of English boroughs, having already risen at one-and-a-half times the rate of incomes in the 10 years to 2007.[23]

Further confirmation can be found below in a discussion of strategies on "buy to let" for "investment:"

> In September, the average rent rose by 0.7% to reach £718 in September, surpassing the previous record high of £713 in August. This represents a 4.3% increase on September 2010's average of £689. The research also shows the average yield rose from 5.2% in August to 5.3% in September. Rents hit record highs in six regions: London, the South-East, Yorkshire and Humber, the East of England, Wales and the East Midlands.
> Rents increased the fastest in the South-East and the East Midlands, where they rose by 1.8% and 1.1% respectively compared to August, while the smallest increases were in the West Midlands and the North East, where rents rose by 0.2% and 0.3%. Over the

---

21 See BBC report, http://www.bbc.co.uk/newsbeat/15035299.
22 See: http://www.bbc.co.uk/newsbeat/15035299
23 See: http://www.bbc.co.uk/news/business-15287743; http://news.bbc.co.uk/today/hi/today/newsid_9614000/9614436.stm.

past year, London's rents have risen at a faster rate than any other region, increasing by 5.8%.[24]

This cannot solely be explained by supply and demand arguments. The government push towards home ownership since the 1980s had led to rising home ownership. Despite the numbers falling since the crisis, 67% of British homes are owner-occupied (down from 71% in 2005). This government policy rather than ensuring renting and provision of social housing has lead to the decline in building of social housing. Add to that increased indebtedness for purchasers due to easy (but very expensive credit) has cost people their homes due to rising unemployment and attacks on income.[25] The contraction of the credit market has made it harder for those trying to get on the housing ladder. Meanwhile, tenancy laws favour the landlords rather than tenants in the UK.[26]

While the government's policy of cutting housing benefits so as to clear out the poor from the centre of London has yet to take effect, this will only compound the problem as displaced people are shifted to the outer boroughs where rents can be covered by housing benefits. However, given rising rents in London the question arises is what will displaced people and current renters be able to obtain given the government's targeted numbers for housing benefit?

Again, benefit cuts are falling harder on women as compared to men. The concentration of women in part-time work leaves them dependent upon government benefits which are also facing cuts. Additional problems arise as cuts to benefits and services are adding further hardship: protection for victims of sexual, domestic and other forms of violence,[27] disability benefits and pensions. Add to these the cuts in benefits that were specifically geared towards women (e.g., maternity benefits, pregnancy benefits). Then, of course, there are the cuts to children's services and benefits (including child tax credit, youth-centres, child-care benefits themselves). Alison Garnham, chief executive of the Child Poverty Action group said:

> Child poverty and the incomes and services women are able to access are intrinsically linked. The vast majority of child benefit is received by women, whether as the main carer in a couple, or as a single parent.

---

24   See: http://www.mortgagestrategy.co.uk/buy-to-let/rents-rise-in-all-regions-for-first-time/1040047.article.
25   See for example: http://www.homepurchaser.co.uk/first-time-buyers/2011/07/05/number-of-england-s-homeowners-takes-a-slight-dip.
26   See for example: http://www.globalpropertyguide.com/Europe/United-Kingdom/Landlord-and-Tenant.
27   See *The Guardian*'s piece on the Fawcett Society report: http://www.guardian.co.uk/society/2011/nov/04/women-equality-clock-back-fawcett.

> It is hugely unfair that such a large burden of the government's cuts should be falling on the shoulders of women and children, and it would be profoundly wrong if these unfair cuts to child benefit became permanent.[28]

The government has insisted that benefits be capped at £500/week for those households with couples and lone parent households (single adult household with no children benefits will be capped at £350/week). This is inclusive: that means, rent (and housing benefit), food, disability payments, and child benefits. As such, people caring for elderly parents can lose carer benefits if their overall benefits exceed this amount.[29] This clearly Benthamite argument based upon the notion of lesser eligibility is trying to ensure that the income of those on benefits must be lower than those that are actually working; as such, benefits are capped at £500/week as that is lower than the average working household income per week. Even the government acknowledges that the impact will fall primarily on women:

> [...] 60% of customers who are likely to have their benefit reduced by the cap to be single females, but only around 3% to be single men. Most of the single women affected are likely to be lone parents, this is because we expect the vast majority of households affected by the policy (around 90%) to have children. Around 60% of those that are capped are single women. Single women form 40% of the overall benefit population.[30]

Finally, there is the re-pegging of benefits and pensions to the CPI (as opposed to the RPI which covers housing costs); this means that increases in benefits and pensions will certainly be at a lower level as the CPI is lower than the RPI. Women live longer than men and they have had lower incomes (both in terms of pay for the same jobs and the fact that "women's work" pays less). As such, their pension contributions and hence pensions will be lower. This is reality; this means that women that are able to retire will be living longer on lower pensions (while women that are married may get their husband's higher pensions upon their deaths; this does nothing for single women or single mothers).

---

28   As cited by *The Guardian*: http://www.guardian.co.uk/society/2011/nov/04/women-equality-clock-back-fawcett.
29   See, Winvisible, "Defend our entitlement to benefits – we're not "workless", http://www.winvisible.org/BEN/Welfare_Reform_Bill_info_%20and_what_we_can do.htm. See also, The Department of Works and Pensions, on the Benefit Cap, http://www.dwp.gov.uk/docs/eia-benefit-cap-wr2011.pdf.
30   DWP, *Household Benefit Cap, Equality Impact Assessment*, October 2011, http://www.dwp.gov.uk/docs/eia-benefit-cap-wr2011.pdf.

Two-thirds of pensioners living in poverty are women, and as many as half of all women are not able to make adequate pension provision for their future. The average pension for a woman working in local government is just £60 per week. Yet changes to the way that state pension contributions are calculated means that millions of public sector workers, the majority of whom are women, will be expected to work longer and pay more in contributions, only to get a smaller pension.[31]

This is a government blinded by its own ideology that poverty exists because the poor are lazy, drunks, immoral and dissolute; their arguments are reminiscent of reading Malthus, Bentham or the reports of the commission of the 1834 Poor Law Reform. Rather than acknowledging reality that capitalist economies cannot sustain full-employment due to the needs of the system for profitability, it is far easier to blame the poor for their poverty. However, the level of employment depends on the capital available for the employment of labour as opposed to machinery; this depends on known techniques of production which are chosen to maximise profits. Competition means reducing wage costs and costs of inputs so as to maximise profitability. Even during the 19th century during periods of continually increasing economic growth, where wage costs were incredibly low and with continual deskilling of labour to drive wage costs down, full employment did not exist. All of the increased growth was absorbed as profits; as such, while there were extremely high profits, full employment was not and has never been consistent with the needs of the system.

Increased exploitation of workers

Employed workers are being forced to take wage cuts to keep their jobs in the face of rising unemployment. Benefits like paid holidays are been attacked. People are being asked to work extra hours for the same wages. All these things are increased exploitation of workers; in this case it is literally an increase of unpaid labour.

Take for example, that public sector workers have been asked to essentially take a wage cut to cover NHS debt caused by cuts to NHS funding by the government.[32] Funding problems for the NHS by

---

31   The Fawcett Society *"A Life Raft for Women's Equality."* http://www.fawcettsociety.org.uk/documents/A%20Life%20Raft%20for%20Women%27s%20Equality%20FINAL%281%29.pdf, p. 2.
32   See for e.g., http://www.bbc.co.uk/news/uk-england-london-15199437 and http://www.guardian.co.uk/society/patrick-butler-cuts-blog/2011/jun/20/public-workers-face-cuts-to-pay-and-conditions.

this government are being compounded by attempts to introduce privatisation of certain parts of the NHS by making contracting open to competition; this will leave the NHS open to EU competition laws which will destroy the system.

Why austerity measures?

We need to keep in mind that in a capitalist economic system, profits are the *raison d'être* of the system; when investment occurs it is profits upon that investment with which investors are concerned, when a business produces a good, it is the return on their costs with which they are concerned.

Given the social subsistence wage, profits are earned upon goods sold at a price over and above their cost of production. How is this obtained? Costs of production relate to the capital, labour and land used in production. Capital can be broken down simply into capital used up in the production process (constant circulation capital) and capital goods that last for more than one period of production (constant fixed capital, this wears out over time and needs replacement when the machinery or building wears out). Rents on land derive from private ownership of land; if land is used in production rents are paid depending on fertility of soil and due to private ownership.

Wages depend on two things: 1) historical social subsistence levels that are dependent upon the subsistence and reproduction of the working class and societal agreement that working people should have certain things as citizen; 2) the level of class struggle. A working class, with high levels of unemployment and low levels of trade union organisation and limited political power means that the wage will be close to, or at, the historical social subsistence level as the power balance lies with the employers. That means that capitalists can appropriate all, or almost all, of the surplus revenues earned on goods as profits. A strong working class with powerful trade unions and political might can demand a portion of the increased revenues earned from economic growth as surplus wages over and above their costs of reproduction. This was the situation that was obtained during the post-war period in the US and EU.

In the absence of economic growth, profits essentially need to come through a wage squeeze. What we are seeing is a deliberate squeeze on wages and incomes for the poor, working and middle class; specifically they are undermining the historical social subsistence level in an attempt to increase profits. This can only be shrunk theoretically back to the biological subsistence level, but the powers that be are pretty certain that the majority of people in the advanced capitalist world will not stand for that, so they are chopping back a bit at a time; first wage stagnation, then relative wage reductions and now absolute reductions in income.

But what happens when we squeeze wages?

Keynes was a very clever man that understood that capitalism was a system prone to economic crises; he came up with am idea to manage or mitigate the crises in a capitalist economic system. Keynesian economic policies do not eliminate crises as they are part and parcel of how the system operates. Keynes focused on the question of effective demand and manipulating it to ensure that demand for goods produced in the system would be sufficient to ensure that they could be sold at a price ensuring a profit. Increased wages, ensuring incomes for the poor, provide for an increase in the effective demand for commodities; this also clearly affects the production not only of final commodities, but also those goods that enter into the production of these final commodities. This does not solve realisation problems in the system (workers on their own cannot sustain sufficient demand to keep the system running), but they certainly reduce tremendously their impact. However, it is important to understand, that realisation problems are not the cause of the crisis, rather they are a part of the crisis.

What is a realisation crisis?

This relates to what was raised earlier concerning the question of capitalists selling goods and services at a price over and above their costs of production. Through the exploitation of labour (in that workers work far more hours than needed to produce the value of their subsistence), capitalists have the possibility of workers producing value over and above that needed for the replacement of capital used up in production and worker's own subsistence and reproduction; this surplus product (or value) if realised by sale of the goods, is net product or surplus which forms the basis of profits.

Insufficient general effective demand means that the goods are sold at a level in which the surplus portion is not realised; that means that profits are lower than expected. In the absence of sufficient effective demand, profits upon investment are not high and this will also affect future investment. If this was only in one industry, capital could move to another one seeking higher levels of profits; but if this is a general problem, investment is nonsensical. Money capital will either be hoarded or invested in short-term speculative investments. If you want to know why banks are not lending or capitalists are not investing, it is because we are in the realisation crisis portion of an economic crisis.

The delusions of neoliberalism

The government in the UK has introduced measures following an economic crash that are growth restricting rather than growth expanding (even if David Cameron does not seem to understand this at all). If growth exists, profits are rising and wages can stay stagnant; increased profitability can be sustained by total increased surplus revenues produced by economic growth being appropriated as profits (rather than divided between workers and capitalists as during the consumer capitalism period from the post-war period until the late 1970s).

What neoliberalism has advocated and pushed for was the shrinkage of the surplus portion going to wages; this was achieved through the destruction of the traditional industrial and manufacturing sectors in the advanced capitalist world to destroy the power of unions. Shifting work first to areas with anti-union laws and then ultimately moving them overseas to areas where wages were kept artificially low due to prohibitions on union organisation and minimal laws on work conditions. The last bastion of organised labour is the public or state sector, the attack on the state sector is partly an attack on organised labour. It is also an attempt to destroy social subsistence levels (wages) by attacking social welfare provisions. Finally, they are trying to shift the services provided by the state to the control of the private sector so as to open up another area of exploitation for capital.

These policies are based upon the rather mistaken belief that it is the wealthy that makes the system work rather than the working class. Both in terms of their labour to produce goods and services and their purchase of goods and services, the working class ensure that the system keeps running. High levels of unemployment caused by the destruction of the industrial and manufacturing goods sectors, the introduction of machinery to reduce wage cost and reduce the labour in use in the economy may have enabled them to destroy trade unions and shift wages downwards, but it has also resulted in decreased demand in the advanced capital world for the goods that they are producing. Their insistence that wages were kept low in the periphery means that the replacement for advanced capitalist world effective demand does not exist as of yet. While they are developing a middle class and a native bourgeoisie, China's economic development is based more on export-led growth than developing the domestic market; the vast majority of incomes are too low and, as such, Chinese effective demand is simply not strong enough to sustain the system.[33]

In the absence of the possibility of profitable investment, capital simply is not invested in productive growth creating investment; money capital is either hoarded or invested in short-term speculative investment which while making them more money does not ensure long-term profitability desperately needed for the system to function.

Conclusion

This is where we are at now: the ideology of neoliberalism justifying increases in income and wealth inequality and the greed of the upper classes on the basis that increased inequality will lead to further investment by the private sector is merely an exercise in political and economic apologetics; it is class warfare, nothing more, nothing less. We are moving towards to the same situation that led to the great depression; the reason for government provision of investment, nationalisation of industry (in Europe), the creation of the social welfare state is that this free-market insanity leads to further and more devastating economic crises. That is where we are heading once again ...

---

33   See, chapter "China's Rise Amidst the Crisis" in this book.

A GREEN INDUSTRIAL REVOLUTION

Towards an ecosocialist industrial strategy

Sean Thompson

It is right and necessary that all men should have work to do which shall be worth doing, and be of itself pleasant to do; and which should be done under such conditions as would make it neither over-wearisome or over-anxious. Turn that claim about as I may...I cannot find that it is an exorbitant claim; yet...if Society would or could admit it, the face of the world would be changed.

William Morris

Introduction

In July 2008, just prior to the collapse of Lehman Brothers, the New Economics Foundation published the *Green New Deal*. While its authors, who included the Green Party's Caroline Lucas, Larry Elliot of the Guardian and Ann Pettifor, took what was an essentially left(ish) Keynesian position, they recognised what most other 'experts' have still signally failed to; that the current crisis is not just financial, but the first of three overlapping and global crises that we face. This 'triple crunch', as they called it, is a combination of the banking crisis we are still experiencing, the ongoing and ever growing threat of climate change and the explosion of energy prices caused by the imminent approach of peak oil.

It probably isn't necessary to rehearse once again the details of the sequence of events that led to the greatest financial crisis for at least eighty years, apart from pointing out that while the deregulation of financial markets that began in the seventies led to the creation of almost limitless credit the led to a huge credit boom and the growth (and eventual rapid popping) of asset bubbles it is the structural instability and impossible unpredictability of the financial system that is the prime mover of the credit crunch rather than the sleight of hand of a relatively tiny number of spivs and hucksters. As the Canadian economist Jim Stanford has said:

> Capitalism is nothing if not creative and the financial industry has lured some of humanity's smartest minds to focus on the utterly unproductive task of developing new pieces of financial paper, and new ways of buying and selling them. Despite the finger pointing at mortgage brokers and credit rate, therefore, the current meltdown is rooted squarely in the innovative but blinding greed that is the raison d'être of private finance[1].

It is also now widely accepted by all but a small coterie of right wing cranks and corporate lobbyists that global warming caused by our ever increasing generation of CO_2, is already starting to make dramatic, and potentially disastrous, impacts on climatic conditions throughout the world. While 2010 was, worldwide, the warmest on record we experienced in Britain the coldest December on record. At the beginning of 2011 we watched much of Australia continue to suffer its longest ever drought while other parts experienced unprecedented flooding and exceptionally powerful tornadoes.

Levels of CO_2 are rising relentlessly. From 1958 to 2001, levels rose from 315 parts per million to 370ppm. In 2009, the total atmospheric concentration of CO_2 was 386.92ppm, in 2010 it was 388.45ppm and in January 2011 it was 391.19ppm.[2]

'Peak oil' is the point where further expansion of global oil production ceases because new production is fully offset by declines in production elsewhere. Beyond that point, global oil supplies will begin to shrink and will become increasingly expensive. That point is imminent, if it hasn't already arrived. The political and economic reaction to the catastrophic pollution caused by the explosion of BP's oil platform in the Bay of Mexico, the recent Wikileaks disclosure that a senior figure in the Saudi oil ministry had admitted that existing

---

[1]   Jim Stanford, *Economics for Everyone*, Pluto Press, 2008
[2]   National Oceanic and Atmospheric Administration, measured at Mauna Loa Observatory, Hawaii.

estimates of Saudi oil reserves were greatly overstated and the effect on world oil prices of the uprising against Gaddafi in Libya, all demonstrate how fragile and susceptible to shock the oil market is. Indeed, Fatih Birol, the International Energy Agency's chief economist, has said that high oil prices could weaken trade balances, add to inflation and put pressure on central banks to raise interest rates. 'Oil prices are a serious risk for the global economic recovery. The global economic recovery is very fragile - especially in OECD [Organisation for Economic Cooperation and Development] countries'.[3]

The authors of the Green New Deal propose that we should deal with these interlocked crises with twin strategies:

First:
    a structural transformation of the regulation of national and international financial systems, and major changes to taxation systems' and

Second:
    a sustained programme to invest in and deploy energy conservation and renewable energies, coupled with effective demand management[4]..

In November 2009 (revised in October 2010) the Campaign against Climate Change Trade Union Group published the pamphlet One Million Climate Jobs, which looked at how the second of these strategies might be implemented. However, useful though the pamphlet is, it is basically a popular tract rather than a more considered assessment of not only what is to be done but how.

Despite their limitations - particularly those of the Green New Deal - I think that both pamphlets provide a starting point for more focussed thinking about alternative strategies. The purpose of this paper is to further develop some of the ideas and proposals sketched out by the authors of those two pamphlets and integrate them into a broader ecosocialist industrial strategy.

Aims and objectives

An ecosocialist industrial strategy has to have aims and objectives quite different from the crude imperative to capital accumulation that is currently the sole driver of economic activity in our society. It must

---

3   *The Guardian*, 22 February, 2011
4   *New Green Deal*, July 2008, p3

recognise not only the inherent instability and brutality of capitalism, but the limits to our ecosystem; that the biosphere on which we depend is finite, closed and constrained by the laws of thermodynamics.

As Caroline Lucas said in October 2010:

> I think the challenge for progressives when it comes to the environment is to accept that our current economic system is economically and morally unsustainable. In other words, it only works by cheating future generations out of their birthright and by exploiting the vulnerable here and abroad. So when we talk of a green recovery, we're not talking about a traditional economic recovery boosted by selling some home insulation or building some windmills. We're not talking about business as usual, with a few green trimmings.
>
> It's not about finding new products to sell, and sticking a green label on them.
>
> We're talking about a recovery based on green principles and insights; one that is rooted in social justice and which balances our needs, against those of the developing world, the natural world, and those of future generations.[5]

We therefore should have five key aims in developing our industrial strategy:
1. The assurance of meaningful employment and a life of dignity and modest comfort for all
2. The development of a low carbon society, and therefore a sustainable low carbon industrial base.
3. Freedom from a reliance on endless growth in the production of commodities and financial transactions.
4. Industrial production based on social needs rather than the maximisation of profit and ever increasing consumption.
5. Democratic control in and of the workplace.

Ten key objectives can be identified to begin to implement those aims:
1. To reduce greenhouse gasses (CO_2, methane and nitrous oxide) emissions by at least 80% within twenty years.
2. To increase electricity production by 80% within twenty years.
3. To retrofit thermal efficiency equipment and materials in all existing homes, public buildings and commercial premises within twenty years.

---

5   Caroline Lucas, October 2010, www.compassonline.org.uk

4. To replace or totally refurbish 20% of existing homes and 50% of public and commercial buildings within twenty years.
5. To increase the use of public transport by 250% within ten years.
6. To reduce real unemployment levels to a maximum of 2.5% within four years.
7. To create at least one million new jobs directly concerned with infrastructural reconstruction over four years.
8. To reduce income differentials within enterprises to a maximum of 10:1 within ten years.
9. To abolish income differentials between men and women within enterprises within five years.
10. To ensure that tertiary education and training/retraining is freely available to all within five years.

The Green New Deal and the Million Climate Jobs campaign

The ideas introduced in the *Green New Deal* and *One Million Green Jobs* pamphlets provide a good starting point for looking at the development of an ecosocialist industrial strategy.

The *Green New Deal* calls for the execution of 'a bold new vision for a low-carbon energy system that will include making every building a power station. Involving tens of millions of properties, their energy efficiency will be maximised, as will the use of renewables to produce electricity.' It also calls for the creation and training of a 'carbon army of workers to provide the human resources for a vast environmental reconstruction programme. We want to see hundreds of thousands of these new high and lower-skilled jobs created in the UK'.[6]

The *One Million Climate Jobs* pamphlet enlarges on these demands and adds detail to them. The pamphlet's authors call for the rapid creation of a million 'jobs that tackle the main sources of emissions. ...We don't mean old jobs with new names, or ones with 'sustainable' inserted into the job title. And we don't mean 'carbon finance' jobs'.[7]

They point out that both New Labour and the Tory/Lib Dem administration share the same approach of encouraging 'the market' to invest in renewable energy by the use of subsidies and tax breaks, and that government policy has also been to give people grants and

---

6 Green New Deal, op. cit.
7 One Million Climate Jobs, 2010, p6

loans to insulate and refit their houses, but that this has proved much too slow and inefficient. *One Million Climate Jobs* argues for direct public involvement ('something more like the way the government used to run the National Health Service') both in the design and funding of the regeneration programme but also in the employment of the workers who will implement it. It is, in effect, a call for the establishment of something like the Work Projects Administration (WPA), of Roosevelt's original New Deal, which provided almost eight million jobs in the USA (it became the largest employer in the country) between 1935 and 1943.

Priority industrial sectors

A massive infrastructural investment and reconstruction programme will require us to prioritise the rapid development of three key sectors; energy generation and transmission, transport and construction. This is for three reasons.

First, because electricity generation and transmission, transport and the heating and cooling of buildings between them account for 83% of the 673 million tonnes of greenhouse gasses (CO_2) emitted in Britain annually[8]. If we are to reduce emissions as rapidly and drastically as we need to then these sectors are clearly of the highest priority.[9]

Second, because these three sectors provide the fundamental underpinnings of all other productive sectors and the essential foundations for the overall infrastructural and social renewal that is vital to our society.

Third, because a major programme of public investment and employment in these sectors will not only lead to major regeneration in other key industrial sectors, such as machine tool manufacturing and electrical engineering but also, if properly funded, lead to rapid growth in R&D in sustainable and socially useful technology and stimulate the demand for graduates from almost all areas of tertiary education and/or training.

Energy

Around 400 terawatt hours (TWh) of electricity is currently generated in Britain every year, and its production annually generates around

---

[8] 2008 data for emissions from Department of Energy and Climate Change (DECC), www.decc.gov.uk
[9] The other two major sources of emissions, agriculture and landfill, are not dealt with in this paper.

420 million tonnes of CO2. We face two linked challenges which we have to deal with together.

First, even though the huge energy conservation programme proposed by the authors of both the *Green New Deal* and *One Million Climate Jobs* is (along with a radical overhaul of transport) the quickest and most effective way to drastically reduce demand for energy, over the next few years we will have to increase the amount of electricity generated in order to provide a substitute for the coal, oil and natural gas currently used in space and water heating and for the diesel and petrol used for transport. We will also face additional demand for electricity as an alternative to CO2 emitting energy sources as we modernise and decarbonise a range of critical industrial processes, such as iron and steel production.

Second, we must simultaneously dramatically reduce the level of CO2 emissions across the board. However, because we reject current nuclear technology for electricity generation we will have to undertake a programme of hugely expanding our generation capacity using other zero carbon technologies based on wind, sun and water. Thus, we have to develop an integrated approach, one which the Centre for Alternative Technology calls 'powering-down' (reducing energy wastage) and 'powering-up' (deploying renewable energies).[10]

Heating buildings and water in Britain generates 102 million tonnes of CO2 a year. A massive programme of insulation and renovation of all homes and public and commercial buildings has the potential to reduce that by about 40% by 2030. This would create 175,000 jobs over the twenty year period, front-loaded, so we will need 200,000 workers initially and this will fall to 100,000 in the last five years.

At the same time, it will be necessary to completely rejig how we generate and distribute electricity. There are several key factors driving this. By far the most important, of course, is the urgent need to reduce CO2 emissions, but three other factors also require us to take urgent action. First, for the first time in over a quarter of a century, the UK has recently become a net energy importer. Second, Britain faces a widening gap between electricity supply and demand, due to the retirement of plant and generation capacity. Third, there is an urgent need to renew and extend the carrying capacity of the National Grid. According to the Institute of Mechanical Engineers (IMEE):

> The UK's electricity supply network was built to connect coalfields to cities. Major redevelopment is required primarily due to new renewable sources of electricity. The priority is for new and

---

[10] Centre for Alternative Technology (CAT), *Zero Carbon Britain 2030*, 2010

strengthened transmission network infrastructure to connect the network with major areas of supply, especially wind energy in Scotland and offshore in the North Sea. Electricity storage has the potential to break the link between supply and demand and in doing so eliminate intermittency as an issue. ... Interconnectors have the potential to balance demand across a 'Supergrid'.[11]

In Britain the flow of electricity is mainly from the north of the country to London and the South-East via the high voltage alternating current (AC) network that we know as the National Grid. The development of very large offshore wind farms creates the opportunity to develop a completely new high voltage direct current (DC) network located on the sea bed to move electricity from the north of the country directly to the centres of demand in the southeast, to complement our present system. In addition, the National Grid has to be adapted to deal with distributed energy sources.

Distributed energy is the term which describes the local supply of both electricity and heat which is generated on or near the site where it is used. It covers a range of technologies at varying scales from the household to the community, which can generate electricity and heat from renewable or fossil fuel energy sources.

Distributed energy can be generated from renewable sources integrated into everyday buildings which are part of any local community, such as supermarkets, offices and hospitals. This includes renewable micro-generation technologies, in other words energy generating devices or systems in homes or in small, single buildings such as schools, which can provide heat and electricity, as well as larger on-site or near-site renewable heat and electricity technologies.

The development of a Supergrid would be a huge civil and electrical engineering project, similar in scale to building two or three motorways simultaneously that would take more than a decade to complete. Little work has been done to estimate the employment it would generate but it would certainly be measured in tens of thousands.

Britain has been extracting gas from the North Sea since 1967 and oil since 1975. However, North Sea oil production peaked in 1999, gas production peaked in 2000 and Britain became net importer of fuel in 2005.[12] In addition, Britain now imports the bulk of its coal. 76% of the coal used in Britain in 2008 was imported.[13] A rough estimate of the effect of replacing North Sea extraction with imports

---

11   Institute of Mechanical Engineers (IMEE), Sustainable energy infrastructure, www.imeche.org
12   Department of Energy & Climate Change (DECC), 2009
13   ibid.

suggests that it would add £53 billion to the trade deficit, not to mention the loss to the government of nearly £13 billion in tax from the offshore oil and gas industry.[14]

The Carbon Trust estimates that 8 of the 29GW of coal generation operating in 2005 will be retired by 2020, due to the need to comply with the EU Large Combustion Plant Directive and flue gas desulphurisation requirements. Over the same period, 8 of the UK's 12GW of nuclear capacity is also scheduled to be retired.[15] The 2007 Energy White Paper estimated that the UK will need around 30–35GW of new electricity generation capacity (equal to more than a third of current capacity) over the next two decades, and around two-thirds of in the next ten years.

CAT estimates that it is possible for us to reduce our energy demands by over 55% through the energy-efficiency retrofitting of homes, offices and industrial premises to maintain more heat in buildings, and by improving transport systems through changes in technology and use.[16] However, even after such a large decrease of total energy demand on current levels, electricity demand will roughly double compared to current demand because of partial electrification in the transport and heat sectors. If this is also to be carbon neutral the need for the dramatic expansion of electricity generation from renewable sources is even more urgent. CAT proposes a mix of zero carbon generation technologies which will be able to produce 842 TWh,[17] which the authors of *One Million Climate Jobs* estimate will create 425,000 jobs.[18]

However, there are a number of problems to be resolved before this generation capacity is put in place and those jobs created. The most important of these are the lack of production capacity, the shortage of skilled mechanical and design engineers and craftspeople and the lack of any strategic programme of research and development.

Engineering and manufacturing based industries are going to be at the core of delivering the equipment, technology and transport needed to the programme outlined above. However, over the last 30 years, the British economy has been increasingly dominated by the finance and service sectors, at the expense of the engineering and manufacturing sector. During the Thatcher and Major years, manufacturing capacity slowly declined from 25% to around 22%. Over the Blair and Brown years, this decline accelerated and today the

---

14	DECC's estimate of 2008 tax income
15	Carbon Trust & LEK Consulting, 2006
16	CAT, op. cit.
17	CAT, op.cit.
18	One Million Climate Jobs, op.cit.

sector now accounts for between 12% and 15% of GDP. However, even with this reduced capacity the UK manufacturing sector is still the world's sixth largest by output, still produces 55% of all exports, funds over 75% of all research and development, and directly employs over three million people.[19]

The IMEE, in a paper discussing the currently planned development of offshore wind power capacity (a relatively modest 32GW of new offshore capacity by 2020), says that 'the UK does not have sufficient numbers of qualified personnel for the development, assembly, operation or maintenance of this emerging offshore technology'.[20] While it says that 'the UK has a substantial heritage in engineering and marine excellence to draw on' it warns that 'to create a big enough pool of skilled workers in the UK to meet the emerging demand, will require support for engineering education at all levels, together with training and apprenticeship schemes'.

Given that the conditions in the seas around Britain are among the best in the world for the production of wind and wave generated electricity, it is absurd to the point of criminality that there is very little wind or wave generator manufacturing capability located in Britain, and that that which does exist is largely owned by large Danish and German companies. Even though the manufacturing and engineering sector (particularly at its 'heavy' end) has been significantly eroded and starved of resources for R&D for much apart from military related production, it has the potential to develop the production capacity and skilled workforce that will be needed - if there is the political will and sufficient funding.

For example, the sustainable renewal of the steel industry will need to be at the heart of a sustainable and socially useful engineering and manufacturing sector. The British steel industry specialises in high quality steel, including that designed for the manufacture of wind turbines. However, it has been in steady decline since its privatisation in 1988. The largest producer, Tata (formerly Corus) has closed or mothballed much of its capacity in Britain since January 2009, with a loss of more than 2,500 jobs. The development of wind power in Britain has the potential to ease the decline of the industry in the medium-term and, over the long-term, it has the potential to contribute to its growth as we export our technology.

While the steel making process currently generates vast amounts of CO_2, research is currently taking place under the aegis of the ULCOS (Ultra–Low Carbon dioxide Steelmaking) programme with the aim of more than halving the levels of CO_2 generated by the manufacturing process. To rapidly scale up this work to an industrial

---

19   IMEE, Engineered in Britain, 2010
20   IMEE, UK Offshore Wind Round 3, 2010

scale will require major R&D resources and process re-engineering on a vast scale, and if we are to develop a sustainable industrial base similar R&D and reinvestment programmes are likely to be needed in many other areas of manufacturing, such as glass and chemical engineering. Investment on such a level will require direct public funding and such funding will require levels of democratic public accountability that can only be guaranteed by public ownership.

The development of such a manufacturing base, along with that required to design and build a whole new distribution system, would, as well as giving us a sustainable zero carbon electricity supply, at a very conservative estimate generate at least 450,000 new jobs in manufacturing and civil and electrical engineering.

Transport

If we include, as we should, the British contribution to shipping and international aviation, transport in Britain currently creates 173 million tonnes of CO_2 a year.[21] Transport accounts for 24% of domestic emissions and while, since 1990, emissions from other sectors have gone down (by modest amounts) those from transport have gone up by 11%. Even as other sectors start, or continue to decarbonise, transport demand is predicted to continue to grow; with vehicle miles forecast to increase by 28% between 2003 and 2025 and air passengers increasing on 2007 levels by 200% by 2030.[22]

There are three ways in which the issue of lowering these emissions can be addressed; first, through better land use planning and redesigning the urban environment, so that less transportation is needed. Second, by a progressive move from oil to (renewably generated) electricity as the major transport fuel. Third, a major shift in the balance between transport modes from cars to public transport. All three have major implications for our industrial strategy.

Motor vehicle traffic volume in 2009 was 313.2 billion vehicle miles. Road transport makes up around 90 per cent of all domestic transport emissions with car travel accounting for just over half and heavy goods vehicle and light van traffic accounting for just under a third. While cars, vans and taxis account for over six times as many passenger miles as public transport (buses, coaches, rail and light rail) they generate thirteen times the emissions.[23] It is therefore clearly essential to undertake a massive development of public

---

21 Department for Transport (DfT), 2008
22 DfT, 2009
23 DfT, Transport Statistics Great Britain, 2010

transport capacity and quality in order to enable a rapid shift from cars to buses, trams and trains.

Around 450,000 people are currently employed directly or indirectly by the 'sustainable transport sector' (public transport plus bicycles).[24] According to the authors of *One Million Climate Jobs*, this figure could be increased to around 800,000 if the modal shift recommended by CAT[25] were adopted. This figure is probably quite conservative, because by their nature, bus/coach and train and rail infrastructure construction tend to be much more labour intensive than car and van production. The creation of 100 direct rail jobs supports 140 indirect jobs, compared with 100 direct motor industry jobs which create 48 indirect jobs. Research into transport investment in America suggests that investing in public transport creates twice as many jobs than investing in roads.[26]

This modal shift would see train travel double, from 7% of miles travelled to 14%, coaches increase their share from under 1% to 10%, local buses and trams increase from just below 4% to 5%, while cars, vans and taxis would decline from 80.% to 54% (with most vehicles being fully or partly electrically powered). It could also see transport CO_2 emissions reduce from the current level of 174 million tonnes p.a. to around 35 million tonnes.

But such a modal shift will require a massive increase in transport and related infrastructure manufacture and maintenance that is quite beyond the current capacity the British motor and locomotive industries. Our domestic capacity to produce the buses, coaches, locomotives and rolling stock we will need, has been shrunk to the point of near invisibility. Alexander Dennis Ltd (ADL) is Britain's biggest bus and coach manufacturer, but with a workforce of only 1,400, is hardly a giant. At least, for what it is worth, Dennis is a British based company; the only remaining train manufacturing in Britain is carried out at the Derby Carriage and Wagon Works, which is currently owned by Bombardier of Canada.

In order to meet the needs of a socially and environmentally sustainable public transport system that meets the needs and aspirations of most ordinary people, it will be necessary to completely reorient and rejig the existing motor vehicle industry in much the same way as the US motor industry was by the Roosevelt administration when the USA entered World War 2. There will be two main drivers to this process; first, the need to move from petrol and diesel powered technologies to emerging electricity based ones and

---

24   Ekosgen for the Campaign for Better Transport et al, *Employment in Sustainable Transport*, 2010
25   CAT, op.cit.
26   Campaign for Better Transport, 2010

second, the need to run down car and van production and expand bus, coach and light and heavy rail vehicle production. Such a radical shift in resources and direction is inconceivable without direct public intervention, both in terms of investment and direction - in other words, public ownership.

In addition, it is inconceivable that the current shambolic and fragmented provision of public transport could be reorganised and dramatically expanded on the basis of the current pattern of ownership. There is complete consensus on the left that the railway system must be brought back into full public ownership, but public ownership of bus and coach services, whether on a municipal, regional or national basis - or, most probably, a combination of the three - is also vital.

At the moment, private bus operators operate routes only where it suits them, or where the local authority can afford to pay them to run a non profitable route for 'social' reasons.[27] Similarly, coach operators only deliver the long distance routes that suit them. A publicly owned and democratically controlled public transport system would not only be able to integrate its various transport modes into a seamless service but would be able to experiment with new and potentially more environmentally benign transport solutions.

For example, in 2006, the economist Alan Storkey suggested how coaches could be part of an integrated transport system, rather than the transport solution of last resort for poor people. His plan would see coach stations established at motorway and major trunk road intersections, linked to their urban and suburban hinterlands by metros and local buses, and a frequent service of long distance coaches running shuttle services between them on reserved motorway lanes. As he said at the Select Committee on Transport:[28]

> Each coach hoovers up a mile of car traffic at 60 mph assuming normal (not full) occupancy. They save road space by a factor of fifteen to twenty, simply by bringing people together and eliminating the space between vehicles. They cut fuel consumption by 80%, but because they cut the congestion and slowness of other vehicles this pushes up towards 90% or more, making them greener than any other possible form of transport. They can tackle congestion where it occurs, because coaches can be put where car traffic is heaviest, on motorways, orbitals and major trunk roads. Because they are smaller units than trains, with reasonable demand it is easy to push up frequency times and offer an on-off service. As the Oxford-London route shows, despite its disabilities, a frequent

---

27 Except in London, where Transport for London determines routes and contractors deliver them.
28 Alan Storkey, Memorandum to the Select Committee on Transport, 5 April 2006

on-off service increases demand fivefold or more, even though the full journey speed is little over 30mph.

What is needed to reform the coach system is a comfortable, fast, frequent network with congestion free transfers into the heavy centres of population. Orbital services round London on the M25, Birmingham and Manchester motorways are crucial.

Coach stations with platforms and flat entry, allowing easy and rapid transfers, need to be moved to motorway and major trunk road intersections. Clearly, this would allow rapid transfer to and from buses and coaches, without getting embroiled in city centre congestion, and would provide a true alternative to the car. Crucial, too, would be systems of coach priority, justified by their efficient use of road space, which would guarantee their journey speeds and reliability.

Compared with all other transport infrastructure, the capital costs of such a reform are remarkably low, because coach reform largely uses existing infrastructure, the road and motorway network, more efficiently by a factor of fifteen and most of the capital is going into vehicles. A full M25 coach and transfer system would possibly cost less than £1 billion.

Such a system could, perhaps, be a relatively cheap transitional system that could provide a practical substitute for medium and long distance car journeys during the two decades or more that will be needed to completely upgrade the rail network, yet it is clearly out of the question that such a bold national initiative could be planned or implemented on the basis of a privatised public transport system.

Construction

The design, construction, maintenance, refurbishment and management of our built environment is central to the achievement of a low carbon society. 27% of UK emissions arise from energy use in the home, while the heating, cooling and powering of non- domestic buildings accounts for an additional 17%.[29]

A nation-wide, street by street programme to retrofit all existing homes is needed, not just to minimise energy use by draught

---

29 DECC, Energy Consumption in the UK, 2009

proofing and insulating, but also, wherever possible, to install high renewable energy sources, such as solar thermal heating, ground source heat pumps and photovoltaic generators. It has been estimated that such a programme (accompanied by a switch over to renewably generated electricity for heating) would reduce greenhouse emissions generated by heating homes from 80 to 24 million tonnes, an overall cut of 70%, while creating at least 200,000 jobs.[30]

There are a total of 22.5 million houses and flats in England and Wales, 21.6 million of which are occupied. If houses last for an average of one hundred years, that means that it will be necessary to replace or radically refurbish 225,000 homes a year, just to maintain the current housing stock. However, not all houses are in the right places for the needs of our current population. Our growing and aging population is increasingly requiring changes in the housing type mix and over the course of the national refit programme some existing housing will prove to be of such poor quality or have such low potential for refurbishment to meet increasingly demanding building regulations, that in practice that percentage is likely to be closer to 1.5%, and the number of houses requiring replacement will be more like 300,000 a year. In addition, there are almost two million households on council housing waiting lists.[31] In order to clear those waiting lists over a twenty year period, an additional 100,000 homes a year will need to be built, giving a total new build/radical refurbishment target of 400,00 homes a year. In addition, it is likely that due to the needs of rising standards and changing use patterns, 50% of non domestic buildings will need to be replaced or totally refurbished over twenty years.[32]

The construction industry, as it is currently organised, is simply not capable of meeting that challenge. At the end of 2006, 1.85 million people worked in the construction industry and there was a chronic shortage of skilled building workers, but by the beginning of 2010 over 400,000 jobs had gone. The Construction Products Association reported a fall of 12% in construction activity in 2009 (the industry's worst decline in more than 35 years) and a 3% fall during the first quarter of 2010 (compared to the economy with 0.2% growth). It was anticipated that by the end of the 2010 the construction industry would have lost £16 billion of work in just three years.[33]

---

30   One Million Climate Jobs.
31   Department of Communities and Local Government, 2010
32   Kingspan Insulated Panels briefing, 2010
33   Editorial in *New Civil Engineer*, 2010

This pattern of boom and bust has been repeated endlessly over the years. As Owen Luder wrote when President of the Royal Institute of British Architects:

> If much has changed [over the last two centuries] some things have not. Bust always followed boom in the 1800s just as it does now. Building was, and still is, a barometer of the economy. The secret of success then, as now, is to be ahead of the growth and get out before the crash.[34]

The result of the construction industry being continually disrupted by sharp cyclical upturns and downturns is that though large, it is highly fragmented and short-termist, with many small under-capitalised and fundamentally unstable firms who are on the whole conservative in both their organisation and use of technology and frequently shoddy (or in some instances downright corrupt) in their business practices. For many years local authority Direct Labour Organisations, inefficient and badly managed and directed though many of them were, provided oases of proper training and regular employment. However, the demise of council house building and the privatisation of housing maintenance has seen a huge reduction in the numbers of DLOs the scale and range of work they undertake and the amount of training opportunities they provide for young people. In the areas of civil engineering and non domestic building construction where large firms like Atkins, McAlpine and Murphy operate, blacklisting of trade union activists is still practiced and the lump is widespread.

In order to undertake the huge building, rebuilding and refurbishment programme that is required it will be necessary for the industry to be able to offer proper training and jobs that offer security and a worthwhile career path. It will be necessary to disseminate and put into practice on a national scale those examples of good practice and innovative technology that can be found, both in Britain and (more frequently) elsewhere in Europe and further afield. And it will be necessary to develop, fund and implement a plan of action both nationally and locally that is democratically accountable to the people whose daily lives will be effected by it.

None of that will be possible in an atomised industry dominated by the continuous scramble for the next job by a multitude of small enterprises and the demands of a much smaller number of large players largely concerned with meeting the demands of property speculation of various kinds. It will be necessary to radically reorganise the industry and introduce a large measure of social enterprise in a range of forms, from the revival of DLOs to the

---

34   Powell, The British Building Industry Since 1800, 1996

establishment of community based environmental refurbishment co-operatives and the development of publicly owned regional and national specialist civil engineering and non domestic construction undertakings.

Research and Development

The lack of properly funded long term R&D in the construction sector is an ongoing scandal. The Building Research Establishment (BRE) was formerly a government owned and funded organisation which was established in 1921 to improve the quality of construction in Britain. It was privatised (by New Labour) in 1997 and is now, very much in tune with the Tories' 'big society' fraud, is owned by a charitable trust and funded by income from its commercial programmes, the BRE bookshop, contracted work, and by bidding for short term research funding. The Timber Research and Development Association (TRADA) is another important R&D organisation in a similar position. Clearly, organisations like BRE and TRADA must be removed from the private sector and properly funded on a long term basis in order to research and develop the low carbon construction technologies that we urgently need to put into practice.

Even worse, perhaps, is the almost complete neglect that R&D in such vital areas of low carbon technology as wave generation of electricity. The Western Approaches - the North Atlantic to the west of the Outer Hebrides, have the potential to generate up to 80 TWh - 15% to 20% of our current electricity consumption.[35] Yet despite the revolutionary 'Salter's Duck' device being developed in the seventies it wasn't until 2001 that the European Marine Energy Centre was established in the Orkneys and not until 2004 that an industrial scale trial that actually put electricity into the national grid went into operation. The National Renewable Energy Centre (NaREC) in Blyth, Northumberland, wasn't established until 2002 and is dramatically underfunded.

At the moment, there are seven Research Councils in Britain, which between them spend around £3 billion annually on funding academic research. These include the Engineering and Physical Sciences Research Council (EPSRC), the Biotechnology and Biological Sciences Research Council and the Science and Technology Facilities Council. Valuable though these institutions are, they are almost entirely concerned with academic research. Unlike many other

---

35 *Future Marine Energy*, The Carbon Trust, 2006

countries (including many, like Ghana, in the Third World) we have no proper Industrial Research Council.

A new body, a Low Carbon Technology Research Council, needs to be established. Such a body would be, like the other seven Research Councils, funded by central government but independent of it, with research strategy developed by a governing body made up of representatives of the sectoral industrial research units, universities and professional bodies that would be undertaking the research. It would need to be funded at the same sort of level as that of the EPSCR and the other big research councils - at least £450million to £500million a year.

Employment, training and redeployment

The programme of infrastructural investment outlined above would lead to a rapid expansion in key industrial sectors and a huge increase in available jobs - indeed, is likely to lead to local labour shortages and more generalised skill shortages in some sectors. At the same time, there would clearly have to be a run-down in other areas, leading to job losses and a consequent need to provide opportunities for redeployment or alternative employment. The ending of the dangerous and expensive farce of the British 'independent' nuclear deterrent is a *sine qua non* on the left, for example, but the closure of the nuclear weapons establishment at Aldermaston and the scrapping of the Navy's fleet of nuclear submarines would lead to several tens of thousands of redundancies in Scotland, Devon and Berkshire. Similarly, the run-down of nuclear power stations would, over a period of years, lead to the loss of highly skilled and relatively well paid jobs in parts of the country where no easy substitute sources of employment are currently available, such as Anglesey, Suffolk, Cumbria, Teesside, North Devon and Scotland. Even in sectors where significant growth could be expected, such as engineering manufacturing, there would probably be a localised run down in some areas, such as the car industry on Teesside and Merseyside and aerospace in Bristol and Derby, that would not be completely mirrored by expansion in new products and processes in those localities.

Disputes within the trade union movement leading to the temporary suspension of Plymouth Trades Council have already occurred over policy towards the Trident submarine fleet in the recent past, and it is clear that any plan for major industrial restructuring would have to deal with the real and legitimate concerns of those workers whose current livelihoods might be adversely affected by them.

Therefore, an iron clad commitment to guaranteed alternative employment and/or training for all affected workers with no loss of wages is essential. Such a commitment would have to include guarantees on the provision of satisfactory housing for redeployed workers, should they have to, or choose to, move away from their homes to take up new jobs.

In order to meet the twin challenges of skills shortages within rapidly growing industrial sectors and the urgent need to retrain workers redeployed from declining sectors, it will be necessary to completely overhaul the provision and organisation of industrial training and technical education.

In 1964, the Industrial Training Act was passed. The act had three objectives:

> to enable decisions on the scale of training to be better related to economic needs and technological developments; to improve the overall quality of industrial training and to establish minimum standards; and to spread the cost more fairly.[36]

The Act allowed the Minister of Labour to set up Industrial Training Boards (ITBs). Each was responsible for overseeing training in its industry, setting standards and providing advice to firms. Most importantly, each paid allowances to trainees that were financed via a compulsory levy on firms in its industry. This levy/grant system was designed to remedy the failure of the labour market to deliver sufficient skilled workers and to end the tendency of employers to poach skilled labour rather than invest in training.

Unfortunately, the Central Training Council that theoretically ran the system never had the power it needed, either to administer the government's training grants or to oversee the levy/grant system, and instead of radically reshaping British industrial training and technical education the ITBs simply consolidated extant training practices, particularly in apprenticeships, rather than becoming an opportunity to expand training into new areas and to broaden the apprenticeship system.

Despite their failure to challenge the failure of employers or the state (or, to some degree, the craft unions) to reorganise and properly invest in industrial training, in the eighties the ITBs were seen as being dangerous intrusions into the freedom of the market by Thatcher and almost all of them were abolished. The sole surviving

---

36   Ministry of Labour, Cmnd.1892, paras. 6-7, 1964

ITB, the Construction Industry Training Board (CITB) is a model of ineffectiveness.

It is clear that what is needed is an effective Central Training Council that would be capable of developing and implementing a national strategy. Such a CTC would have to be run by those who are the main actors in that strategy; democratically elected trade union representatives along with representatives of the colleges and their staff and those of the industries involved, (who would, with central government, be the funders of training) most probably representatives of sectoral industrial strategy boards or similar industrial co-ordinating bodies.

Not only has technical education (which should be seen as encompassing vocational or industrial training) long been undervalued and underfunded by the British state; it has always been seen by the ruling class as simply the process of giving hewers of wood and drawers of water those limited skills they need to carry out their allotted tasks. The culture of British class society is nowhere as apparent as in the distain shown for 'the rude mechanicals', for those who allegedly work with their hands rather than their brains, within the education system. We have to break down the division between 'brain work' and 'hand work, and part of how we do that is to break down the division between 'vocational' and 'non vocational' education. One contribution to doing that would be to guarantee free access to tertiary level education all

Planning and investment

The massive infrastructural investment programme sketched out above, along with a dramatic expansion of R&D and the renewal of our post 19 education and training system will be hugely expensive. It will also require a whole new way of planning what we do and how we do it, at national, regional, local and individual enterprise level. We will need to replace the current failed market mechanisms with a democratic planning system that has at its heart a recognition that it is ultimately accountable, not to banks or speculative financial institutions, not bureaucratic institutions like regional development corporations or regeneration partnerships, no matter how benevolent their intentions, but the people whose homes and jobs are involved at a local level and the local institutions that can be made to be democratically accountable to them.

It isn't possible to go into any detail in discussing the structures and processes of a democratic planning system, for to do that would require an article at least as long again as this and would involve looking at, among other examples, the great debate on socialist planning in Cuba led by Che Guevara in the sixties. Suffice it to say that planning processes would have to be democratic to a degree not seen before and that input into them would have to be shared at all levels, so that workers' representatives from individual enterprises or representatives of specific localities would have as much say as Ministers or their 'experts'.

One possible actor in a new democratic planning process might be the Industrial Strategy Board. Each industry or each significant sector of each industry could have a Strategy Board, which would be responsible for drawing up an action plan in conjunction with the Government and for regularly reporting on the plan's progress to the government, the workers in the enterprises concerned and the communities directly or indirectly affected by the plan. The boards might be made up of representatives from relevant government departments, from relevant research institutions and educational bodies, from elected representatives of relevant local communities and, most importantly, elected representatives of the workers in the industry concerned.

There is no doubt that rebuilding our society will be very expensive. The energy conservation and renewable energy development plan outlined in *The Green New Deal* has been costed at between £50billion and £70 billion a year and the additional programme proposed above would add between £40 billion and £60 billion a year to that, so we are talking about finding something like £110 billion, or around 5.5% of GDP.

Increasing government borrowing by a mere 5.5% of GDP doesn't sound like too big a deal. However to try to fund a significant part of that 110 billion pound by extra borrowing would be an extraordinarily difficult task for a socialist government seeking to dramatically redistribute power and wealth. Therefore, we would need to look to funding the programme from our own resources.

Taken together, the Green New Deal Group estimate that more than £100 billion a year is lost at present because of abuse of loopholes in the tax system, tax bills remaining unpaid and from illegal non-payment of tax.[37] The social democratic pressure group Compass has suggested that measures could include: abolishing the domicile rule; abolishing tax havens; taxing investment income equally to income earned through labour; introducing a new wealth tax for all those earning over £250,000; introducing a new tax on bonuses; adopting a general anti-avoidance rule; removing secrecy from all British-controlled tax havens and increasing the number of tax inspectors to allow more thorough investigation.

---

37   The Green New Deal Group, *The Great Tax Parachute*, 2010

There are a number of modest and straightforward ways by which the government could both make tax fairer and increase the tax take. First, the government could raise nearly £24 billion a year by introducing new tax bands of 50% on incomes above £100,000, 65% above £250,000, 75% above £500,000 and abolishing the national insurance cap so that contributions are paid at 11% all the way up the income ladder. Cutting major road building programmes (we would need the resources for the infrastructural renewal programme anyway) would save £3 billion a year and cutting Trident, along with other defence cuts, would save around £5.5 billion a year. In addition, Air Passenger Duty could be substantially increased and would generate an additional £9 billion annually.

In June 2010, Greg Philo suggested a very elegant way of both attacking inequality and generating income for social and economic reconstruction. He wrote:

> The total personal wealth in the UK is £9,000billion, a sum that dwarfs the national debt. It is mostly concentrated at the top, so the richest 10% own £4,000bn, with an average per household of £4million. The bottom half of our society own just 9%. The wealthiest hold the bulk of their money in property or pensions, and some in financial assets and objects such antiques and paintings.
>
> A one-off tax of just 20% on the wealth of this group would pay the national debt and dramatically reduce the deficit, since interest payments on the debt are a large part of government spending. So that is what should be done. This tax of 20%, graduated so the very richest paid the most, would raise £800billion. A major positive for this scheme is that the tax would not have to be immediately paid. The richest 10% have only to assume liability for their small part of the debt. They can pay a low rate of interest on it and if they wish make it a charge on their property when they die. It would be akin to a student loan for the rich.[38]

Unlike Britain, where the state retirement pension is funded on a year to year basis solely by tax receipts, most European countries have established some sort of ring fenced fund which builds up over time. In Ireland there is a National Pension Reserve Fund. Under the agreement with the EU and the IMF signed by the previous Fianna Fail government, part of this would be used to underwrite the massive bailout received by the Irish banks. Sinn Fein, on the other hand, has advocated committing €7 billion of the Reserve Fund to a jobs stimulus package.

---

38   Greg Philo, *The Guardian*, August 2010

When its oil and gas fields in the North Sea first began to be exploited over thirty years ago, Norway established the *Oljefondet,* a fund to underpin its state pension scheme, and all the government income from the oil and gas fields went into it. It is now worth $325 billion and is the second largest pension fund in the world. Since 1998 the Norwegian fund has been allowed to invest up to 40% of its portfolio in the international stock market. It is forecast that the fund will reach $681 billion by the end of 2014.

If National Insurance payments were channelled into a similar national pension and investment fund in Britain, which would, over a period of time, incorporate existing state and private occupational pensions, it would both provide the necessary financial underpinning for a new universal SERPS (State Earnings-Related Pension Scheme) and provide the funding for direct public investment programmes. Through this vehicle we could invest in both necessary public works and our green industrial revolution, building the new, low carbon manufacturing base that is the vital prerequisite for a socially just low carbon economy. If a British National Pension and Investment Fund was to avoid the route that the Norwegian scheme has taken and invested solely in the development and acquisition of industrial enterprises in Britain it would generate the bulk of funding for the desperately needed extensions of public ownership and provide a solid base for public enterprise and endogenous social and industrial development.

If we are to free ourselves from the three interconnected threats to the future of humanity - the anarchic brutality of globalised capitalism, dependence on a shrinking supply of oil and gas and a warming world which threatens destructive and unpredictable climate change - there will have to be revolutionary change to society and how it is organised. As part of that wider change, we need a new industrial revolution; a revolution which will see low carbon technology powering the development of production for social good rather than for capital accumulation. We should be starting to model it now.

MARXISM AND THE CRISIS

John Rees

Every economic crisis has its own peculiarities. No individual crisis conforms exactly to our general theory. Specific work is necessary to comprehend the pattern of each crisis. The left's analysis of the crisis has much strength but in some important respects it has failed to chart accurately the shape of this crisis as it has emerged.

If this were a shallow crisis perhaps this would be no more than regrettable. Weaknesses could be addressed over time without much harm being sustained. But this is not, as everyone now agrees, a shallow crisis. It is the most serious crisis of our lifetimes even if it does not, as many think it will, become a double-dip recession.

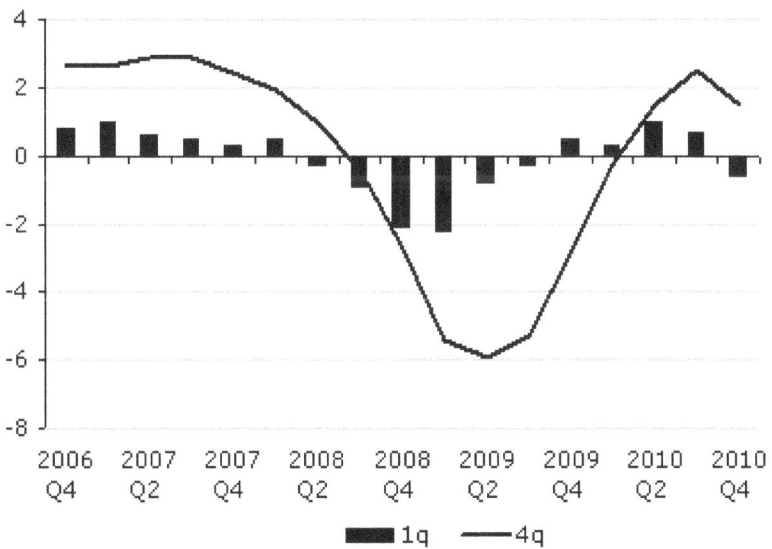

ONS: Real GDP quarterly growth in the UK

Mistaking important aspects of the crisis will have immediate and possibly long-lasting consequences. So it is important that we swiftly identify those elements of our analysis that are wrong and correct them. This short article aims to contribute to that discussion.

Use and abuse of the falling rate of profit

What is the purpose of the theory of the falling rate of profit in Marx's political economy? The main purpose of the theory is to demonstrate why, over time, the capitalist system is not a self-correcting mechanism. Its point is to show why economic crises are endemic but cannot restore the viability of the system.

If there were no such thing as the falling rate of profit the defenders of the capitalist system could argue that however regrettable the damage caused by slumps might be they restore the conditions of economic growth. They could then claim that over time the system is progressive since although the cathartic moments of crisis are unfortunate they lead to renewed periods of growth. There would be no reason why the system could not go on forever simply passing through phases of expansion and contraction.

What the theory of the falling rate of profit points out is that this rosy picture is false. The falling rate of profit means that the system finds it more and more difficult to cleanse itself through crises. It underlines the fact that the measures that must be taken in order to accomplish this cleansing are ***increasingly*** damaging and destructive. The most obvious of these is the attempt to drive down the cost of labour power in order to raise the level of profit. But this is not the only aspect of the law. Marx's law also outlined the various counter-acting tendencies that worked to restore the rate of profit.

Marx was adamant that the tendency of the rate of profit and the counteracting influences be treated as a single process and that a long historical timescale was necessary in order to judge their effects. As he wrote in *Capital Vol. III*:

> We have thus seen in a general way that the same influences which produce a tendency in the general rate of profit to fall, also call forth counter-effects, which hamper, retard, and partly paralyse this fall. The latter do not do away with the law, but impair its effect. Otherwise, it would not be the fall of the general rate of profit, but rather its relative slowness, that would be incomprehensible. Thus, the law acts only as a tendency. And it is only under certain circumstances and only after long periods that its effects become strikingly pronounced.[1]

---

1   K Marx, *Capital, Vol. III* (London, 1954) p.239.

It follows that we should not treat the question of the increasing cost exacted by the system for restoring its profitability as simply one which refers to the depth of each *slump*. Other methods that the system has developed for dealing with the decline in the rate of profit, for instance the permanent arms economy that underpinned the long post war boom can be as destructive as a slump but in ways which are social, political and imperial as well as narrowly economic.

The operation of the falling rate of profit and the measures taken to offset it can therefore tell us about the long-term tendencies in the system, its historic limits. It can, at a closer level of analysis, also tell us about the nature of whole phases of capitalist development the post war boom, for instance. What it cannot tell us is why a particular slump is more serious than the one which preceded it. For this purpose a much closer, more specific and more mediated analysis is necessary.

Trotsky applied this approach in his writings on booms and slumps in the 1920s. These articles are often treated as if the only point that Trotsky was making was that crises do not necessarily have a radicalising effect on workers. This certainly an important point, but it is not the only important point that Trotsky makes. Crucially he outlined two broad considerations that are vital in understanding the relationship between the longer term phases of capitalist development and the pattern of booms and slumps.[2]

First, following Marx, he argued that we have to look at the boom and bust cycle against the longer term background of capitalist development. Second, Trotsky argued that we have to look at the economic crisis in a wider political framework. We have to look at the way in which imperialism, the crisis in the governmental system, party politics and, crucially, the consciousness and combativity of the working class all interact with economic downturns. We can think of the recession as a beam of light and the political conditions with which it interacts as a prism. The same beam of light can be refracted in very different ways depending on the kind of prism it hits.

Trotsky looked first at the relationship between the broader phase of capitalist development and individual recessions. Trotsky compared the economic upswing that he was analysing in the early 1920s with the upswing analysed by Karl Marx and Frederick Engels in the aftermath of the 1848 revolutions across Europe. In the 1850s the upswing marked the beginning of a prolonged period of capitalist

---

2 For Trotsky's views see:
http://www.marxists.org/archive/trotsky/1924/ffyci-1/ch19b.htm, and
www.marxists.org/archive/trotsky/1924/ffyci-2/06.htm, and
www.marxists.org/archive/trotsky/germany/1932/320914.htm

expansion – "an entire epoch of capitalist prosperity which lasted till 1873", as Trotsky described it.

But, he added, the period after the Russian Revolution and the First World War was a period of capitalist decline in which "upswings can only be of a superficial... character, while crises become more and more prolonged and deeper going". Trotsky's general point was this:

> The movement of economic development is characterised by two curves of a different order. The first and basic curve denotes the general growth of the productive forces...
> On the whole, this curve moves upward through the entire development of capitalism. This basic curve, however, rises upward unevenly. There are decades when it rises only by a hair's breadth, then follow other decades when it swings steeply upward... In other words, history knows of epochs of swift as well as more gradual growth of the productive forces.

Trotsky argued that the second curve showing the boom and bust cycle must be "superimposed" on this first curve if we are to correctly understand the likely impact of an economic crisis.

Trotsky's analysis makes clear why the transition from boom to bust needs an analysis in a different register to the falling rate of profit. Crises tend to cleanse the system of its immediate crisis of profitability; they temporarily restore the conditions for profitable investment, as Marx makes clear in *Capital Vol. III*. But an individual crisis is not **caused by** the declining rate of profit in an immediate sense.

An analysis based on the theory of the declining rate of profit can tell us whether we are in a period of generally more severe crises (as we have been since the 1970s) or of less severe crises (as we were during the long boom). But it cannot be used in a mechanical and immediate way to explain why this particular crisis is just so deep or not so deep. This is for two reasons. Firstly the theory of the rate of profit has to be understood in all its complexity. Marx discussed the general abstract tendency to depress rates of profit as a result of the rising organic composition of capital (dead labour replaces living labour and this depresses the rate of profit because living labour is the only source of surplus value).

But the law also contained a discussion of the countervailing tendencies ~ the ways in which the system attempts to mitigate this downward pressure on profit. Crises were one such mechanism because they destroy capital and restore the rate of profit. But so, Marx argued, was financial speculation and colonial expansion. Building on an insight by Tony Cliff, Mike Kidron developed the

Permanent Arms Economy theory to explain how arms production can under certain historical conditions also have this effect.³

So it is obvious that we should not treat this approach as a general law which then has certain 'exceptions'. Something like the permanent arms economy that lasts for 30 years and defines a whole imperial epoch can hardly be described as an 'exception'. These are parts of the law not exceptions to it. This is how the system works and the 'exceptions' are the normal malignant functioning of the system, as much part of its inhumanity and destructiveness as economic crises.

What is necessary is to examine for each era how the whole law, the tendency of the rate of profit to decline and the tendencies that the system develops to deal with this pressure, define the political economy of that epoch. It is a mechanical, reductionist and economistic reading of Marx to diminish his **political** economy to mere 'economics' by attempting to simply read the movement of the business cycle from the declining rate of profit and to fail to use the broader conceptual framework that Marx gave us to describe the economic, social, political and imperial dimensions of the crisis.

Secondly the immediate oscillations of the business cycle are determined by causes other than the falling rate of profit: the shortage of labour and the overproduction of commodities at the peak of the cycle and by the opposite at the pit of the cycle. The precise factors governing the severity of any particular slump must be examined specifically in order to explain the depth and nature of each crisis and cannot be simply read-off from the general tendency of the rate of profit to fall.

Some current defences of Marx's theory are too narrow. They refer to some of the countervailing tendencies but they do not make them central to our analysis. Repeated references to the general tendency of the rate of profit to fall as a direct cause of this economic crisis are a mistake -a bit like referring to the law of gravity to explain why this particular apple fell from this specific tree at this precise moment. At the very least we need to know about a few other things: the season of the year, the ripeness of the apple, the force of the wind, the age of the tree and so on. If we rely too much on (at the right level perfectly correct) generalities we end up explaining everything...and nothing. If the rate of profit has been falling since the 1970s why is it this crisis, rather than the crisis of 2001 for instance, that has been the deepest for a generation?

---

3   Michael Kidron, *Western Capitalism since the War* (London, 1970), Michael Kidron, *Capitalism and Theory* (London, 1974).

Let us look at two factors that Marx analyses as counteracting tendencies to the fall in the rate of profit which have both postponed a more serious crisis since the 1980s and prepared the depth of the crisis which is now upon us. The first is speculation, including financial speculation. Marx argues:

> If the rate of profit falls, ...there appears swindling and a general promotion of swindling by recourse to frenzied ventures with new methods of production, new investments of capital, new adventures, all for the sake of securing a shred of extra profit which is independent of the general average and rises above it.[4]

The second, says Marx, is foreign trade:

> ...foreign trade develops the capitalist mode of production in the home country, which implies the decrease of variable capital in relation to constant, and, on the other hand, causes overproduction in respect to foreign markets, so that in the long run it again has an opposite effect.[5]

In modern parlance Marx is pointing to the effects of financialisation, globalisation and imperialism. It is to the credit of some Marxists, like Costas Lapavitsas and John Bellamy Foster for instance, that they have been tracking the effects of financialisation[6]. But we need more work that also ties in the imperial dimensions of the crisis. Marx himself was clear that when it comes to the conflict over how the crisis will be resolved and exactly whose capital will be destroyed, this will be a struggle involving political power as well as economic strength:

> How is this conflict settled and the conditions restored which correspond to the 'sound' operation of capitalist production? The mode of settlement is already indicated in the very emergence of the conflict whose settlement is under discussion. It implies the withdrawal and even the partial destruction of capital... Although, as the description of this conflict shows, the loss is by no means equally distributed among individual capitals, its distribution being rather decided through a competitive struggle in which the loss is distributed in very different proportions and forms, depending on special advantages or previously captured positions, so that one capital is left unused, another is destroyed, and a third suffers but a relative loss, or is just temporarily depreciated, etc..[7]

---

4   K Marx, *Capital Vol. III*, p.259.
5   Ibid. p239.
6   See, for instance, John Bellamy Foster and Fred Magdoff, *The Great Financial Crisis, Causes and Consequences* (New York, 2009).
7   K Marx, *Capital Vol. III*, p253.

From re-visiting Marx's original account of the falling rate of profit we can see that its effects are cumulative *and* result in the periodic destruction of capital values, which then restores the rate of profit by lowering the ratio of fixed to variable capital once more. The point about seeing the law as a whole is that this can either be done by an economic crisis (bankruptcies, slashing the value of capital, cheapening capital goods) or by war (physical destruction of capital) or by waste production (arms production in the case of Permanent Arms Economy) which diverts capital that would otherwise lower the rate of profit into non-productive use. One of the ways the system ages is that the methods of destroying capital become increasingly malignant, increasingly 'political' as well as purely economic. This is one sense in which the crises in the system get 'worse' as it ages.

Thus the effect of the falling rate of profit is cumulative but not in a narrowly economic sense (i.e. the slumps are always deeper) since the long boom shows that this is not true. But the overall cost of maintaining profitability (slumps, plus waste production, plus war) does increase over time. This then leads us back to a conjunctural analysis of a period of crisis when the economic cost, the waste factor and the imperial register coincide in a malignant form (unlike the Cold War when they, arguably, coincided in a less explosive form for the system).

Confusion over the role of state spending

The left's attempts to explain the nature of the current crisis have been hamstrung by an inability to describe whether or not the state has the power to mitigate the crisis by essentially Keynesian methods. Even *International Socialism* argued:

> The increased importance of state expenditures—and the willingness of central banks and government to spend rapidly in trying to cope with the crisis—means there is a base level of demand in the economy which provides a floor below which the economy will not sink, which was not the case in the early 1930s'.[8]

---

8   C Harman 'The Slump of the 1930s and the Crisis Today' *International Socialism 121*, p37.

If this were true, however, a Keynesian solution to the crisis would be viable. Marxists wish to reject this conclusion. So the article goes on to say:

> But there is an important second difference that operates in the opposite direction. The major financial and industrial corporations operate on a much greater scale than in the inter-war years and therefore the strain on governments of bailing them out is disproportionately larger.[9]

So should we then conclude that, although the state has more resources to deal with the crisis, this will ultimately be unsuccessful because the size of the units of capital is so great that even the increased resources of the state will not be enough to save them? Apparently not, otherwise what would be the meaning of the phrase in the first quotation which says "there is a base level of demand in the economy which provides a floor below which the economy will not sink". And the figures given for the share of state spending in national wealth indicate that even though corporations are larger, state spending is larger still. In the end, in spite of these figures, the analysis in the *International Socialism* concludes:

> For the moment all we can do is extend the 'bail out' metaphor: the pails being used are bigger than ever in the past but the pool of debt they have to dispose of is also much deeper.[10]

On the one hand the state has great resources to mitigate the crisis, on the other hand the crisis is very deep...but then again the state has great resources...but then again the crisis is very deep! This is an explanation which is no explanation at all. Keynesianism might work...or it might not! It is this confusion which led *Socialist Review* to argue in 2008 that:

> The response of capitalist governments and their central banks has been to look for some desperate ploy to keep borrowing going. One way to do so is to cut interest rates so as virtually to give money to the banks to lend to people... Another way is to increase government borrowing...". "It is just possible", the argument ran, that despite the difficulties for the capitalist governments, "that such measures will defer the crisis, as they did at the end of the 1980s and 1990s. But they will not be able to do more than that.[11]

---

9   Ibid.
10 Ibid, p45.
11 *Socialist Review*, February 2008.

In fact the crisis was not deferred at all but rapidly deepened. The problem here lies in seeing the crisis as mainly 'economic' and the state as its possible 'saviour'. In fact the crisis is both economic and political. It engulfs both the economy and the state. And the state itself is both an economic and political entity. The left's analysis of the crisis would be stronger if we centred it on the fact that any really deep crisis must become a crisis for the state as well as an economic event.

This is true in two senses. It must become a crisis for the state because the scale of intervention required can threaten to undermine the stability of the state economically. This has subsequently made clear by the collapse in Iceland and the depth of the crisis engulfing Ireland, Greece, Portugal and Spain. This crisis also threatens the current ideological defences of the state because it raises the issue of nationalisation.

The state is also threatened in a second sense by the increased tension between it and rival states during a severe recession. This has become clear in the increased tension between the US and China over both economic issues and political issues like climate change. Thus we should not see the crisis as primarily affecting the economy and then see the state as the force which can bail it out. We should see the crisis as one which effects both economy and state simultaneously, although differently.

Nothing however could have more dramatically demonstrated the linkages between the economic, political and imperial dimensions of the crisis than the explosion of revolution in the Arab world in 2011. Those revolutionary explosions in Tunisia, Egypt, Libya and elsewhere were of course in part a response to the world economic crisis. Tunisia's growth rate more than halved between 2008 and 2010. Egypt's growth rate collapsed by more than a third between 2009 and 2010. Economic demands were at the heart of opening phase of the Tunisian revolution and central to the strikes which both preceded the Egyptian revolution and re-emerged in the two days before Mubarak fell. But this is certainly not the whole story. Long term political discontent was also a central cause of the Arab revolutions. And the imperial dimension of politics can never be ignored, either as cause or consequence, in the Middle East. This explosion of revolutionary energy points us back to the fundamental elements of Marx's political economy: the long term interaction of economics and politics as the key causal relationship in any explanation of the current crisis.[12]

---

12   For a more detailed analysis see J Rees, *Imperialism and Resistance* (Routledge, 2006).

Strategic thinking

Some of these theoretical weaknesses are reflected in the recent lack of strategic thinking about what the left should be doing. After the Seattle demonstration of 1999 it was clear that although the recovery in the industrial struggle was slow, there was a political upturn. This was demonstrated by the rise of the anti-capitalist movement, the anti-war movement, activism around global warming and third world debt and active disillusion with Labourism. The correct strategy for revolutionaries was to use the tactic of the united front to build this resistance, carry socialist argument to a wider audience and, crucially, to use the growing political confidence of the class to lift its confidence in the industrial sphere. This was the origin of the idea of 'political trade unionism.'

The onset of the recession and the recent increase in struggles related to it show how correct this approach was and is. Many of the struggles against the recession have been as much political struggles as narrowly economic strikes. They have involved political issues, been motivated by political activists and have campaigned using the very same types of organisations as the political movements.

It would be strange then if at precisely this moment the left should choose to move away from this perspective. We need to stand back and take serious stock of where we are. The essential points are these:

- The political radicalisation that began in 1999 is, under the impact of the recession, spreading more widely throughout society and helping to lift the level of industrial resistance. There is a threat from the right, but it will only become dominant if the left fails to provide leadership on the central question of the recession.

- We need a wider theoretical debate so that our analysis of the crisis is broadened to effectively integrate the new dimensions of the economic crisis and its social and imperial dimensions into our analysis.

- Politics remains central. But this does not simply mean socialist propaganda, however valuable this is. It means a renewed commitment to united front work on political and economic issues.

- Imperialism, as the demonstrations over Gaza in January 2009, the continued crisis over Afghanistan and the outbreak of the Arab revolutions all show, is central to British politics. It will remain central to any notion of political trade unionism.

- The recession requires an initiative on a class wide, national basis which tries to involve the widest possible layers in the labour movement in generalising the resistance to the recession.

- Resistance will always be stronger if it is connected to an already existing nationally organised network of the kind that the Coalition of Resistance is attempting to build.

Such a network would provide a much wider audience for revolutionary ideas than can be obtained by propaganda means alone. The creation of such a network is the best possible guarantee that the recession will not pass the left by without there being any qualitative increase in its size. In the years ahead the creation of such a network is likely to be crucial in raising the level of working class resistance and building mass support for socialist politics in the face of the greatest crisis of world capitalism since the 1930s.

112

A FISCAL CRISIS OR A CRISIS OF DISTRIBUTION?

A transitional program for an alternative Europe

Özlem Onaran

Introduction

We are in a new episode of the global crisis: the struggle to distribute the costs of the crisis. This crisis has been an outcome of increased exploitation and inequality, since the late 1980s across the globe. Neoliberalism tried to solve the crisis of the golden age of capitalism via a major attack on labour. The outcome was a dramatic decline in labour's bargaining power and labour's share in income globally in the period since the 1980s. However, the decline in the labour share has been the source of a *potential realization crisis* for the system – one of the major sources of crisis in capitalism according to Marxian economics. The decline in the purchasing power of workers limited their potential to consume. Demand deficiency and financial deregulation reduced investments despite increasing profitability. Thus neoliberalism simply replaced the profit squeeze and over-accumulation crisis of the 1970s with the realization problem. Financialisation and debt-led consumption seemed to offer a short-term solution to this potential realization crisis. Since the summer of 2007 this solution has also collapsed. The crisis was tamed via major banking rescue packages and fiscal stimuli. Now the financial speculators and corporations are re-labelling the crisis as a "sovereign debt crisis" and pressurizing the governments in diverse countries ranging from Greece to Britain to cut spending to avoid taxes on their profits and wealth. The pressure on wages associated with budget cuts is great news for the corporations! However the push for public debt reduction is the biggest threat to recovery.

The realization crisis at the origin of the crisis based on wage suppression was deeply connected to global imbalances. In the European context, the wage suppression strategy and current account surpluses of Germany in particular created imbalances within Europe in the form of current account deficits, public or private debt in the periphery of the eurozone, in particular in Greece, Portugal, Spain, and Ireland or in Eastern Europe, in particular in Hungary, the Baltic States, Romania, and Bulgaria. The crisis laid bare the historical divergences within Europe, and led to a European crisis and a new stage in the global crisis. The limited policy framework, which is based on strict inflation targeting, and which lacks a common fiscal policy has failed to generate convergence within the EU in the first place. In countries of the periphery like Greece where both public debt and the budget deficit to GDP ratio are high and are coupled with a high current account deficit, the attack of the speculators asking for dramatically higher yields has brought the country to the edge of a sovereign debt crisis in 2010. Indeed before Greece, in 2009 Hungary, the Baltic States, and Romania were under attack. It looked as if the euro saved Slovakia and Slovenia from the turbulence in the currency markets, but their problem will be a permanent loss of international competitiveness as is unfortunately illustrated by the problems of the periphery of the eurozone. Initially Eastern Europe was seen the only problem zone in Europe. However, together with Greece, the attention of the speculators turned to the public debt and deficits in Portugal, Spain, Ireland, and then towards the core to Italy, Britain and Belgium.

The governments agreeing to the cuts are avoiding taxing the beneficiaries of neoliberal policies and the main creators of the crisis. The public debt would not be there, if it were not for the bank rescue packages, counter-cyclical fiscal stimuli, and the loss of tax revenues during the crisis. Finally, the crisis would not have happened without the major pro-capital redistribution and financialisation. Thus this is a crisis of distribution and a reversal of inequality at the expense of labour is the only real solution, which in turn needs to connect the demands for equality with an agenda for change beyond capitalism.

This chapter focuses on the crisis in Western Europe as another chapter in this book by Catherine Samary analyses the situation in

Eastern Europe. The rest of the chapter is structured as follows: Section two analyses the main pillars of neoliberalism and the road to the global crisis. Section three discusses the crisis in Western Europe in both the core and the periphery. Section four outlines the costs of the crisis. Section five concludes with a transitional program for an alternative Europe.

The crisis of the neoliberal era of capitalism

Neoliberal economic policies have been the answer of the capitalists to the crisis of the 1970s. Since the 1980s, the world economy has been guided by deregulation in labour, goods and financial markets at the domestic and international level. Since the 1990s, the transformation of the Soviet Union and Eastern Europe opened up new markets for consumption and a wide global reserve army of cheap labour and relieved the pressure on the welfare states of the West to maintain a certain living standard for the working masses. This has led to a decline in labour's bargaining power, and in the share of labour in national income since the early 1980s in not only the major capitalist economies but also the developing economies of Latin America, Asia, as well as Eastern Europe, who have all shared similar neoliberal policy guidelines.

The increase in globalization, in particular the mobility of capital, and the stagnation in aggregate demand and rise in unemployment have been the central factors behind this pro-capital redistribution of income. Furthermore as a result of the very high wages of the CEOs and other top managerial income earners, the share of high income groups in total labour income has increased dramatically at the expense of the rest of the wage earners in the last two decades. Thanks to increased rates of exploitation, profit rates had already recovered by the late 1990s or early 2000s in the US and in most EU countries back to the levels of the early 1970s (Figure 1). The profit rate has indeed recovered not only in the aggregate economy but also in the non-financial sector as well as in manufacturing, albeit at a lower degree in the latter due to intensive intra-capitalist competition. The recovery in the profit rate has been combined with both the decline in the wage share, i.e. higher rates of exploitation, and a lower investment rate out of profits in both the EU countries and the US.

Figure 1: Profit rate in different sectors (net returns on net capital stock.)

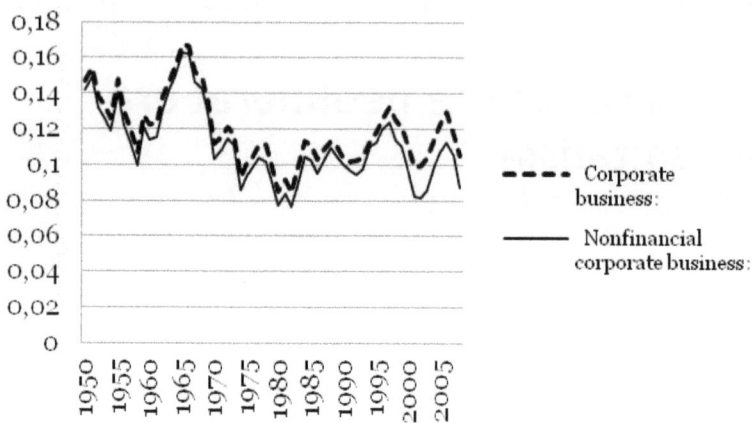

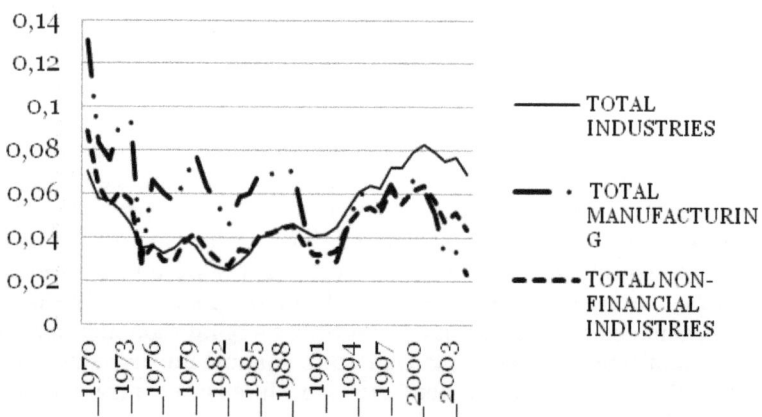

A fiscal crisis or a crisis of distribution? 117

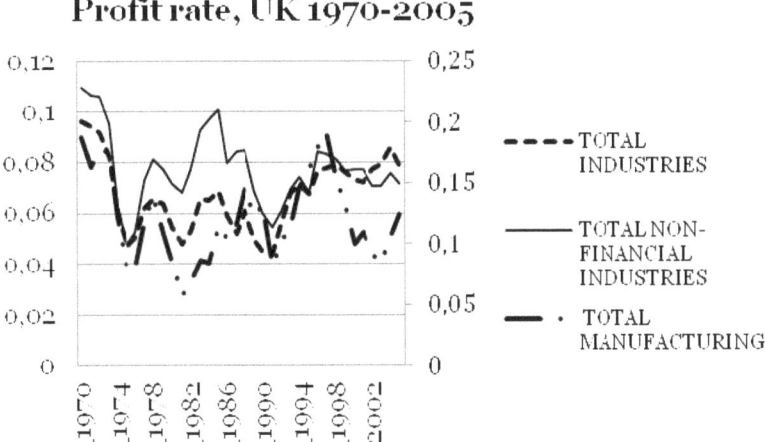

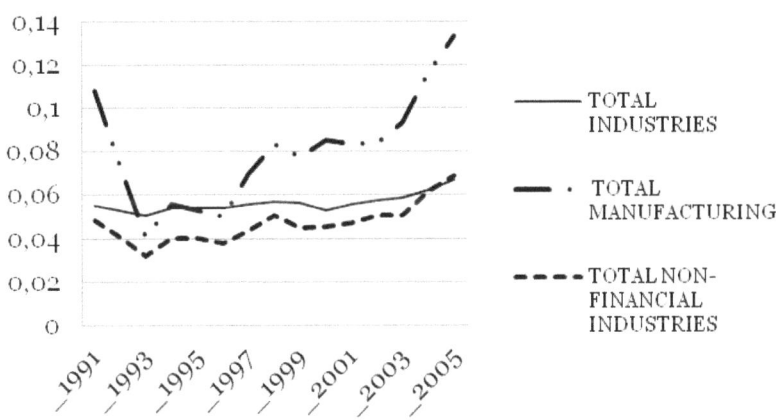

Source: Bureau of Economic Affairs for US, and EUKLEMS for Europe

Here lie the two important long term contradictions of the neoliberal era of capitalism. Firstly, the neoliberal era has generated higher profits for multinational firms, and especially for the financial sector. However, the high financial returns have replaced profits from real activity in many cases. As the finance dominated regime rose, the investment behaviour of firms was significantly affected by the rising shareholder value orientation. Lazonick and O'Sullivan (2000) argue that a shift in management behaviour from 'retain and reinvest' to 'downsize and distribute' has occurred. Financial market-oriented remuneration schemes based on short-term profitability increased the orientation of management towards shareholders' objectives. The unregulated financial markets and the pressure of financial market investors have created a bias in favour of asset purchases as opposed to asset creation. At the same time most of the effort of macroeconomic policy makers has been going to policies to retain the confidence of volatile financial markets. Markets have been deregulated mainly to support the interests of the rentier-capitalists. The same process has limited the demands of workers. In a way, the loss in labour's share has prevented the profits in the real sector from being eroded by increased interest payments. Consequently the relationship between profits and investment has changed; thus higher profits do not automatically lead to higher investment. The share of dividends and interest payments in profits increased substantially in the last two decades; thus retained profits for investment declined. In spite of higher profit rates and a boom-euphoric business environment, not only in the USA, but also in the major advanced capitalist economies (Germany, France and the UK), as well as some developing countries (e.g. Latin America, Turkey), economic growth rates have been well below their historical trends. In a deregulated financial environment, it would be irrational for the capitalists to give up the short term high profit options in financial speculation and engage in long term irreversible and uncertain physical investment. At this point it has to be emphasized that the reference point for the capitalists since the 1980s was not the profit rates of the early 1960s in manufacturing, which might be higher than currently, but was the high return offered by short-term financial assets. Thus, it is unconvincing to see this crisis as an outcome of a long-term declining trend in the profit rates due to an unavoidable rise in the organic composition of capital (as suggested by Choonara, 2009; Harman, 2009; Kliman, 2009) or increased international competition (as suggested by Brenner 2009).

Secondly the decline in the labour share has been a potential source of realization crisis for the system. Profits can only be realized, if there is sufficient effective demand for the goods and services. But the decline in the purchasing power of labour has a negative effect on consumption, given that the marginal propensity to consume out of profits is lower than that out of wages. This affects investments negatively, when they are already under the pressure of share holder value orientation.

Exactly at this point the financial innovations seemed to have offered a short-term solution to the crisis of neoliberalism in the 1990s: debt-led consumption growth. It is important to note that without the unequal income distribution the debt-led growth model would not have been necessary or possible. Particularly in the US, but also in UK, Ireland or even some continental European countries like Netherlands and Denmark household debt increased dramatically in the last decade. The increase in housing loans and house prices fuelled each other; then the increased housing wealth thanks to the housing bubble served as collateral for further credit, and fuelled consumption and growth and maintained high profit rates. This phase, despite growth rates lower than in the 1960s, deserves to be named as a new expansionary long wave with the peculiarity of profits without investment and growth without jobs and with an increased financial fragility. Financialisation leads to a debt-led growth by fuelling consumption in the short-run, but debt has to be serviced in the future. Because of high debt levels, the fragility of the economy to the possible shocks in the credit market also increases.

The deregulation in the financial markets and the consequent innovations in mortgage backed securities, collateralized debt obligations and credit default swaps facilitated the debt-led growth model. These innovations and the "originate and distribute" model of banking have multiplied the amount of the credit that the banks could extend given the limits of their capital. The premiums earned by the bankers, the commissions of the banks, the high CEO incomes thanks to high bank profits, the commissions of the rating agencies all created a perverse mechanism of investments that led to short-termism and ignorance about the risks of this banking model. In the short-run in the sub-prime credit segment, even if the risk of default were known, this was not perceived as a major issue: first, most of these credits were anyway sold to other investors in the form of mortgage backed securities with high ratings. Second, when there is a credit default, the houses, which serve as collateral, could be taken over and as long as the house prices kept increasing this was a profitable business for the creditor. However this approach to banking led to a very risky economic model and a time bomb, which was destined to explode eventually. The bad news from the sub-prime markets triggered the explosion eventually, and first the market for CDOs and then the interbank market, and finally the whole credit market collapsed at a global scale.

It is interesting to ask, why it took so long for the time bomb to explode. The reason is the endogenous evolution of expectations: as the debt-led growth model produced high short-term growth and profits, optimism was stimulated via a self-fulfilling prophecy, and risks were more and more underestimated even by those who were more conservative at the beginning. In a world of coerced competition (Crotty, 1993) even those who see the risks are forced to take risky positions, if they are to keep their jobs as dealers, bankers, or CEOs, since the burst of the bubble is a matter of time, and it can take longer than the short-term evaluation of the profits by the share holders, who fail to value more secure investment behaviour. Just a couple of weeks before the big collapse in July 2007, the ex-CEO of Citibank, Chuck Prince, had said "when the music stops, in terms of liquidity, things will be complicated. But as long as the music is playing, you've got to get up and dance" (Elliott, 2007). When the shock came, credit crunch and the collapse of the debt-led growth model was inevitable.

A more important explanation is the distributional aspect behind this risky model: the prevention of the crisis required the solution of the distributional problems behind the debt-led growth model, i.e. redistribution of income and wealth; however the powerful global elite, who have influence over global policy making through their nation states would not agree with this solution. Therefore the policy institutes hoped for a "soft-lending" that would correct the bubbles without effectively touching the distributional conflict.

From wage suppression to sovereign debt crisis in Europe

The mirror image of the debt-led consumption model was global imbalances and export-led growth strategy: the debt-led consumption model created a current account deficit in the US that exceeded 6% of the GDP. This deficit was financed by the surpluses of some other developed countries like Germany and Japan, developing countries like China and South Korea, and the oil rich Middle Eastern countries. In Germany and Japan the current account surpluses and the consequent capital outflows to the US were made possible by wage moderation, which has suppressed domestic consumption and fuelled exports. Thus this is again an outcome of the crisis of distribution. On the side of the developing countries like China and South Korea, the experience of the Asian and Latin American crises stimulated a policy of accumulation of foreign reserves as a bail-out guarantee against speculative capital outflows. Here the international dimension of inequality plays an important role: these countries, threatened by the free mobility and volatility of short term international financial flows, invested their current account surpluses in US government bonds instead of stimulating their domestic development plans. Similar imbalances took place within Europe between the surplus countries in the core and the periphery of Europe. The wage suppression strategy and current account surpluses of Germany were matched by current account deficits, public or private debt in countries like Britain and Italy in the core as well as Greece, Portugal, Spain, and Ireland in the periphery of the eurozone or in Eastern Europe.

At the root of the problem of these divergences within Europe is the neoliberal model that turned the periphery of Europe into markets for the core countries without any prospect of catching up. The lack of a sufficiently large European budget and significant fiscal transfers targeting productive investments in the periphery led to persistent differentials in productivity. Stability and Growth Pact as well as EU competition regulations limited the area for manoeuvre for the implementation of national industrial policy. In the absence of industrial policy and productive investments to boost productivity, and unable to devalue, the strategy of competitiveness was based mainly on wage moderation, and increased deregulation and precarisation in the labour markets, which further eroded labour's bargaining power throughout the EU. In Ireland the integration to the core took the form of attracting Foreign Direct Investment based on low wages; and consequently despite productivity booms in the 1990s, real wage increases remained much lower than productivity increases until the 2000s. Overall labour's share in income declined sharply in that period (see Figure 2).

The decline in the wage share does not reflect the full dimensions of increase in inequality in some countries. In both Ireland and Britain, the share of top 1% in total income (before tax) increased dramatically from the post-war low levels of 6-8% respectively to 10-13% as of 2000 (Atkinson and Piketty, 2007). While this is very similar to the trends in the US, in the other continental European countries, such a rise in top incomes did not take place or has been at a much more modest rate as in the case of Germany. Part of this increase is related to the hike in managerial wages, which makes the fall in the wage share look more modest than it is in reality for the majority of the wage earners.

Figure 2a and 2b: Adjusted wage share, selected western EU MS, 1960 – 2008 (compensation per employee as percentage of GDP at factor cost per person employed).

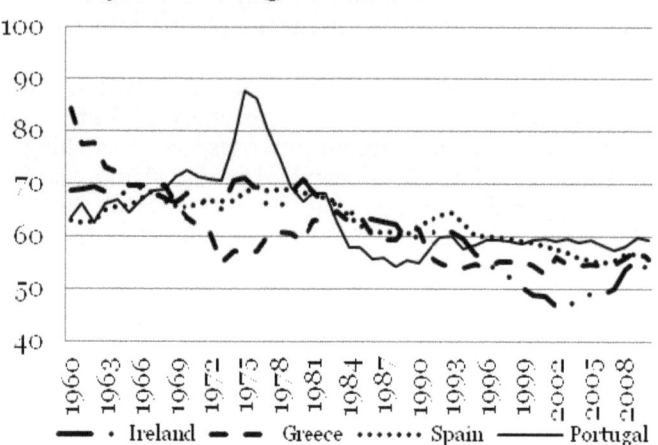

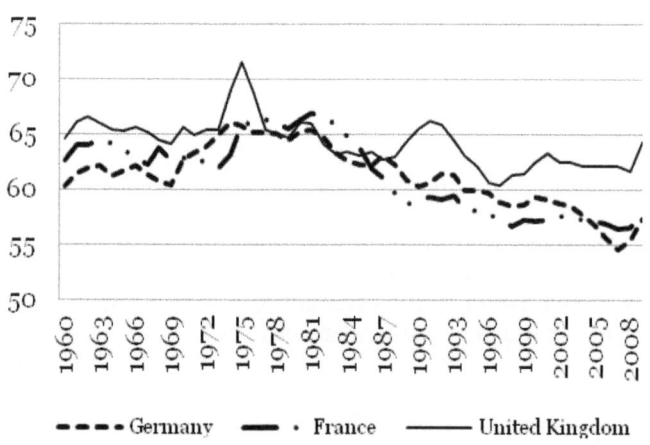

Source: AMECO, 2010 (Economic and Financial affairs, Annual Macroeconomic Indicators online database, updated in November 2010)

However, wage moderation also did not save the countries in the periphery of the eurozone, like Greece, Portugal, Ireland, Spain, since Germany was engaged in a much more aggressive wage and labour market policy: in the 1990s and 2000s productivity increases exceeded changes in real wages in all Western EU countries (except Portugal), with the gap being largest in Germany and Ireland (see Table 1). In Germany and Spain real wages even declined in the 2000s. Thus the gap between wages and productivity in Germany in the 2000s was due to real wage decline, and not necessarily high productivity. Moreover, in the periphery nominal labour costs have increased faster than in Germany due to a higher rate of inflation.

Table 1: Average annual % (compound) in real wages and productivity, 1997-2007

	France	Germany	United Kingdom	Greece	Ireland	Portugal	Spain
Real wages	1.09	0.48	1.91	1.56	1.98	2.00	0.19
Productivity	1.23	1.35	2.08	1.97	2.88	1.70	0.6

Real wages = Labour compensation/number of employees/private consumption price deflator. Productivity = GDP/number of employed persons

Source: OECD national Accounts, 2010, online database

The low investments despite a high profit share explain the stagnant productivity and low rates of GDP growth in Germany. The German case is also in striking contrast to France, where the gap between real wage and productivity growth is the smallest. France did not have Germany's export boom, but domestic demand and employment growth has been much stronger.

With weak domestic demand due to low wages, exports were the main source of growth in Germany, but this has been detrimental for the exports of the peripheral countries due to both loss of competitiveness and the contraction of domestic demand in Germany. Indeed Germany is like the China of Europe with a large current account surplus, high savings and low domestic demand. This neo-mercantilist policy has also been a model for some other countries like Austria and the Netherlands. In Spain, Greece, and Portugal consumption led by private debt has filled in the gap that low exports and high imports have created. In Ireland the effects of the core-periphery relationship have manifested themselves differently: Ireland has had a trade surplus but a current account deficit due to massive repatriation of profits by the Multinational Enterprises. A construction boom, real estate bubbles, and private debt have been a typical feature particularly in Spain and Ireland in maintaining growth and consumption in an era when wage share was falling.[1] In Greece and to a lesser extent Portugal a fiscal deficit also played a compensating role along with the debt of households and corporations. This is the background of the divergences between the periphery and the core in Europe, which has led to serious sovereign debt problems in the periphery.

There have been significant differences in the effects of the crisis in different European countries due to these divergences, which already existed prior to the crisis. In the core, Britain had a deep recession due to dependence on the financial sector, its own overextended banks, over-indebted private sector, and housing bubble, and GDP contracted by 6.4% peak to trough (between the first quarter of 2008 and the third quarter of 2009), and the recession has lasted longer than in Germany and France. The exposure of the domestic banks to the toxic assets in the US financial markets has been one of the earliest transmission mechanisms of the crisis to the other core European countries like Germany and France. Germany did not have a household debt problem, but has particularly suffered from the curse of its neo-mercantilist strategy of export based growth via wage dumping, as export markets shrank. From peak to trough (from 2008.Q1 to 2009.Q1) German GDP declined by 6.6%, while French GDP contracted by just 3.9% in the same period. Contrary to Germany, in France a better developed system of automatic stabilizers, a larger state sector and a better position in terms of income inequality made the conditions of the crisis more moderate at the onset, since the weakening of international demand was less important (Fitoussi and Saraceno, 2010).

In the periphery of Europe, Ireland, with its disproportionately large banking sector and the bust of its housing bubble has had the deepest recession. The contraction in Ireland's GDP has reached 14.3% from peak to trough (between 2007.Q4 and 2009.Q4). The recession also hit Spain hard with the collapse of the housing bubble and the consequent contraction in construction, and GDP has contracted by 4.9% from peak to trough (from 2008.Q1 to 2009.Q4). Most importantly the imbalances between the core and periphery of Europe, and the limited fiscal capacity of the periphery to tame the crisis evolved into a sovereign debt crisis in Greece followed by Ireland, Portugal, and Spain in 2010. As of the second quarter of 2010 (the latest available data), the recession in Greece was still deepening,

---

1   In Ireland, the wage share has recovered slightly during 2002-2007 from 46.6% to 50.1%; it nevertheless remained lower than its peak level of 71.2% in 1975.

and the economy has contracted by 5.7% compared to the peak in 2008.Q3. Ireland, Greece, and Spain are expected to end 2010 in a recession. The length of the recession has also been longer (7-8 quarters as of 2010.Q2) than in the core countries.

Following speculations about Greece's default and exit from the Euro, the eurozone governments' first decision came at the end of March 2010 after months of hesitation and worries about Germany's constitutional court, who could rule out any bailout as being against the EU treaties. As part of a package involving substantial IMF financing and a majority of European financing via coordinated bilateral loans, euro area member states declared their readiness to support Greece subject to strong conditionality based on an assessment by the European Commission and the ECB and at a penalty interest rate. In April 2010, as the IMF and the eurozone technocrats were bargaining over the conditions of the credit, the interest rate of two-year Greek government bonds increased to 19%; the cost of the Credit Default Swaps (CDS) for the Greek bonds was hiked as speculation about default spread; and Greek bonds were downgraded to junk status. The contagion started to threaten Spain and Portugal, whose bonds were also downgraded slightly; in Ireland the interest rates on bonds increased and eyes turned to the sovereign debt problem in the core countries like Italy, Belgium, Britain, and even the US. Worries also rose about the solvency of the private banks holding government bonds. Under pressure the initial amount of €30 billion turned out to be the first part of a larger 3-year bailout package of €110 billion. EU unveiled later in May a further surprise package of €500 billion to be supported by a €250 billion IMF facility to defend all eurozone countries. The eurozone governments are indeed protecting their own banks that are holding Greek bonds against a default; the bulk of the Greek bonds are held by German and French banks.

Germany, backed by the Netherlands, Austria, and Finland, all current account surplus countries, initially resisted the €750 billion package. Axel Weber, the Bundesbank president, did not hide his critique of the ECB's new decision. The package was pushed by France and the deficit countries like Spain, Italy, Portugal, and most importantly by the external intervention of the US with the fear of a second "Lehman Brothers" turning point in the global economy. Interestingly the information about Sarkozy's threat to leave the euro to stop Merkel's block was leaked to the press by the Spanish Prime Minister Zapatero's colleagues. Barroso, the head of the European Commission, is also pushing for moving the monetary union in the direction of a fiscal union. Life for Germany's ruling elite is not easy: Merkel's party lost in a local state election amid the Greek crisis. Her liberal coalition partner (the FDP) complains that transfers to imprudent eurozone members have a higher priority than tax cuts. The social democrats (the SPD) oppose the fact that banks are again being bailed out. The German technocracy is expressing its fears about fiscal federalism and the euro turning into a French Euro; the German media is spreading fears of inflation. However, one thing is clear: the eurozone's ruling elite is committed to defending the euro in ways which may also involve a creditor-led debt restructuring in order to avoid a possible debtor-led default. Obviously the plan here is to manage the orderly future repayment of debt via an acceptable hair cut for the creditors while still imposing austerity policies on working people.

Outside the eurozone, Britain is also troubled: it tried to stay out of the large defence scheme; however this proved to be premature after the attacks on the bond markets of Ireland. As a result of the involvement of the Banks in Britain in the Irish banking industry, British tax payers in Britain will finance up to £10 billion of the rescue package as a result of the government's attempts to bailout the Banks in Britain. This is in striking contrast to the cuts in spending in Britain. Financial regulation is another issue that Britain tries to resist to protect the City of London.

At the beginning of the crisis the ECB acted merely as a lender of last resort to the private European Banks, and did not fulfil the same function in the case of the eurozone governments during the initial phase of the sovereign debt crisis, and remained loyal to the neoliberal policy framework of the EU treaties, which did not allow it to buy the government bonds of the Member States (MS). Even when countries of the periphery faced excessively high interest rates and borrowing hardships, the ECB statute was preserved; thus the function of lender of last resort to the governments was not permitted. This course was abandoned only in May 2010 when the markets speculated fiercely about a default in Greece. In 2007-10, unlike the US or Britain, eurozone governments had to finance their rescue plans in financial markets, which raised the costs of the rescue packages. Ironically the ECB's quantitative easing policy helped the banks to acquire cheap funding for their operations. From 2007 summer to October 2008 European banks shifted their lending towards the peripheral countries in the eurozone, assuming that the toxic assets in those countries' banks were limited (Lapavitsas et al, 2010). Government bonds with higher yields in the periphery were also seen as an attractive and safe alternative. Even more ironically, it was the same banks that later fled to US government bonds, and cut lending to the periphery in 2009 as they became more risk averse. These same banks were not only bailed out by the ECB, but also the macroeconomic environment in which they are operating was supported by expansionary fiscal policy to prevent the recession turning into a great depression. Eventually the rescue packages, fiscal expansion, and the decline in tax revenues due to the recession led to a significant increase in the budget deficit. Now it is again the same banks who are asking for high risk premiums from the governments with high budget deficits and public debt. They are asking for cuts in spending, in particular in public wages and employment, and threatening to stop lending to the governments who fail to do so.

Only after the market pressures on sovereign debt increased to unsustainable levels, the ECB announced in March 2010 that it would continue to accept from the banks bonds with ratings as low as triple-B-minus as collateral; later it even accepted the Greek bonds after they were downgraded to Junk status. Finally in May under the pressure of banks and the European Commission, the ECB made a U-turn and launched a programme of buying up the bonds of the peripheral eurozone countries from the banks.

Who pays the costs?

In the following, we will discuss the costs of the crisis and their distributional effects under two headings: public finance and labour market outcomes, i.e. wages and employment.

Public finance

The most obvious cost of the crisis has been the increase in public debt and budget deficits. The increase in budget deficits would not be there, if it were not for the bank rescue packages, counter-cyclical fiscal stimuli to tame the crises, increases in social protection spending due to the rise in unemployment, and the loss of tax revenues during the crisis. The crucial question is then who will carry the burden of the debt either in the form of increases in taxes or decreases in public spending. Thus the question of distribution of the costs becomes a question of changes in the composition of taxes and spending.

Table 2a shows the budget deficit/GDP during 2006-2010 in selected countries. In all countries there is a significant increase after the crisis, but most notably in both Spain and Ireland as well as in Germany the budget surplus of 2007 turned into a deficit. In Ireland the change has been the most dramatic. Ireland's major problem has been the guarantees of the government for the whole debt of the banks. As the housing bubble bust and international funding became scarce, the banks engaged in leveraged property lending found themselves in the edge of bankruptcy and the state had to support the capital of the banks beyond initial expectations. This will hike the budget deficit of the government to 32.4% of GDP as of 2010. The crisis had already led to an initial budget deficit of 7.3% of GDP in 2008 and 14.3% in 2009. Faced with the new needs to support its leveraged banking sector with a disproportionate size relative to the size of its small economy, Ireland had to accept a bailout package of €85 billion from the IMF and EU.

Table 2a: Budget deficit/GDP (%)

	2006	2007	2008	2009	2010
Germany	-1.64	0.19	0.04	-3.3	-4.95
France	-2.32	-2.73	-3.34	-7.58	-7.98
United Kingdom	-2.73	-2.79	-4.89	-11.4	-11.8
Ireland	2.96	0.14	-7.26	-14.3	-32.3
Greece	-3.84	-5.37	-7.67	-13.5	-9.37
Spain	2.02	1.91	-4.06	-11.2	-9.8
Portugal	-3.94	-2.65	-2.9	-9.43	-8.53

Table 2b: Public debt/GDP (%) and change in debt in 2010-2007 (%-points)

	2006	2007	2008	2009	2010	2010-2007
Germany	67.6	64.9	66.3	73.4	75.7	10.8
France	63.7	63.8	67.5	78.1	83	19.2
United Kingdom	43.4	44.5	52.1	68.2	77.8	33.4
Ireland	24.8	25	44.3	65.5	97.4	72.4
Greece	106.1	105	110.3	126.8	140.2	35.2
Spain	39.6	36.1	39.8	53.2	64.4	28.3
Portugal	63.9	62.7	65.3	76.1	82.8	20

Source: Ameco

Table 2b shows the ratio of public debt to GDP. Again debt/GDP ratios were modest in all cases except Greece until the crisis. Between 2007 and 2010, the cost of the crisis has been an increase in public debt by 10.8% in Germany, 19.2% in France, and 33.4% in Britain. In the periphery the cost has ranged between 20.0% in Portugal to 35.2% in Greece and the most dramatic increase is by 72.4% in Ireland. Britain in the core and Ireland in the periphery stand out with the highest increases in public debt due to their overextended banking sector.

This is the background of the financial crisis, which is now being repackaged as a public debt crisis by the governments. How the governments will change the composition of their tax revenues and spending in order to deal with the debt problem is the next question in terms of the distribution of the costs of the crisis. Even before the austerity measures most of the tax burden fell on labour income, or consumption –a regressive type of taxation. The two categories together make up 68.4% (in Britain) to 81.6% (in Germany) of total tax revenues in 2007 according the latest data available. Austerity measures, which will be discussed in more detail below, will lead to further shifts in this direction due to increases in VAT. Perversely some countries like Britain and Greece are decreasing corporate tax rates along with increases in the VAT, which will increase the share of labour taxes in financing the costs of the crisis further.

Regarding the changes in the composition of public spending, the planned cuts aim at a tightening of the conditions of unemployment benefits or freezes in benefits. Yet if these measures result in a deepening of the recession, despite a worsening in the conditions of the unemployed, the total unemployment benefit payments or other welfare spending may paradoxically increase. Another change we will observe in the medium run will be a fall in state pension payments along with cuts/freezes in pensions and increases in the retirement age. In general we can expect a shift in the composition of spending from public goods, which benefit labour, towards spending, which favours capital, i.e. the mobile factor of production, as countries try to compete in attracting firms during a global recession given the current state of the political balance of power relations between labour and capital. In addition to social protection spending, expenditures in education, health, culture, and recreation fall under this category of public goods that will be the targets of cuts or privatization efforts.

The most dramatic indicator of the distribution of the costs of the crisis is the details of the austerity measures announced so far in the selected countries. Ireland, until recently, had been the role model pointed out by the EU politicians for Greece in spring 2010, as it had already smashed public sector wages between 5-15%, cut social welfare spending and other spending in order to decrease its budget deficit to 10% in 2011 and 2.9% in 2014. These brutal spending cuts and the detrimental pro-cyclical fiscal policy in Ireland had been praised, since they had at the time restored market confidence without aid from the EU. However, now as the new problems with the banking sector have emerged, the government has further committed itself to a new round of austerity policies (Burke, 2010): real spending on education and health will fall by 7.5% and 12.5% respectively. Expenditure on other programmes will drop by 27.5%. The social welfare budget will be cut between 5-10%. There will possibly be public sector job cuts despite the former consensus between the unions and the government (McDonald, 2010). The minimum wage will be cut by 12%. In the meantime, Ireland is resisting any increase in its record low corporate tax rate of 12.5%.

The list of measures implemented in Greece are similar: Greece committed to cut its budget deficit from 13.5% of GDP in 2009 to 3% in 2013 via dramatic cuts in spending, public sector employment and wages and pensions, an increase in the retirement age, cuts in unemployment benefits, tax hikes in indirect taxes and reduction in corporate taxes, along with a fight against tax evasion. Public sector wages are to be cut by 20-30%, and frozen for three years; only one out of five retired employees in the public sector is to be replaced (Lapavitsas et al, 2010). There are also efforts to increase the use of temporary labour contracts. Finally a large privatisation programme is planned for public land, ports, airports, railways, finance, energy and utilities (Lapavitsas et al, 2010).

Portugal and Spain have also committed to austerity packages with higher taxes on consumption, decreases in social spending and pensions, and freezes/cuts in wages and employment in the public sector. Spain has cut public sector wages by 5% and passed a new labour code to increase labour market flexibility.

In the core of Europe, Britain is leading austerity policies. The aim is to cut the budget deficit, which is 11.4% of GDP in 2009 and 11.8% in 2010, to 1.1% of GDP by 2015-16. Dramatic cuts in the welfare budget and the tightening of the conditions of eligibility for the job seekers allowance, cuts in most government expenditures including higher education and housing, pay freezes in the public sector and planned restructuring in public sector pension schemes are supposed to make up three quarters of the decrease in the deficit. Only one quarter of the decrease in the deficit is via increases in taxes. The government has increased VAT in 2011 while it is decreasing the corporate tax rate from 28% to 24% by 2014 starting from 2011. There is a levy of 0.04% on bank balance sheets in 2011; however the decline in corporate tax rates will possibly more than offset this levy. No new levy is introduced on bank bonuses or profits. Capital gains tax has been increased slightly and the income tax threshold for personal allowances raised to £7,475. Overall the measures will reduce the income of lower income households more than that of higher income households (Emmerson, 2010).

Although the deficit in Britain is one of the highest in the EU, the average maturity of the debt is 13.7 years, the interest rate is at a historical low, and the ratio of debt to GDP is 68.2% in 2009 and 77.8% in 2010 despite the significant increase after the crisis. Public sector cuts at this stage will turn stagnation into a double dip recession. The talk about a fiscal crisis looks more like an excuse of the business lobbies to avoid tax increases to finance the budget deficit, and make the wage earners pay the costs of the crisis through cuts in income, jobs, and social services, to create a situation of "national emergency" to smash the remaining power of the trade unions, particularly in the public sector, and to decrease the size of the public sector. This situation shows a striking resemblance to the motivations of the Thatcher government as described by Sir Alan Budd - a monetarist economist and a Treasury civil servant in the 1970s, chief economic adviser to the Treasury during 1991-1997- in an interview in 1990: "many in the Thatcher government never believed for a moment that [monetarism] was the correct way to bring down inflation. They did however see that this would be a very good way to raise unemployment. And raising unemployment was an extremely desirable way of reducing the strength of the working classes... What was engineered - in Marxist terms - was a crisis of capitalism which re-created the reserve army of labour, and has allowed the capitalist to make high profits ever since" (cited in Cohen, 2003).[2] If we replace "monetarism" by "tight fiscal policy" and "inflation" by "public debt/budget deficit", this can fit well the discourse of the current government of Britain.

In the other core countries of Europe budget deficits have also increased, but not as dramatically as in the periphery or in Britain. However, there is still talk of tight fiscal policy. France and Germany have just increased the retirement age. Another major problem in the core will be the costs of the bailout packages for the periphery.

The speculators also now worry that these measures are not a solution to the problems: first they think that the default of Greece or other countries in the periphery may be inevitable given the popular resistance, the size of the debt and the recession. Second, in a contradictory way, they are also worried that austerity measures will deepen the recession in not only Greece or Ireland but also core countries like Britain, and create a double dip in the global economy, decrease tax revenues, and make it even harder to pay the debt back. They are right; there is a major inconsistency in this austerity plan: as the recession becomes deeper, tax revenues will become lower and despite severe cuts, budget deficits do not improve as much as

---

2   The author is grateful to Robert Wade for the reference in his presentation at the Global Labour Conference in Berlin, October 15-16, 2010.

planned as can already be seen. The estimates of IMF indicate that if Greece reduces its budget deficit to 2.6% of GDP by 2014, its GDP will contract so much that its debt to GDP ratio will rise above 150%. The latest developments in Ireland are also very telling: despite being the poster boy of austerity measures at the beginning of 2010, in less than one year the banking crisis put Ireland once again under focus; the austerity plans are now creating the conditions of a deepening recession in both Greece and Ireland, and it is unclear how the austerity plans will rescue the public or private sectors from insolvency. Finally, the worries about private debt, which may make further rescue packages necessary, are growing.

A long global recession seems very likely without the support of strong and coordinated fiscal stimuli. The uncertainty about the strength of the recovery is making new investments as well as hirings less likely. Declines in income and confidence, job losses and the pressure to pay back debt are restraining household consumption. Both investment and consumption will not return back to normal even when the banks relax credit. The presumed positive effect of a reduced budget deficit on private investment is based on the argument that lower government borrowing leads to lower interest rates and higher private investment and spending. Under the current conditions where consumers and firms are trying to reduce their debt and interest rates are already low, this channel has no relevance. Instead higher spending in public investment in the right areas, like renewable energy, infrastructure, housing, education, care, could crowd in private investment and consumption as well as help to meet the long term targets of sustainability and full employment.

Wages and employment

These conditions are turning the public debt crisis into a jobs crisis. Table 3 shows the cumulative change in GDP, employment, and hours worked (all seasonally adjusted) from the peak to trough of each variable as well as the second quarter of 2010 (the latest data available in the OECD National Accounts) compared to the peak.

Table 3: % Cumulative change in GDP, employment, and hours worked (seasonally adjusted)

	France	Germany	UK	Greece	Ireland	Portugal	Spain
	GDP						
peak/trough	-3.88	-6.62	-6.39	-5.66	-14.26	-3.84	-4.89
10.2/peak	-2.16	-2.7	-4.55	-5.66	-11.98	-1.82	-4.58
peak/trough dates	09.1/08.1	09.1/08.1	09.3/08.1	10.2/08.3	09.4/07.4	09.1/08.1	09.4/08.1
length	4	4	6	7	8	4	7
	Employment, total						
peak/trough	-1.73	-0.29	-3.19	-3.55	-12.53	-4.16	-9.64
10.2/peak	-1.55	-0.08	-2.54	-3.55	-12.53	-4.16	-9.64
peak/trough dates	09.4/08.2	09.4/08.4	10.1/08.2	10.2/07.4	10.1/07.4	10.2/08.2	10.2/08.1
length	6	4	7	10	9	8	9
	Hours worked, total						
peak/trough	-2.12	-3.39			-13.9	-4.03	-8.68
10.2/peak	-1.81	-1.42			-11.45	-3.27	-8
peak/trough dates	10.1/08.1	09.2/08.2			09.3/07.3	09.3/07.4	10.1/08.2
length	8	4			8	7	7

Source: OECD National Accounts, 2010

In Germany, France, Britain, and Portugal employment started falling one to three quarters after GDP. The fall in employment has lasted longer than that in GDP in all countries except Germany, and although the fall has stopped in the core countries, it is still going on in the periphery. In Germany after the initial job losses, employment has recovered, and the overall decline in employment is just 0.1% in 2010.Q2 compared to the peak. France has also had a modest fall in employment of 1.7% in 2010 compared to the peak. These outcomes in France and in particular in Germany are related to the adjustment of hours worked due to the short working time arrangements supported by government subsidies (Leschke and Watt, 2010). Hours worked started to decrease earlier and have fallen more than employment in Germany and France. Interestingly in Ireland, Spain, and Portugal the reverse is true: hours have decreased more than employment from the peak to 2010 second quarter. This can be explained by the lack of fiscal capacity to support short time work arrangements. In all countries except Portugal there has been a rise in part-time employment. Unfortunately there is no data for hours worked for Britain and Greece.

In Germany, France, Britain, and Greece the fall in employment in cumulative (as of 2010.Q2 compared to the peak) has been less than the fall in GDP (compared to its own peak); however the reverse is true for Spain, Portugal, and Ireland. The higher share of temporary contracts in Spain and Portugal (31.7% and 22.4% as of 2007 compared to 14.4%-14.6% in France and Germany), the concentration of the crisis in the construction sector in Spain and Ireland, and the lack of short time working arrangements have contributed to this fact. Britain did not have a government subsidized short working time arrangement; however voluntary unpaid leaves, wage freezes, or nominal wage cuts have led to a less severe fall in employment compared to the fall in GDP.

As a result in Germany short working time arrangements have significantly moderated the rise in the unemployment rate, which has increased by a mere 0.5%-point at its peak in 2009.Q2 compared to 2008.Q4 (see Figure 3). The unemployment rate in Germany is now even lower than its pre-crisis level. However it is yet to be seen what will happen to unemployment in Germany when the short working time arrangements are eventually terminated and the export-led recovery loses steam as the advanced economies stagnate. The termination of short working time arrangements may spread the problem of unemployment from lower skilled temporary workers to higher skilled workers.

Figure 3: Unemployment rate, %

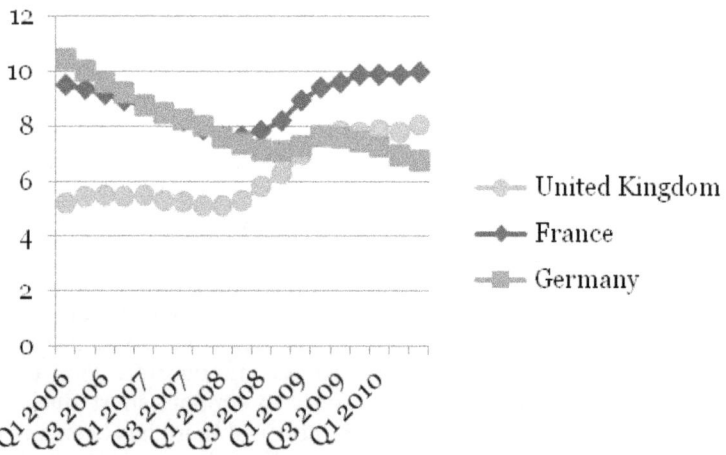

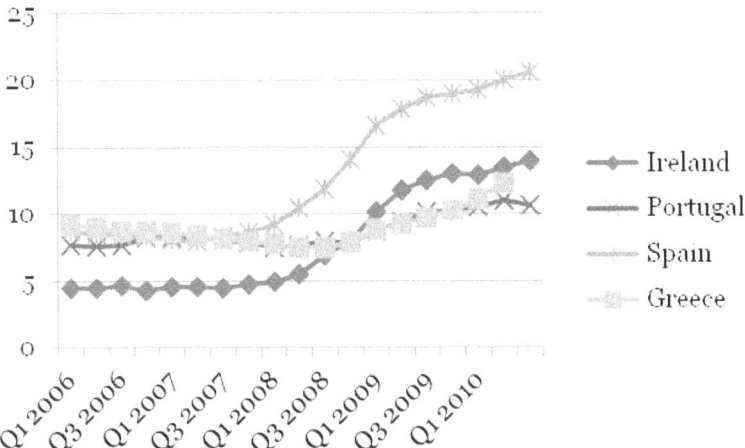

Source: OECD Main Economic Indicators, 2010

France and Britain have experienced increases of 2.3%-points and 3%-points in unemployment respectively as of the third quarter of 2010 (compared to the trough point), and the increase has been persistent and continuing during the weak recovery in 2010. The increases in Greece and Portugal have been 4.7%-points and 3.2%-points respectively as of 2010 (the second quarter in Greece and third in Portugal compared to the trough point). Particularly high increases took place in Ireland and Spain: 9.5%-points and 11.4%-points respectively (as of 2010.Q3 compared to the trough point). The unemployment rate is now as high as 20.6% in Spain and 13.9% in Ireland. Unemployment is expected to increase further and display a significant persistence in all countries. ILO (2010) estimates that employment rates will not return back to the pre-crisis levels before 2014.

Firms might want to make use of the recession to rationalize a strategy of increasing productivity and start a new wave of firing or engage in hiring freezes long after the recovery. As firms increase the working hours and delay hiring, this worsens the job chances of the unemployed and the young first time job seekers, and may lead to an increase in discouraged workers who drop out of the labour market. The crisis has already led to an increase in long term unemployment as well as the youth unemployment rate. The share of long term unemployed in total has increased in all countries except Germany in 2009 compared to 2008 (see Figure 4). The increase had started already in 2007 in Spain, Ireland and Britain. The sharpest increases have been in Ireland and Spain with 1.7%-points and 2.3%-points respectively. Youth unemployment has increased in all countries, although in Germany the change is very modest at the moment (see Figure 5).

Figure 4: The share of long term unemployed, %

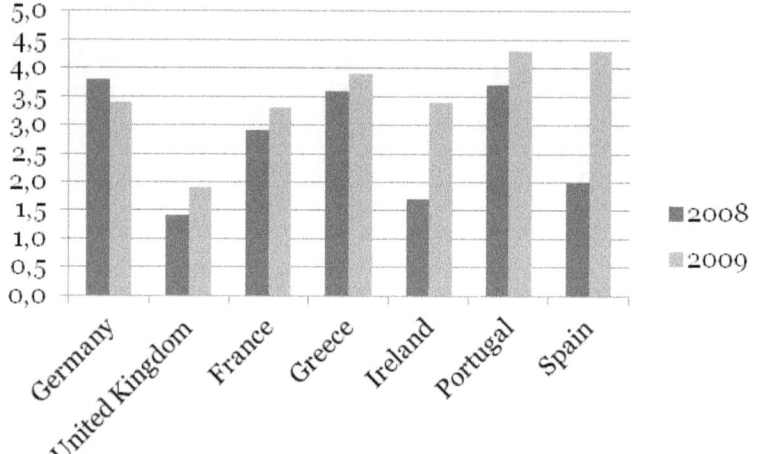

Source: Eurostat, 2010

Figure 5: Youth unemployment rate (<25), %

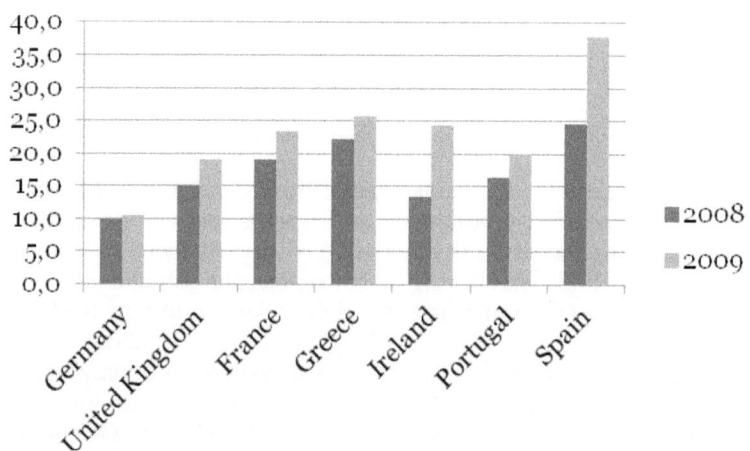

Source: Eurostat, 2010

The increase has been 4%-point in France and Britain in 2009 compared to 2008. Again the most dramatic rise took place in Ireland and Spain with the youth unemployment rate reaching to 24.4% and 37.8% respectively in 2009. There are also structural problems of unemployment in sectors like the automotive industry and construction, where the crisis only uncovered the already existing bottlenecks. Recovery of the aggregate economy will not necessarily create jobs in these sectors.

It can be argued that the unemployed have been the first victims to pay the costs of the crisis. The effects on the living conditions of the rest of the working population is only starting to be felt through cuts in spending in social services and the consequent rise in the cost of living in countries like Britain, Greece, Ireland, Spain, and Portugal, who have started major austerity programmes in 2010. Wage cuts/freezes in the public sector, which are either planned or already under way, will also hurt the wage earners in the private sector as public sector wages play a signal role for bargaining. The effects of increased unemployment on the bargaining power of workers will also be increasingly felt. However most of these effects on wages will be realised with a lag. Moreover wages are often bargained in the previous year, and there is a time lag until labour market and macroeconomic conditions are reflected in future contracts. In particular, the crisis has come after a period of increasing consumer price inflation in late 2007 and early 2008 following the food and energy price shocks. In several countries real wages had decreased in 2008 (France, Britain) or stagnated (in Germany, Ireland, Portugal) partly due to unexpected inflation (own calculations based on OECD National Accounts data). The wage bargains for 2009 had reflected the persistence of these expectations or the correction of the previous losses (O'Farrell, 2010). As a consequence, in 2009 real wages[3] in the aggregate economy have increased in all countries but Germany, where they were just stagnant (own calculations based on OECD National Accounts). The private sector wages have decreased in Germany and Britain in 2009 (own calculations based on OECD Economic Outlook).

Table 4 shows the latest developments in real wages for 2010. The real wage data for the aggregate economy is available as of the second quarter of 2010 in the OECD National Accounts; however there is no data for private sector wages in the National Accounts. The real wage data in the private sector is calculated based on the forecast for labour compensation in OECD Economic Outlook (June 2010[4]), which however only reports annual data for wages in the private

---

3   Compensation per employee deflated by private consumption deflator.
4   The November 2010 detailed data appendix is not available yet.

sector. Since the data sources are different and the private sector data is based on forecasts from June 2010, a comparison of the private and public sector wages is not possible.

Table 4: Cumulative % change in real wages (Compensation per employee deflated by the private consumption deflator)

		France	Germany	UK	Greece	Ireland	Portugal	Spain
Total economy*	2010.2 / peak**	-	-0.13	-1.75	-7.10	-1.14		-2.02
Total economy***	2010 2 quarters average / 2009 average	0.94	0.28	-0.24	-6.06	-0.50		-1.01
The private sector***	2010	0.27	-1.38	-0.83	-3.28	-2.47	-0.48	-0.34

*OECD National Accounts, quarterly, November 2010. The data for Ireland ends in 2010.1
**Peak wage was in 2009.1 in Germany; 2009.3 in Greece and Ireland; 2009.4 in Spain and the UK.
***annual data, OECD Economic Outlook, November 2010.

In France in 2010 real wages are stagnating in the private sector, and decreasing slightly in the aggregate economy; thus despite unemployment real wages have been preserved in 2010. In Germany real private sector wages have fallen in 2010, and the aggregate wages as of 2010.Q2 are slightly lower than in their peak (in 2009.Q1). This fall is due to lower hours of work rather than a fall in hourly wages. In Britain in 2010 both total and private sector wages are falling; the fall in aggregate wages as of 2010.Q2 has reached 1.75% compared to the peak (in 2009.Q4). Also in the periphery both aggregate and private sector wages are falling.[5] The cumulative decline in aggregate wages in Greece has been particularly high by 7.1% as of 2010.Q2 compared to 2009.Q3. Sharp and long-lasting increases in unemployment are likely to make the wage losses much stronger in the future.

Data on personal income inequality is released with a time lag; however in 2008 compared to 2007 the ratio of the income share of the top 20% to the bottom 20% has already increased in France, Britain, and Spain. There is a decrease in the other countries. In Britain, data is also available for the income share of the top 10% to the bottom 10%, which has increased from 7.04 in 2007 to 7.28 in 2008. The Gini coefficients in 2008 have also increased in France and Britain compared to 2007 (from 26 to 28 in France and from 33 to 34 in Britain). Although the increases in inequality in this first year of the crisis are modest, it is still striking given the hikes in top income shares on the way to the crisis. In Britain between December 2009 and April 2010, bonus payments increased by 16% in the aggregate

---

5   In Portugal quarterly wage data for the aggregate economy is not available.

economy, and 25% in the financial sector. Although bonus payments still remain below the levels seen in 2006-07 and 2007-08, they are still 50% higher than they were in 2000 across the whole economy. Again in Britain the number of High Net Wealth Individuals (with investable assets above $1 million) has increased by 23.8% in 2009 indicating a partial even if not complete recovery in the wealth of the HNWI.

Finally Figure 2 shows the trends in the adjusted wage share after the crisis. In 2008 and 2009 the share of wages in GDP has increased in a counter-cyclical fashion as a result of decreases in productivity, with the exception of Britain in 2008 where the wage share fell. However, in 2010 in all countries both in the core and the periphery the wage share is expected to decrease according to the estimates of the European Commission Economic and Financial Affairs (AMECO, November 2010 forecasts). The sharpest decreases are taking place in Ireland (2.2%-points) followed by Greece (1.8%-points), Britain (1.2%-points), Portugal (0.7%-points), and Spain (0.6%-points).

It is usual that during a recession, labour's income share slightly increases. However, the long recession of Japan is indicative how wages may develop if the recession persists. In Japan, in the later years of the recession, not only wage freezes but also nominal wage declines took place as deflation persisted (in 1998-99, 2002-04, and 2007). The firing of many workers in the first half of the 2000s has been influential in this process. After the recession, the institutionalized wage co-ordination mechanism was almost broken down (Uemura, 2008). As a measure against labour hording in large Japanese firms, the number of non-regular workers increased dramatically; there has also been a shift towards unstable service jobs (Uemura, 2008). All these developments have led to a weakening in the bargaining position of unions and the suppression of nominal wage growth. Overall the wage share decreased by 6.9%-points as of 2007 compared to 1998, and 6.6%-points compared to 1992. The decline in the wage share contributed to a decline in domestic demand, and exports became an important source of demand again in Japan, which also increased the pressure of international competition with the other Asian countries and the increasing number of foreign affiliates of the Japanese multinational firms (Uemura, 2008).

The long recession of Japan led to a strong and continuous increase in unemployment from a level of 2.1% in 1991 to 5.4% in 2002. Despite the recovery since 2003, unemployment as of 2007 was still higher than in 1997. Adverse developments in total unemployment, long term unemployment and youth unemployment took place despite a strong decline in the male as well as female labour force participation rate, which declined from 64.1% in 1992 to 59.6% in 2007. Although the unemployment rate in Japan in its peak point is still lower than in most other advanced countries, it is important to realize that drastic increases in unemployment can radically change the industrial relations and wage bargaining process in a persistent way.

The experience of Japan shows that the episodes of crisis intensify the distributional struggle. The crisis also creates a hysteresis effect that destroys the bargaining power of labour for a long period afterwards. Diwan (2001) defines crises as episodes of distributional fights, which leave "distributional scars". Needless to say, the global dimension of this crisis will make these effects stronger.

A transitional programme for an alternative Europe

The existing policies in Europe have three fundamental flaws: First the approach of the EU is assuming that the problem is a lack of fiscal discipline and repeats the old faith in strengthening the surveillance of budget deficits; it does not question the reasons behind the deficits; it ignores all the structural problems regarding divergences in productivity, imbalances in current accounts due to the "beggar my neighbour" policies of Germany. The austerity packages throughout the EU are pushing countries into a model of chronically low internal demand based on low wages. The deflationary consequences of wage cuts may turn the problem of debt to insolvency for the private as well as the public sector. In the past in Germany low domestic demand was substituted by high demand for exports. But it is not possible to turn the whole eurozone into a German model based on wage suppression and austerity, since without the deficits of the periphery the German export market will also stagnate. Particularly for the periphery of Europe contraction in domestic demand means prolonged recession. Second, the mainstream policies are based on the argument that Europe has a sovereign debt crisis, which ignores the fact that public debt would not have increased at the current rates if it were not for the financial crisis, which was prevented by unprecedented bank rescue packages; which in turn increased the budget deficits along with lost tax revenues and increased social spending because of the crisis. Therefore the banking sector, which has generated the crisis, should pay for the effects of the crisis on the public budget –the current policies in Europe aim at exactly the opposite. Third, the underlying reason behind the crisis was unequal distribution of income and wealth. Thus a fundamental reversal of this process requires redistribution in favour of labour.

The existing wage suppression policies hurt all working people alike. The popular discontent in Germany about Greece misses the fact that the German workers' loss of wages, unemployment benefits, and pension rights created part of the problem. Uncovering this fact along with the idea of unequal distribution as the main cause of the crisis is an important step towards building a progressive alliance for an alternative Europe. The attack is international: multinational bank and business lobbies are determining the policies of the governments and EU institutions by using boycotting of government bonds as a threat; thus the opposition also needs to be internationally organized. A pro-labour solution of the public debt crisis in the periphery as well as the core countries like Italy or Britain requires debt default, and a joint struggle can create a stronger counter to this multinational lobby. In that respect a European network of movements could be turned into a lever to bring together peoples' opposition to the budget cuts in different countries. An internationalist solution might generate a more powerful front in the core and the periphery compared to national alternatives. Moreover in the current situation, anti-European and anti-euro positions are more likely to mobilize nationalist, right-wing currents. Nationalism is certainly a problem among the working class in the core (e.g. the discourse of "PIGS"); however the far right is also quickly mobilizing the discontent in the periphery. Last but not least, the solution to the problems in the periphery of Europe would be tremendously facilitated by fiscal transfers within the EU as opposed to isolated national solutions in small countries, which can easily lead to a persistence of underdevelopment. This position is also consistent with the interests of the working people in the core countries: a low wage periphery as an alternative location for MNEs is a threat to the wages and jobs in the core as well.

Regarding the issue of the euro and the peripheral countries, there are two positions among Marxist economists: a position, which promotes the exit from the eurozone as suggested by e.g. Lapavitsas et al. (2010) or de Santos (2011), and a position, that primarily calls for alternative policies for Europe rather than seeing the currency as the core of the debate as suggested by e.g. Husson (in this book), Samary (2011) or the author of this article. I would prefer to push for an alternative Europe and changes in the economic policy framework within which the euro operates for the reasons mentioned above. Furthermore I do not share the optimism about the competitiveness effects of devaluation, which would follow an exit from the eurozone.

Devaluation means an increase in the costs of imported inputs, and the pass-through effect of import prices in an import dependent country soon erodes the competitiveness effects; furthermore it leads to devastating real income losses for workers. Tactically a better starting point for advocating change is an alternative policy framework for Europe accompanied with debt default rather than a focus on exit from the eurozone. If an anti-capitalist revolutionary change is initiated in one single country in the periphery and if this wave does not spread to the rest of Europe, and thus the existing EU institutions become an obstacle to debt restructuring and change, exit from the euro can be the outcome of this process, but the starting point for change should still be a push for an alternative Europe and debt default.

Such a radical transformation of the EU requires a major change in the institutions and policy framework that builds a bridge from the urgent demands of people for decent living standards and a sustainable environment to an alternative anti-capitalist agenda. As the economic crisis intermingled with the ecological crisis demonstrates that capitalism is economically, ecologically, and politically unstable and unsustainable, policies for a change beyond capitalism offer themselves as opposed to reforms to "save capitalism from itself." Such policies build the bridge from today's urgent demands to the alternative of a democratic, participatory socialism.

In the following we discuss alternatives for fiscal policy, monetary policy, incomes and labour market policy, finance, and decision making within such an anti capitalist agenda for Europe.

The most important obstacle today in initiating any progressive economic policy in Europe is the speculation on public debt and the governments' commitment to satisfy the financiers. Public finance has to be unchained via debt default in both the periphery and the core following a process of debt audit. This has to be coordinated at the European level as part of a broader public finance policy to make the responsible pay for the costs of crisis and to reverse the origin of the crisis, i.e. pro-capital redistribution. A debtor-led default is fundamentally different from the current creditor-led debt restructuring plans of the European Elite, which are attached with further austerity policies. Debt default is also not just a question of solvency as in the case of Greece or Ireland; but it is also a question related to the origins of the public debt: thus the question is not only "can we pay the debt?", but "should we pay the debt?" In Britain the newly generated debt because of the crisis that amounts to 33.4% of GDP still raises the question why taxes of working people should be used to pay this debt. The recognition of the need for default is also important given the ecological limits to growth, which poses a constraint to higher growth to ease debt repayment.

Along with debt default, a radical restructuring of public finance involves a highly progressive system of taxes, coordinated at the EU level, on not only income but also wealth, higher corporate tax rates, inheritance tax, and a tax on financial transactions. A progressive income tax mechanism could also introduce a maximum income with the highest marginal tax rate increasing to 90% above a certain income threshold in relation to the median wage. To cite a recent historical case from Britain, between 1974 and 1979 the top income tax rate was 83% on annual incomes above £90,500 in today's prices (£24,000 in 1979). Indeed, with additional taxes of 15% on unearned income such as dividends and interest on investments, the top rate could increase to 98% in 1979! This is a striking comparison to the current top income tax rate of 50% above an annual income of £150,000 in Britain. This would make the banks, the private investment funds, and high wealth individuals pay the costs of the fiscal crisis, and reverse the pro-capital income distribution.

Economic policy and public spending should aim at full employment, ecological sustainability, and equality. This is a feasible but challenging task. First, if the use of environmental resources is to maintain a certain 'sustainable' level, economic growth in advanced capitalist countries, in the long term, has to be zero or low, i.e. equal to the growth rate of 'environmental productivity'.

Second, advanced capitalist countries of Europe need to slow down to create space for development in the Global South as part of a broader strategy of climate justice. This type of zero-growth or even de-growth, however, has nothing to do with the disastrous recession caused by the crisis. This is a managed zero-growth economy that redistributes existing wealth, which should be sufficient to maintain a life with dignity and creativity for all, if resources were used sustainably and in accordance with the needs of the majority. Growth in past decades has not brought jobs, equality, prosperity, or happiness. We can create prosperity and equality without growth. Consumerism and conspicuous consumption would also decrease in a more equal society.

The reconciliation of full employment with zero growth and a low carbon economy requires two policies: creating more labour-intensive jobs, and ecological investments. First, public spending should generate public employment in labour-intensive social services such as education, child care, nursing homes, health, community and social services. The need for social services is not met under the present circumstances, where they are provided either at very low wages (to ensure an adequate profit) or as a luxury service for the upper classes or via invisible unpaid female labour within the gendered division of labour in the private sphere. To avoid this deficit they can be provided by the state or by non-profit/community organizations. The gender aspect of public employment programmes should also be carefully designed in order not only to avoid disadvantages for women but also to increase women's employment share.

Second, for the purpose of ecological sustainability, there is need for a shift in the composition of aggregate demand towards long-term green investments; this cannot be achieved without new strategic tasks for active public investment. Public investment in ecological maintenance and repair, renewable energy, public transport, insulation of the existing housing stock and building of zero-energy houses can create jobs as well as a low carbon economy.

To maintain full employment without growth, a substantial shortening of working time in parallel with the historical growth in productivity is also required. Reduction in weekly working hours should take place without loss of wages, which means an increase in hourly wages. Again this is not unrealistic. Compared to the 19th century, we are all working part-time today. But the shortening of working hours has slowed down since the 1980s, with the notable exception of France. This is also the way to break the illusion among working people of the need for growth and to make a zero-growth economy socially desirable by guaranteeing work with dignity and an equitable distribution of income. The minimum wage should also be adjusted upwards to a living wage level, and a basic income for all residents should be introduced.

Regarding employment in the private sector, it is important to prevent firms from making use of the crisis to implement their long-term downsizing strategies. The alternative is legal measures to ban firing during the crisis: if the firing ban leads to bankruptcy in certain firms, these firms can be re-appropriated and revitalized under workers' control, supported by public credits. Widespread examples of that were seen in Argentina after the crisis in shut-down companies.

In cases of sectors that are under the threat of structural problems and mass layoffs, like the auto industry, nationalization of the firms and restructuring of these public firms should be considered, e.g. in the auto industry a shift of focus towards the production of public transport vehicles, and a gradual transfer of labour towards new sectors.

This programme requires a public banking sector. Financial regulation is important but not enough. Finance is a crucial sector which cannot be left to the short-termism of the private profit motive.

This sector has already been de facto nationalized, but without any voice for society and with a commitment to privatization as soon as possible. Yet the challenge is the finance of socially desirable large new investments, e.g. in the energy sector. Large private banks exploit their advantage of being "too big to fail". Instead, what needs to be done is to nationalize the banking sector with the participation of the workers and other community representatives in decision making and transparency of the accounts.

On the international front, speculative financial flows should be prevented via capital controls and a stable world monetary system based on fixed exchange rates with the possibility of managed adjustments. The nationalization of banks is a natural complement to debt default. This can prepare the ground for a policy of debt restructuring for working people by linking their debt payments to national banks to a reasonable share of their income.

The implications of these policies for an alternative European policy framework are to completely abandon the Stability and Growth Pact on the fiscal policy front and to align monetary policy with fiscal policy targets. The ECB should be turned into a real central bank with the ability to lend to member states. Higher public spending financed by monetary expansion does not pose a threat of inflation today given the recession, low demand, and deflationary environment. However it is important that monetary expansion serves the priorities of development, sustainability, full employment, and equality.

On the incomes and labour market policy level, there is need for a fundamental correction of the wages in both the periphery and the core of Europe to reflect the productivity gains of the past three decades fully. To facilitate convergence a minimum wage should be coordinated at the EU level. Higher productivity growth in poorer countries of the EU will help to create some convergence in wages, but regional convergence should be supported by fiscal transfers and public investments to boost productivity in poorer regions. Furthermore a European unemployment benefit system should be developed to redistribute from low to high unemployment regions. This requires a significant EU budget financed by EU level progressive taxes.

Last but not least, the crisis calls for a major shift in decision making to facilitate economy-wide coordination of important decisions. This requires public ownership and the participation and control by workers in the firms, of consumers, and regional representatives in other critical sectors such as housing, energy, infrastructure, the pension system, education, and health. Such a transformation will build the bridge to a democratic, participatory, feminist ecosocialism.

References:

AMECO, 2010, *Economic and Financial affairs, Annual Macroeconomic Indicators online database.*

Atkinson, A.B. and Piketty, T. 2007. *Top Incomes over the Twentieth Century: A contrast between European and English speaking countries.* Oxford: Oxford University Press.

Brenner, R., 2009. *What is good for Goldman Sachs is good for America: the origins of the current crisis*, Prologue to the Spanish translation of Economics of Global Turbulence, Akal

Burke, M. 2010. 'Who is being bailed out?' *The Guardian*, 27.11.2010, p. 43

Choonara, J., 2009. 'Marxist accounts of the current crisis', *International Socialism, 83,* http://www.isj.org.uk/?id=557

Cohen, N. 2003. 'Gambling with our future', *New Statesman*, 13 January, http://www.newstatesman.com/200301130012

Crotty, J. 1993. 'Rethinking Marxian investment theory: Keynes-Minsky instability, competitive regime shifts and coerced investment', in: *Review of Radical Political Economics*, 25(1), 1-26

de Santos, Raphie, 2011. 'Portugal: the prospect of a full bailout and more austerity looms in 2011', *Socialist Resistance*, January 2011.

Diwan, I., 2001. *Debt as sweat: Labor, financial crises, and the globalization of capital*, Mimeo, The World Bank, Washington D.C.

Elliott, L. (2007): 'After the orgy, let's clean up', *Guardian Weekly*, August 3, p. 18.

Emmerson, C. 2010. *Opening remarks at the Institute of Fiscal Studies briefing on the October 2010 Spending Review*, 21 October 2010. http://www.ifs.org.uk/budgets/sr2010/opening_remarks.pdf

Eurostat, 2010, online database

Fitoussi, J.P. and Saraceno, F. (2010). 'Europe: how deep is a crisis? policy responses and structural factors behind diverging performances', *Journal of Globalization and Development,* 1(1), article 17.

Harman, Chris, 2009, 'The Slump of the 1930s and the Crisis Today', *International Socialism* 121 (winter 2009), www.isj.org.uk/?id=506

ILO, 2010. *World of Work*, ILO, Geneva.

Kliman, Andrew, 2009, *'The Destruction of Capital' and the Current Economic Crisis*, from http://akliman.squarespace.com/crisis-intervention/

Lapavitsas C., Kaltenbrunner N., Lambrinidis G., Lindo D., Meadway J., Michell J., Painceira J.P., Pires E., Powell J., Stenfors A. , Teles N. (2010). *The eurozone between Austerity and Default, Research on Money and Finance*, Occasional Report, September 2010.

Lazonick, W., and O'Sullivan, M. 2000. *Maximizing shareholder value: a new ideology for corporate governance*, Economy and Society, 29, 13-35

Leschke, J. and Watt, A. 2010. *How do institutions affect the labour market adjustment to the economic crisis in different EU countries?* ETUI Working Paper 2010.04

McDonald, H. 2010. *Lame duck PM likely to get budget passed*, The Guardian, 27.11.2010, p. 24

O'Farrell, R., 2010. *Wages in the crisis*, ETUI Working Paper 2010.03

OECD Economic Outlook, 2010, November, online database

OECD Main Economic Indicators, 2010, online database

OECD National Accounts, 2010, online database

OECD National Accounts (quarterly), 2010, November, online database

Samary, C. 2010. *Which money? Is it really the question?* (in French), Tout Est À Nous.

Uemura, H. 2008. *Growth, Distribution and Institutional Changes in the Japanese Economy: Faced by Increasing International Interdependence with Asian Countries*, Annual conference of Evolutionary Political Economy, November 2008, Rome.

From the Global North to the Global South: debt in its many states[1]

THE DEBT IN THE NORTH: SOME ALTERNATIVE PATHS[2]

Éric Toussaint (CADTM)

Debt over the last few decades:

The debt in the North, i.e., in the most industrialized countries[3], began to reach high levels in the 1980s. This is with good reason. Following the first oil crisis and the 1973-1975 economic crisis, governments tried giving a Keynesian boost to the economy and resorted to borrowing. Debt servicing then soared when the US Federal Reserve suddenly raised interest rates (October 1979) thus marking a break from the past 46 years of Keynesian policy initiated in 1933 during Franklin Roosevelt's first term.

From the late 1980s to the early 2000s, the state of public finances deteriorated to different degrees depending on the countries considered. The main reason for this was the "tax counter-reform" implemented in favour of companies and high-income households; this resulted in declining revenues derived from corporate and individual income tax. This was offset, on the one hand, by a rise in indirect taxes (VAT) and, on the other hand, by increased borrowing.

---

1   This is the second part of an article on the debt. The first part is entitled: "The debt in developing countries: a dangerous unconcern", http://www.cadtm.org/The-debt-in-developing-countries-a
2   This text is a largely revised and extended version of the introductory lecture delivered for the workshop "Public debt in the South and North" during the National Conference of the Local Committees (CNCL) of ATTAC France held on 16 and 17 October 2010 at the University of Saint-Denis (Paris VIII) in Paris. A similar version was delivered during training sessions organized in Liège by the International Debt Observatory with CADTM on 29 and 30 November 2010 (see www.cadtm.org/Dette-publique-dans-les-pays-du,6103) as well as during the 4th workshop of CADTM South Asia held in Colombo, Sri Lanka, on 9 and 10 December (see http://www.cadtm.org/CADTM-South-Asia-meets-in-Colombo) and during a conference given in Nagercoil in Tamil Nadu, India on 28 December 2010.
3   The term "North" in this text refers to the most industrialized countries.

With the current crisis, which started in 2007, the state of public finances suddenly and tragically worsened, in particular owing to State interventions to bail out the bankrupt banks. In countries like the United Kingdom, the Netherlands and Ireland, governments committed huge amounts of public money to rescue the banks. In the medium term, the Spanish government is likely to do the same in order to bail out regional savings banks which have been virtually bankrupted by the real estate crisis. Ireland is crippled by the debts of several large private banks that were nationalized by the State without recovering the cost of the bailout from shareholder assets. The policies carried out since 2007 have dramatically worsened the state of public finances[4].

The creditors of European debts are mainly European bankers

With the considerable amount of liquid assets placed at their disposal by the central banks in 2007-2009, the banks of Western Europe (especially the French and German banks[5], but also Belgian, Dutch, British, Luxembourg and Irish banks) lent huge sums (especially to the private sector but also to the public authorities) to the countries of the "EU periphery" such as Spain, Portugal and Greece (the banks thought it was risk-free) as well as to the former Soviet bloc countries of Central and Eastern Europe (in particular Hungary). This resulted in a sharp increase in the debt of these countries, especially private debt. It must be noted that euro membership earned some countries of the EU's periphery the confidence of the Western European bankers. The latter then granted them massive loans, thinking the big European countries would help them if they found themselves in trouble.

The three charts below show the nationality of foreign holders of the private and public debt securities of Spain, Portugal and Greece

---

[4] I had raised and denounced this fact as early as December 2008 in an article entitled "A holy union for a deuce of a swindle" http://www.cadtm.org/A-Holy-Union-for-a-Deuce-of-a There is almost no amendment to make to its content. The predictions made at the time have been entirely confirmed and the solutions put forward remain valid, though one should add the solution of debt audit resulting in repudiations/cancellations (see below in the present article).

[5] The German and French bankers alone own up to 48 % of the Spanish debt securities (the French banks holding 24% of these securities), 48% of the Portuguese debt securities (the French banks accounting for 30% of the total) and 41% of the Greek debt securities (the French banks being the largest creditors with 26%). See the figures below.

(which represent a large part of the external debt of the three countries)[6]:

Chart 1: Foreign holders of Spanish debt securities (end of 2008)

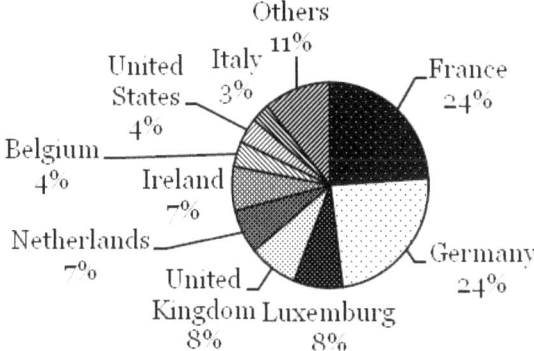

Chart 2: Foreign holders of Portuguese debt securities (end of 2008)

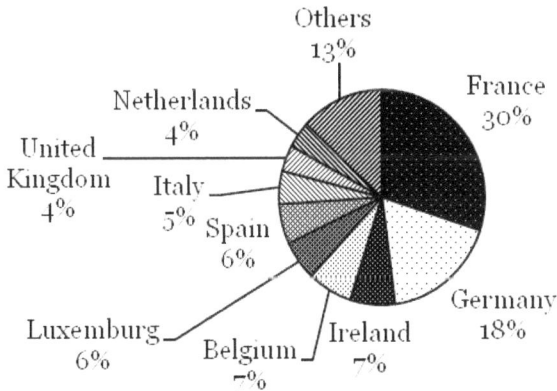

---

6   Taken from C. Lapavitsas, A. Kaltenbrunner, G. Lambrinidis, D. Lindo, J. Meadway, J. Michell, J.P. Painceira, E. Pires, J. Powell, A. Stenfors, N. Teles: *"The eurozone between austerity and default"*, September 2010. Source: CPIS.

Chart 3: Foreign holders of Greek debt securities (end of 2008)[7]

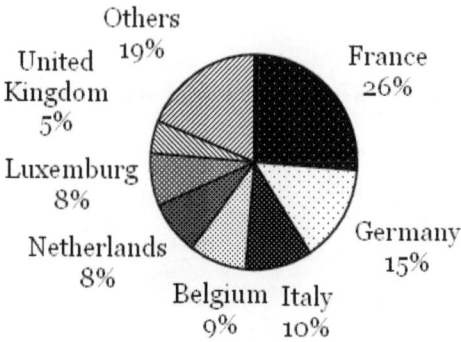

It should be emphasized that in the case of Portugal and Spain, the securities held by France and Germany alone represent almost 50% of the total; in the case of Greece, they represent 41%. This casts a special light on the "leadership" of these countries and their devotion to the European cause.

There has also been a substantial increase in internal debt over the past ten years, and a large financialisation of the economy in these three countries. The private sector debt has grown: borrowing for households, private companies and banks was cheap (interest rates have been low and inflation higher than in the most industrialized countries) and this private debt has been driving the economy in the three countries; the banks, thanks to a strong euro, were able to expand their activities abroad and fund their domestic activities at lower cost.

Rescuing US and Western European banks

The piling up of debts in the eurozone's periphery threatened the banks of the core. This threat of a bank crisis was behind the intervention of the eurozone authorities in May 2010, this was then followed by the one designed for Ireland in November 2010. The exposure of EU (and Swiss) banks to the so-called PIIGS countries[8] (Portugal, Ireland, Italy, Greece, Spain) is very high, as shown in the table below.

---

7   According to the BIS in December 2009, the French banks owned $31 billion of the Greek public debt, the German banks $23 billion.
8   This acronym is sometimes used in a derogatory, or even racist, way.

Debts held by banks as a percentage of creditor countries' GDP

Debts held by banks in:	Credits to:					
	Greece	Portugal	Spain	Ireland	Italy	Total PIIGS
Austria	1.3	0.8	2.5	2.4	7.2	14
Belgium	0.8	0.7	5	14.1	6.9	28
Denmark	0.1	0.1	0.8	7.3	0.2	8
France	3.1	1.8	8.9	2.5	20.8	37
Germany	1.5	1.5	6.2	6	6.2	21
Greece	0	0	0.1	0.3	0.2	1
Ireland	4	2.6	14.5	0	22.1	43
Italy	0.4	0.3	1.6	0.9	0	3
Netherlands	1.6	1.7	16.4	4.2	9.4	33
Portugal	4.7	0	13.4	10.3	2.5	31
Spain	0.1	6.4	0	1.2	3.5	11
Sweden	0.2	0.1	1.6	1.3	0.7	4
Switzerland	0.8	0.9	4	3.6	3.6	13
United Kingdom	0.8	1.2	5.7	9.4	3.8	21
European banks	1.3	1.7	6	4.5	7.3	21

Source: BIS- Consolidated foreign claims of reporting banks – end of 2009 (as a % of GDP)

Taken together, the credits held by the banks of the countries listed in the first column over the PIIGS amount to 21% of the creditor countries' GDP. The exposure of the French banks to the PIIGS represents 37% of the French GDP, mainly concentrated on Italy and Spain. The Irish banks' exposure represents 43% of the Irish GDP (mainly concentrated on Italy and Spain). The Dutch banks' exposure amounts to 33% of the Dutch GDP (mainly concentrated on Spain and Italy). The Belgian banks' exposure represents 28% of the Belgian GDP (mainly concentrated on Ireland and Italy). The British banks' exposure represents 21% of the British GDP (mainly on Ireland and Spain). This data shows to what extent the European financial sectors are intertwined and the propagation risk involved. A domino effect can rapidly and inexorably be triggered unless banks are forced to write off a considerable amount of credits from their balance sheets through debt cancellations.

In May 2010, US President Barack Obama put pressure on Angela Merkel, Nicolas Sarkozy and the other European leaders because US banks were also highly exposed. They had used the aid provided by

Washington from the end of 2008 to increase their positions in the EU, mainly in Germany and France where the banks were themselves heavily exposed to the periphery. If a crisis had broken out in the EU, the US banks would have definitely been hit by the boomerang effect.

In the chart below, the solid curve (UE-US) shows the evolution of European bank assets in the United States between March 2005 and December 2009 (the unit being $1,000 billion). The dashed curve (US-EU) shows the assets of US banks in the EU. It is clear that from December 2008, US bank assets in the EU increased whereas from September 2008 (Lehman Brothers' bankruptcy), the European banks began to withdraw (even if their exposure to the US remains very high).

Evolution of bank assets between the EU and the US

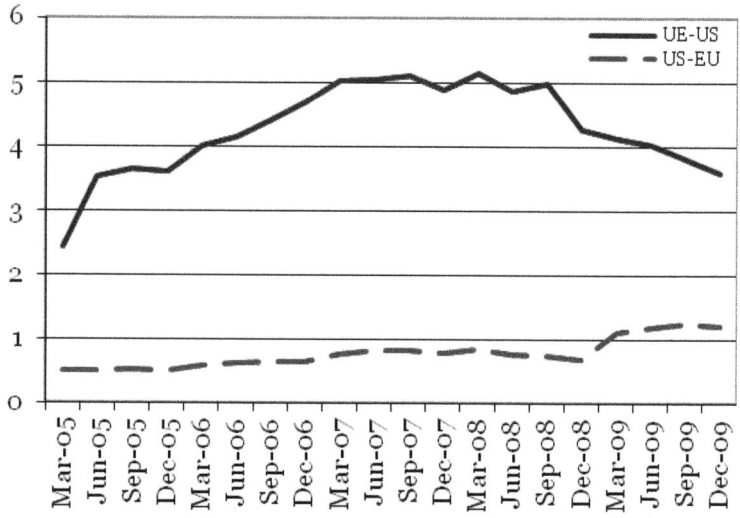

Source: BIS - Consolidated foreign claims of reporting banks - ultimate risk basis[9]

The price to pay for EU (and IMF) intervention comes in the form of austerity plans, in the EU periphery as well as in its core countries, which will have five major consequences:

1. they will prolong the crisis by compressing global demand;

---

9   Taken from C. Lapavitsas et al., op. cit., p. 30

2. they will weaken social protection mechanisms, and aggravate the poverty and precariousness of the victims of the crisis; they will strengthen the domination of the financial corporations, and thus of Capital, over society and States through the pressure (or even blackmail) they never fail to exert thanks to their position as creditors;
3. they will reduce the States' capacity to comply with their obligations with respect to basic human rights and intensify the trend to use repression as a response to social protests; they will also reduce the States' capacity to comply with their international obligations in the field of official development aid, of providing relief assistance to the victims of natural disasters in the South and contributing to the struggle against climate change.

Austerity measures will plunge one million British people into poverty, a study says.

The stringent austerity measures taken by the British government will plunge nearly one million people into absolute poverty, says the Institute for Fiscal Studies (IFS), an independent and highly respected research institute.

By the end of 2014, 900,000 people will fall into the "absolute poverty" category, consisting of households having real incomes of less than 60% of the 2010-2011 average income, according to IFS calculations.

This serious deterioration will result among other things in growing poverty among children for the first time in fifteen years: in 2012-2013, there will be 200,000 more of them living in "absolute poverty". Another 300,000 children will fall into that category in 2013-2014, according to the IFS.

"This finding is at odds with the government's claims that its reforms will have no measurable impact on child poverty in 2012-2013", says the IFS study. The government of Tory Prime Minister David Cameron has implemented a far-reaching austerity plan, considered to be the harshest of the big EU countries, which aims at saving £81 billion (about €92 billion) in less than five years. The plan also includes a tax increase of £30 billion to bring back the deficit to 1.1% of GDP by 2015, down from 10.1% this year.

The austerity plan includes cuts in social benefits, especially in housing.

The Exchequer considered the IFS study contained "considerable uncertainties".

Source: Agence France Presse (AFP). Dispatch of 17 December 2010.

Greece: the very symbol of illegitimate debt

The Greek public debt made the headlines when the country's leaders accepted the austerity measures demanded by the IMF and the European Union, sparking very significant social struggles throughout 2010.

But where does this Greek debt come from? As regards the debt incurred by the **private sector,** the increase has been recent: the first surge came about with the integration of Greece into the eurozone in 2001. A second debt explosion was triggered in 2007 when financial aid granted to banks by the US Federal Reserve, European governments and the European Central Bank was recycled by bankers towards Greece and other countries like Spain and Portugal.

As regards **public debt**, the increase stretches over a longer period. In addition to the debt inherited from the dictatorship of the colonels, borrowing since the 1990s has served to fill the void created in public finances by lower taxation on companies and high incomes.

Furthermore, for decades, many loans have financed the purchasing of military equipment, mainly from France, Germany and the United States. And one must not forget the colossal debt incurred by the public authorities for the organization of the Olympic Games in 2004. The spiralling of public debt was further fuelled by bribes from major transnationals to obtain contracts, Siemens being an emblematic example.

This is why the legitimacy and legality of Greece's debts should be the subject of rigorous scrutiny, following the example of Ecuador's comprehensive audit commission of public debts in 2007-2008. Debts defined as illegitimate, odious or illegal would be declared null and void and Greece could refuse to repay them; At the same time, they can demand that those who contracted these debts be brought to justice. Some encouraging signs from Greece indicate that the re-challenging of debt has become a central issue and the demand for an audit commission is gaining ground.

Factors proving the illegitimacy of Greece's public debt

Firstly, there is the debt contracted by the military dictatorship and which quadrupled between 1967 and 1974. This obviously qualifies as odious debt[10].

---

10   According to Alexander Sack, who theorized the doctrine of odious debt, "If a despotic power incurs a debt not for the needs or in the interest of the State, but to strengthen its despotic regime, to repress the population that fights against it, etc, this

Additionally, we have the Olympic Games scandal of 2004. According to Dave Zirin, when the government proudly announced to Greek citizens in 1997 that Greece would have the honour of hosting the Olympic Games seven years later the authorities of Athens and the International Olympic Committee planned on spending $1.3 billion. A few years later, the cost had increased fourfold to $5.3 billion. Just after the Games, the official cost had reached $14.2 billion[11]. Today, according to different sources, the real cost is over $20 billion.

Many contracts signed between the Greek authorities and major private foreign companies have been the subject of scandal for several years in Greece. These contracts have led to an increase in debt. Here are two examples which have made the main news in Greece:

1. Several contracts were signed with the German transnational Siemens, accused - both by the German as well as the Greek courts - of having paid commissions and other bribes to various political, military and administrative Greek officials amounting to almost one billion euro. The top executive of the firm Siemens-Hellas[12], who admitted to having "financed" the two main Greek political parties, fled in 2010 to Germany and the German courts rejected Greece's demand for extradition. These scandals include

---

debt is odious to the population of all the State. This debt is not an obligation for the nation; it is a regime's debt, a personal debt of the power that has incurred it, consequently it falls with the fall of this power" (Sack, 1927). For a concise overview, see (in French) *"La dette odieuse ou la nullité de la dette"*, a contribution to the second seminar on International Law and Debt organized by CADTM in Amsterdam in December 2002, http://www.cadtm.org/La-dette-odieuse-ou-la-nullite-de. See also "Topicality of the odious debt doctrine", http://www.cadtm.org/Topicality-of-the-odious-debt,3515 and http://www.cadtm.org/Topicality-of-the-odious-debt

11   Dave Zirin, *"The Great Olympics Scam, Cities Should Just Say No"*, www.counterpunch.org/zirin07052005.html : "But for those with shorter memories, one need only look to the 2004 Summer Games in Athens, which gutted the Greek economy. In 1997 when Athens "won" the games, city leaders and the International Olympic Committee estimated a cost of 1.3 billion. When the actual detailed planning was done, the price jumped to $5.3 billion. By the time the Games were over, Greece had spent some $14.2 billion, pushing the country's budget deficit to record levels."

12   See a detailed summary of the Siemens-Hellas scandal at http://www.scribd.com/doc/14433472/Siemens-Scandal-Siemens-Hellas. The charges made by the German courts against Siemens were so undeniable that in order to avoid a sentence in due form, the company agreed to pay a fine of €201 million to the German authorities in October 2007. The scandal has tarnished Siemens's image to such an extent that, in an attempt to redress the situation, the transnational company conspicuously announces on its web page that it has contributed €100 million to an anti-corruption fund. See: http://www.siemens.com/sustainability/en/compliance/collective_action/integrity_initiative.php

the sales, made by Siemens and their international associates, of Patriot antimissile systems (1999, €10 million in bribes), the digitalization of the OTE - the Hellenic Telecommunications Organization - telephone centres (bribes of €100 million), the "C41" security system bought on the occasion of the 2004 Olympics and which never worked, sales of equipment to the Greek railway (SEK), of the Hermes telecommunications system to the Greek army, of very expensive equipment sold to Greek hospitals.

2. The scandal of German submarines (produced by HDW, later taken over by Thyssen) for a total value of 5 billion Euro, submarines which from the beginning had the defect of listing to the left (!) and which were equipped with faulty electronics. A judicial enquiry on possible charges (of corruption) against the former defence ministers is currently under way. It is absolutely reasonable to presume that the debts incurred to clinch these deals are founded in illegitimacy, if not illegality. They must be cancelled. Beside the above-mentioned cases, one must also consider the recent evolution of the Greek debt.

The rapid rise in debt over the last decade

Debt in the private sector has largely developed over the decade of the noughties. The banks and the whole private commercial sector (mass distribution, the automobile and construction industries, etc.) offered very tempting conditions to households, whom then went massively into debt. The same happened to the non-financial companies and the banks which could borrow at low cost (low interest rates and higher inflation than for the most industrialized countries of the European Union like Germany, France, the Benelux countries and Great Britain). This private debt was the driving force of the Greek economy. Thanks to a strong euro, the Greek banks (and the Greek branches of foreign banks) could expand their international activities and cheaply finance their national activities. They took out loans by the dozen. The chart below shows that Greece's accession to the eurozone in 2001 has boosted an inflow of financial capital, which can be in the form of loans or portfolio investments (*Non-FDI* in the chart, *i.e.,* inflows which do not correspond to long term investments) while the long term investments (FDI- Foreign Direct Investment) have remained stagnant.

Flow of financial capital into Greece (in million dollars)

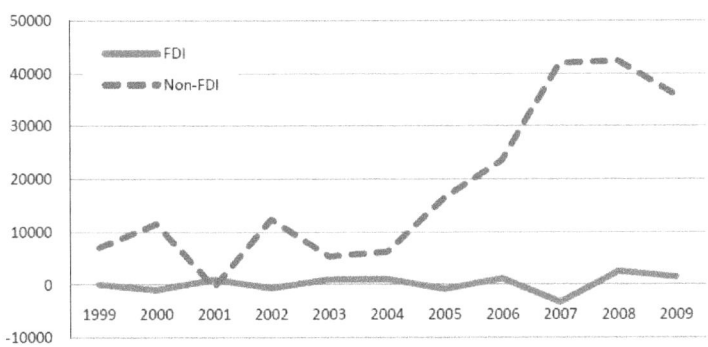

Source: IMF[13]

In the chart below we see that the countries of Western Europe first increased their loans to Greece between December 2005 and March 2007 (during this period, the volume of loans grew by 50%, from less than $80 billion to $120 billion).

Evolution of Western European banks' exposure to Greece (in billion dollars)

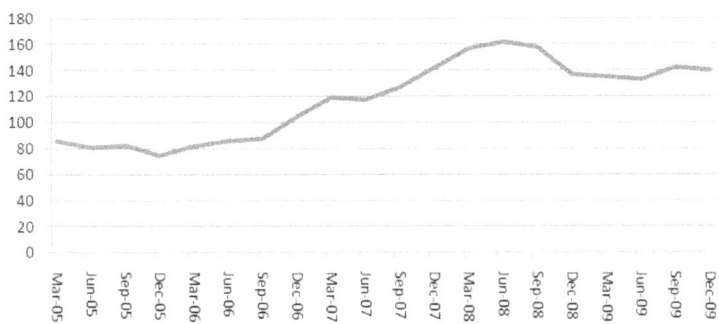

Source: BIS consolidated statistics, ultimate risk basis[14]

After the subprime crisis started in the United States, the loans increased dramatically once again (+33%) between June 2007 and the summer of 2008 (from 120 to 160 $billion). Then they stayed at a

---

13 Taken from C. Lapavitsas, A. Kaltenbrunner, G. Lambrinidis, D. Lindo, J. Meadway, J. Michell, J.P. Painceira, E. Pires, J. Powell, A. Stenfors, N. Teles : *"The eurozone between austerity and default"*, September 2010. http://www.researchonmoneyandfinance.org/media/reports/RMF-Eurozone-Austerity-and-Default.pdf.
14 Taken from C. Lapavitsas et al., op. cit.

very high level (about $120 billion). This means that the private banks of Western Europe used the money which was lent in vast quantities and at low cost by the European Central Bank and the US Federal Reserve in order to increase their own loans to countries such as Greece[15]. Over there, where the rates were higher, they could make juicy profits. Private banks are therefore in large part responsible for Greece's excessive debt.

Greek citizens have every right to expect the debt burden to be radically reduced, which means that the bankers must be forced to write off debts from their ledgers.

Infringement of social rights and neo-liberal measures implemented in Greece since 2010

• Reduction of public sector wages by 20 to 30 %. Cuts in nominal wages that could reach 20%, 13th and 14th month salaries replaced by an annual lump sum, the amount of which varies according to wages. A freeze on wages over the next 3 years. In the public sector, 4 out of 5 workers who retire will not be replaced. In the private sector, massive wage cuts up to 25%.
• Unemployment benefits have been cut, and a poverty support scheme implemented in 2009 has been suspended. Drastic cuts in benefits for large families.
• Plans to end collective bargaining and impose individualized contracts instead. The existing practice of extended very low paid or even unpaid internships has been legalized. Resorting to temporary workers is now permitted in the public sector.
• Employment: Drastic cuts in subsidies to municipalities, leading to mass lay-offs of workers. Sacking of 10,000 workers under fixed term contracts in the public sector. Public companies showing a loss to be closed down.
• Taxes: Increased indirect taxation VAT raised from 19% to 23% and special taxes on fuels, alcohol and tobacco introduced). Increase from 11% to 13% of the lower VAT rate (this concerns staple goods, electricity, water, etc.). Increased income tax for the middle brackets, but reduced corporate tax.
• Privatizations: Intention to privatize the ports, airports, railways, water and electricity supply, the financial sector and the lands owned by the State.
• Pension schemes: Pensions are to be cut and then frozen. The legal retirement age has been increased, the number of years' contributions required to be entitled to full pension benefits will be set at 40 in 2015 up from 37, and the amount of pension will be calculated on the average wages of the total working years and no longer on the last pay. For retired workers in the private sectors, the 13th and 14th month pension payments have been abolished. Spending related to pension has been capped to a maximum level of 2.5% of GDP.
•   Public transport fares: Price of all public transport fares increased by 30%.

---

15   The same occurred at the time for Portugal, Spain, and countries of Central and Eastern Europe.

The odious attitude of the European Commission

After the crisis broke, the military-industrial lobby supported by the German and French governments and the European Commission ensured that hardly a dent was made in the defence budget while at the same time, the PASOK (Socialist Party) government set about trimming social spending (see the box on austerity measures below).

At the beginning of 2010, at the height of the Greek crisis, Recep Tayyip Erdogan, Prime Minister of Turkey, a country which has a tense relationship with its Greek neighbour, visited Athens and proposed a 20% cut in the military budget of both countries. The Greek government failed to grab the line thrown to them. They were under pressure from the French and German authorities who were anxious to safeguard their weapons exports.

In proportion to the size of its economy, Greece spends far more on armaments than the other EU countries. Greek military spending represents 4% of its GDP, as compared to 2.4% for France, 2.7% for the United Kingdom, 2.0% for Portugal, 1.4% for Germany, 1.3% for Spain, and 1.1% for Belgium.[16] In 2010, Greece bought six frigates (€2.5 billion) and armed helicopters (€400 million) from France. From Germany it bought six submarines for €5 billion. Between 2005 and 2009, Greece was one of Europe's five largest weapons importers. The purchase of fighter aircraft alone accounted for 38% of its import volume, with, for instance, the purchase of sixteen F-16 (from the United States) and twenty-five Mirage 2000 (from France) – the latter contract amounting to €1.6 billion. The list of French equipment sold to Greece goes on: armoured vehicles (70 VBL), NH90 helicopters, MICA, Exocet and Scalp missiles as well as Sperwer drones. Greece's purchases have made it the third biggest client of the French military industry over the past decade[17].

From 2010, increasingly high interest rates charged by bankers and other players in the financial markets, supported by the European Commission and the IMF, have triggered the usual "snowball effect": the Greek debt has followed an upward trend as the country's authorities take out loans in order to repay interest (and part of the previously borrowed capital).

The loans granted as from 2010 to Greece by EU member countries and the IMF will not serve the interests of the Greek people; quite the opposite. The austerity measures implemented entail

---

16   2009 figures. Among the NATO members, only the United States spends more than Greece (4.7%) in proportion to its GDP.
17   Some of the data mentioned is taken from François Chesnais, "Répudiation des dettes publiques européennes!" in Revue Contretemps n°7, 2010, which is itself based on the data of the Stockholm International Peace Research Institute (SIPRI), www.sipri.org/yearbook

numerous infringements of the people's social rights. On these grounds[18], the notion of "illegitimate debt" should be applied and its repayment contested.

The demand for an audit is gathering momentum

In December 2010, the independent MP Sophia Sakorafa made a speech in the Greek Parliament proposing the creation of a Parliamentary Commission to audit the Greek public debt. This proposal attracted a great deal of attention.[19] Sophia Sakorafa, who was a member of the government party PASOK until a few months ago, voted against the 2011 budget[20] partly because of the heavy debt repayments. When justifying her brave position, she extensively referred to the audit carried out in Ecuador in 2007-2008 which resulted in a significant reduction of the country's debt. She proposed that Greece should follow the Ecuadorian example and asserted that there was an alternative to submitting to creditors, whether IMF or bankers. In making her case she placed stress on the "odious debt" that should not be repaid. This stance was widely covered by the media. Again in the Greek parliament, the leader of Synaspismos (one of the radical left parties) Alexis Tsipras also asked for an audit commission to be set up *"so that we know which part of the debt is odious, illegitimate and illegal."* Greek public opinion is changing and the media are watching.

Trade unions, several political parties and many intellectuals support this proposal as a means of finding a solution to debt through cancellation on the one hand, and penalization of companies and people responsible for this illegitimate debt on the other. It should be noted that a Greek anti-debt committee was set up in 2010.[21]

---

18   At least one argument can be added for that new debt to be declared illegitimate or void: for a contract between two parties to be valid, according to Common Law, the principle of contractual autonomy, of the voluntary consent of both parties, must be fully respected. This means that each party to the contract must be in a position to say no or refuse any clauses of the contract which go against its interests. When in March-April 2010 the financial markets started to blackmail Greece and when the European Commission and the IMF united to impose draconian conditions on Greece (very harsh austerity measures that infringe social and economic rights), it can be considered that Greece was not really in a position to exert its autonomy and refuse them.
19   See http://tvxs.gr/node/73861/450287
20   http://www.hri.org/news/greek/eraen/last/10-12-22.eraen.html
21   See its website http://www.contra-xreos.gr/. This committee joined the CADTM international network in December 2010.

The Irish crisis: a complete failure for neo-liberalism[22]

For a decade, Ireland was heralded by the most ardent partisans of neo-liberal capitalism as a model to be imitated. The Celtic Tiger boasted a higher growth rate than the European average. The tax rate on companies had been reduced to 12.5%[23] and the rate actually paid by TNCs that had set up business there was between 3 and 4% - a CEO's dream! Ireland's budget deficit was nil in 2007, as was its unemployment rate in 2008. In this earthly paradise, everybody seemed to benefit. Workers had jobs (though often highly precarious), their families were busy consuming, benefiting as they were from the prevailing abundance, and both local and foreign capitalists were enjoying inordinate returns.

In October 2008, a couple of days before the Belgian government bailed out the big "Belgian" banks Fortis and Dexia with taxpayers' money, Bruno Colmant, head of the Brussels stock exchange and professor of economics, published an op-ed in *Le Soir*, the French-language daily newspaper of record, stating that Belgium imperatively had to follow the Irish example and further deregulate its financial system. According to Colmant, Belgium needed to change the legal and institutional framework so as to become a platform for international capital, just like Ireland. A few short weeks later the Celtic Tiger was crying mercy.

In Ireland, financial deregulation had triggered a boom in loans to households (household indebtedness had reached 190% of GDP on the eve of the crisis). This is particularly so in real estate, a factor that helped boost the island's economy (the building industry, financial activities, etc.). The banking sector had experienced exponential growth with the establishment of many foreign companies[24] and the increase in Irish banks' assets. Real estate and stock market bubbles started forming. The total amount of stock market capitalizations, bond issues and bank assets was fourteen times bigger than the country's GDP.

---

22   The present section is largely drawn from a slide show by Pascal Franchet, "Actualité de la dette publique au Nord", (www.cadtm.org/IMG/ppt/Actualite_de_la_dette_publique_dans_les_pays.ppt)
23   The tax rate on company profits is 39.5% in Japan, 39.2% in the UK, 34.4% in France and 28% in the US.
24   The problems experienced by the German Hypo Reale Estate (bailed out by Angela Merkel's government in 2007) and the collapse of the US business bank Bear Sterns (bought over by JP Morgan with the help of the Bush administration in March 2008) were partly due to dodgy hedge funds located in Dublin.

What could not possibly happen in such a fairytale world then happened: in September-October 2008 the (house of cards?) card castle collapsed and the real estate and financial bubbles burst. Companies closed down or left the country, unemployment rose from 0% in 2008 to 14% in early 2010. The number of families unable to repay their creditors swiftly increased too. The whole Irish banking system teetered on the edge of bankruptcy and a panic-stricken government blindly guaranteed bank deposits for €480 billion (that is, about three times an Irish GDP of €168 billion). It nationalized the Allied Irish Bank, the main source of financing for real estate loans, with a transfusion of €48.5 billion (about 30 % of GDP).

Exports slowed down. State revenues declined. The budget deficit rose from 14% of GDP in 2009 to 32% in 2010 (more than half of this due to the massive support given to the banks: 46 billion in equity and 31 billion in purchases of toxic assets).

At the end of 2010 the European bail-out plan with IMF participation amounted to €85 billion in loans (including 22.5 billion from the IMF) and it is already clear that it will not be enough.

In exchange, a radical cure was enforced upon the Celtic Tiger in the form of a drastic austerity plan that heavily affects households' purchasing power, with a resultant decrease in consumption, in public expenditure on welfare, in civil servants' salaries, in infrastructure investments (to facilitate debt repayment), and in tax revenues. On the social level, the principal measures of the austerity plan are nothing short of disastrous:

1. suppression of 24,750 positions in the civil service (8% of the workforce, which would mean 350,000 positions in France);

2. newly recruited employees will earn 10% less;

3. reduction of social transfers resulting in lower family and unemployment allowances, a significant reduction in the health budget, a freeze on retirement pensions;

4. a rise in taxes, to be borne mostly by the majority of the population, already a victim of the crisis: notably a VAT increase from 21% to 23% in 2014; creation of a real estate tax (affecting half of the households that were formerly tax-exempt); a 1 euro reduction in the minimum hourly wage (from 8.65 to 7.65 euro, or 11% less).

The rates for loans to Ireland are very high: 5.7% for the IMF loan and 6.05% for "EU" loans. These loans will be used to repay banks and other financial bodies that buy bonds on the Irish debt, borrowing money from the European Central Bank at a rate of 1% - another windfall for private financiers. According to AFP, IMF managing director Dominique Strauss-Kahn claimed that it would work, though of course "it would be difficult because it is hard for people who will have to make sacrifices for the sake of budget austerity".

Both in the streets and in parliament, opposition has been very determined. The *Dail*, or lower house of parliament, voted the 85 billion euro rescue plan by a mere 81 to 75. Far from relinquishing its neoliberal orientation, the IMF declared that among Ireland's priorities it is counting on the adoption of reforms to do away with structural obstacles to business, so as to support competitiveness in the coming years. "Socialist" Dominique Strauss-Kahn said he was convinced that a new government after the elections in early 2011 would not change anything: "I'm confident that even if the opposition parties, Fine Gael and Labour, are criticizing the government and the programme [...], they understand the need to implement the programme (where does this quote come from?)."

In short, the economic and financial liberalization aimed at attracting foreign investments and transnational financial companies has utterly failed. To add insult to the damage the population must bear as a result of such a policy, the IMF and the Irish government are persevering in the neoliberal orientation of the past two decades and, under pressure from international finance, are subjecting the population to a structural adjustment programme similar to those imposed on Third World countries for the past three decades. Yet these decades should show what must not be done, and why it is high time to enforce a radically different logic that benefits people and not private money.

Contrary to popular belief, private debt is much higher than public debt

Major media and governments claim that in the North, *the* issue is the burden of public debt while in fact in most countries, private debt is much heavier. For instance, private debt accounts for 83% of Spain's, 85% of Portugal's and 58% of Greece's total debt[25]. Also for 89% in

---

25   See C. Lapavitsas, A. Kaltenbrunner, G. Lambrinidis, D. Lindo, J. Meadway, J. Michell, J.P. Painceira, E. Pires, J. Powell, A. Stenfors, N. Teles : *"The eurozone between austerity and default"*, September 2010, 72 pages,
http://www.researchonmoneyandfinance.org/media/reports/RMF-Eurozone-Austerity-and-Default.pdf

Britain, 76% in France, 66% in Italy, 75% in Germany, 79% in the US and 59% in Japan[26]. This huge private debt, particularly that of private companies, may well turn into part of our public debt tomorrow, as happened in 2007-2009, unless we watch out. Now a heavier public debt is used by current governments as an argument that would account for adopting new austerity plans primarily affecting social expenditure.

Proportion of external debt that is the government's responsibility (in % of the total external debt)

Austria	27.29%
Belgium	22.41%
Canada	23.62%
Czech Republic	22.54%
Denmark	6.90%
France	27.10%
Germany	25.45%
Iceland	4.70%
Ireland	4.61%
Italy	46.22%
Japan	31.81%
South Korea	8.77%
Netherlands	13.75%
Norway	16.17%
Poland	31.49%
Portugal	21.76%
Spain	16.72%
Sweden	7.79%
United Kingdom	5.16%

Source: FMI, http://dsbb.imf.org/Pages/SDDS/ExternalDebt.aspx. The figures are for the second term in 2010.

Let us look at the case of Ireland. If you ask people who get their information from the mainstream media whether Ireland's external debt is mainly public debt, they are very likely to give a positive answer. Yet Ireland's public external debt accounts for only 4.6% of the total external debt of the dying 'Celtic Tiger.' The chart above gives the proportion of external debt that is the government's responsibility[27]. Note that the share of private debt in total debt has risen steeply since the end of the 1990s.

---

26 Daily paper *El Pais*, "La deuda externa atenaza a España", 28 February 2010, on the basis of data from the IMF and the McKinsey Global Institute.
27 What is left of the external debt can be considered to be completely private.

Joseph Stiglitz and other economists support the position of those who argue for suspension of debt repayment

Joseph Stiglitz, 2001 laureate of the Sveriges Riksbank Prize in Economic Sciences in Memory of Alfred Nobel, chair of President Bill Clinton's Council of Economic Advisors from 1995 to 1997, chief economist and vice-president of the World Bank from 1997 to 2000, gives strong arguments to those who seek a suspension of public debt repayment. In a collective book published by OUP in 2010[28], he claims that Russia in 1998 and Argentina in the 2000s are proof that a unilateral suspension of debt repayment can be beneficial for countries that make this decision: "Both theory and evidence suggest that the threat of a cut-off of credit has probably been exaggerated (Herman et al. (2010), p.48)."

When a country succeeds in enforcing debt relief on its creditors and uses funds that were formerly meant for repayment in order to finance an expansionist tax policy, this yields positive results:

> Under this scenario the number of the firms that are forced into bankruptcy is lowered, both because of the lower interest rates[29] and because of the improved overall economic performance of the economy that follows. As the economy strengthens, government tax revenues are increased – again improving the fiscal position of the government. [...] All this means that the government's fiscal position is stronger going forward, making it more (not less) likely that creditors will be willing to again provide finance (Herman, et al., 2010, p. 48)." He adds: "Empirically, there is little evidence in support of the position that a default leads to an extended period of exclusion from the market. Russia returned to the market within two years of its default which was admittedly a 'messy one' involving no prior consultation with creditors [...] Thus, in practice, the threat of credit being cut off appears not to be effective (Herman, et al., p.49).

---

28   Herman, Barry, Ocampo, José Antonio, and Spiegel, Shari, 2010, *Overcoming Developing Country Debt Crises*, OUP Oxford, Oxford, ISBN: 9780191573699.
29   Indeed one of the conditions set by the IMF when it helps a country about to default is that it raises local interest rates. If a country is free not to comply with IMF conditions, it can lower its interest rates so as to prevent bankruptcies.

Joseph Stiglitz considers that those who believe that one of the central functions of the IMF is to impose the highest possible price on countries that wish to default are wrong.

The fact that Argentina did so well after its default, *even without* an IMF program, (or perhaps *because* it did not have an IMF program) may lead to a change in these beliefs (Herman, *et al.*, 2010, p.49).

Joseph Stiglitz also clearly challenges the part played by bankers and other creditors who granted massive loans without checking the (solvency?) of borrowing countries or, worse, who granted their loans while knowing full well that there was a high defaulting risk. He adds that since creditors demand high rates from some countries to compensate for risk it is only right that they should accept losses due to debt cancellation. Those creditors should have used the high interests they received as a provision against possible losses. He also exposes 'raider' loans all too lightly granted by bankers to indebted countries (Herman, *et al.*, 2010, p.55).

In short, Stiglitz argues that creditors should take responsibility for the risks they run (Herman, et al., 2010 p.61). Towards the end of his contribution he claims that countries that choose to default or renegotiate debt relief will have to enforce a temporary control on currency exchange and /or taxes to prevent a capital drain (Herman, *et al.*, 2010, p.60). He is in favour of the doctrine of odious debt and claims that such debt must be cancelled (p.61).[30]

In an article published in *Journal of Development Economics*[31] under the title 'The Elusive Costs of Sovereign Defaults,' Eduardo Levy Yeyati and Ugo Panizza, two economists who worked for the Inter-American Development Bank, set out the findings of their thorough enquiry into defaulting in some forty countries. One of their main conclusions is that '*Default episodes mark the beginning of the economic recovery.*' It couldn't be better put.

Alternatives

In August 2010, CADTM put forward eight measures related to the current crisis in Europe[32]. The central proposal as far as debt is concerned is a unilateral moratorium on debt repayment allowing the

---

30   Joseph Stiglitz has defended this position on several occasions over the past ten years. See his book *Globalization and Its Discontents*, 2002.
31   Journal of Development Economics, 94 (2011), 95-105.
32   http://www.cadtm.org/IMG/pdf/Debt_a_boon_for_creditors_30aout.pdf

debtor country to carry out **an audit of the public debt** under citizen scrutiny.

Below are the 8 measures proposed by CADTM and submitted for discussion to all movements and parties that believe a popular riposte is needed to counter Capital's opportunistic exploitation of the debt explosion.

1. **Announce a unilateral moratorium (without accrual of interest on overdue payments) on debt repayments, while an audit of the public debt is carried out (with citizen participation).**
   On the basis of the results of this audit, debt identified as illegitimate will be cancelled. With its experience in analyzing the debt issue in the South, CADTM warns against making insufficient demands such as the mere suspension of debt repayment. There must be a moratorium on all repayments including overdue interest on sums not repaid. The moratorium will be used to conduct a review of loans in order to identify illegitimate debts. Citizen participation is an essential requirement to ensure the objectivity and transparency of the audit. The audit commission should be composed of experts in auditing public finances, economists, trade unionists and social movement representatives among others. The audit will make it possible to identify the different responsibilities in the debt process and demand that those responsible be held publicly accountable. Debts identified as odious or illegitimate will be cancelled.

2. **Expropriate the banks without compensation and transfer them to the public sector under citizen control.**
   There is no sustainable regulation possible with private financial institutions. States must recover their capacity to control and direct economic and financial activities. The cost of taking over virtually bankrupt private banks must be recovered from the general assets of the major shareholders. The private companies that have shares in the banks and led them to the verge of ruin while making juicy profits have assets in other economic sectors. The general assets of the big shareholders must therefore be tapped. The idea is to avoid making the people pay for losses. The Irish example is emblematic: the way the Irish Allied Bank was nationalized is unacceptable. Lessons must be learned from it.

3. **Establish true European fiscal justice and fair redistribution of wealth. Ban legal and illegal tax havens. Tax financial transactions heavily.**
Together with a harmonization of European taxation in order to stop tax dumping, a radical reform of taxation is needed. The goal is increased public revenues, particularly through income and corporate tax, and a rapid decrease in the prices of basic goods and services (food, water, electricity, heating, public transport, etc.) by a sharp, targeted reduction of VAT on these vital goods and services. Since 1980, the rates of direct taxation on the highest incomes and the big corporations have been falling. For instance, in the EU between 2000 and 2008 the higher income tax rate and corporate tax rate fell by 7 and 8.5 points respectively. Those hundreds of billions of euros in tax breaks have been largely oriented toward speculation and the accumulation of more wealth by the richest. There must be a ban on all transactions passing through tax havens, which causes the countries North and South to lose resources each year that are crucial for social development. The G20 countries have repeatedly refused, despite their declarations of intent, to effectively tackle legal and tax havens. These dark chasms of financial corruption, crime and high level illicit trafficking must be banned. As well as the gradual increase in taxation, there should be dissuasive taxation on speculative transactions and on the income of debt creditors.

4. **Fight the massive tax evasion of big business and the rich.**
Tax evasion considerably reduces public resources and deprives the community of employment opportunities. Adequate public resources must be allocated for the effective repression of this type of fraud. The results should be made public and the perpetrators severely punished.

5. **Rein in the financial markets, particularly by creating a register of security holders and prohibiting short sales.**
Worldwide speculation represents several times the wealth produced on the planet. The highly complex nature of this financial engineering makes it totally uncontrollable The mechanisms that are put into motion deconstruct the productive economy. Opacity in financial transactions is the rule. To tax the creditors at the source they must be identified. The dictatorship of financial markets must cease.

6. **Drastically reduce working time to create jobs and increase wages and pensions.**
   Spreading the wealth differently is the best response to the crisis. The share of produced wealth going to employees has decreased significantly, while creditors and businesses have increased their profits and levels of speculation. Increasing wages not only allows people to live with dignity; it also enhances the means of providing social protection and pension schemes. Reducing working time without reducing wages and creating jobs also enhances the quality of life of the population.

7. **Re-socialize the many businesses and services privatized over the past 30 years.**
   A feature of the past 30 years has been the privatization of many businesses and public services. From the banks to industry, postal services, telecommunications, energy and transport, governments have delivered whole sections of the economy to the private sector, losing all possibility of control and regulation. These public goods and services, produced by collective effort, must be returned to the public domain. New public services must be created according to the people's needs, and particularly in response to climate change (creation of a public insulation service).

8. **A constituent assembly of the peoples for a different European Union.**
   The EU forced on European populations through constitutional treaties is a powerful war machine serving capital and finance. It must be completely re-shaped by a constituent process where the voices of the peoples are finally taken into account. This new democratized Europe must work, in CADTM's opinion, towards upward harmonization of fiscal and social justice, encourage a higher standard and quality of life for its inhabitants, withdraw its troops from Afghanistan, leave NATO, slash military spending, ban nuclear weapons, firmly commit itself to disarmament, end the 'siege mentality' policy towards potential immigrants, and become a fair and supportive partner in solidarity with the peoples of the South.

Breaking the domination of big business

The financial institutions behind the crisis enrich themselves and speculate on sovereign debts with the active complicity of the European Commission, the European Central Bank and the IMF to meet the interests of big shareholders and creditors. This private gain, allowable through tax breaks and regressive social legislation and then accelerated by government austerity plans, must cease.

The reduction of public deficits should not be achieved by reducing social spending, but by increased tax revenue through higher taxes on capital (business and financial capital) and income, on the assets of the wealthy and on financial transactions. This means breaking with capitalist logic and imposing radical social change. As opposed to the capitalism we currently live under, the new logic will break with productivism, integrate new ecological factors, and fight all forms of oppression (racial, patriarchal, etc.).

Our demands work towards an effective response to the crisis, in the interest of the people. Cancelling illegitimate debt is a matter for State sovereignty.

In a united anti-crisis front, we plan to assemble the various energies required, not only at European level but also locally, to create a balance of power favourable to the implementation of radical solutions focused on social justice.

Abolishing[33] illegitimate debt is possible, and is in the interest of the people!

Throughout history there have been numerous examples of debt abolition in countries in the South and North, sometimes unilaterally, sometimes as a result of court decisions, sometimes granted under pressure by the dominant powers.

International law is full of doctrines and jurisprudence that can facilitate, and in fact have facilitated, debt cancellation or repudiation.

A casebook example: CADTM actively participated in the audit of the debt of Ecuador in 2007-2008. This audit enabled the Ecuadorian government to force its creditors to sell securities to the State worth $3.2 billion with a 70% discount (put simply, the State bought back for $30 a bond whose face value was $100). This represented a 30 percent reduction of its external public debt[34]. This also enabled the State to save $300 million a year in interest for 20 years - a very substantial sum. This money is now spent on improving public health and education and on new jobs. In recent years other countries have successfully imposed unilateral moratoriums on the repayment of their debt: Russia in 1998, Argentina in 2001-2005 with $80 billion of debt securities sold to banks and other foreign investors (mainly German, Italian, and US). Since 2001 Argentina has suspended payments to the Paris Club for an amount of $6.5 billion

---

33   In abolishing a debt, the initiative can come from the creditor (cancellation) or the debtor (repudiation).
34   This concerned bonds falling due in 2012 and 2030 and were mainly owned by US banks.

and is in excellent health. It was as late as October 2010 that it officially resumed negotiations with its bilateral creditor members of the Club, imposing a condition that the IMF stays out of the negotiations.

These measures, insufficient though they may be, mark significant advances that can be used by social movements in the South and North to demand total and unconditional cancellation of illegitimate debt.

This cancellation is now a necessity and a matter of urgency, given how seriously the sums spent in servicing debts restrict the economic, social and cultural rights of populations, while reinforcing Capital's nuisance potential.

A process of convergence is currently under way

Fortunately, since September 2010, we have been witnessing a process of convergence between CADTM and other movements on ways to confront the issues of public debt and its exploitation by governments to introduce veritable structural adjustment plans. Here are some examples of this process:

In the "Manifesto of the appalled economists"[35] launched in September 2010 and signed by more than 2,700 economists as well as various activists, among the 22 concrete proposals for getting out of the crisis, two are partially in line with those put forward by CADTM:

> Measure 9: Conduct a public, citizen audit of public debts in order to determine their origin and identify the main holders of debt securities, as well as the amounts held.

> Measure 15: If necessary, restructure the public debt, for example by capping the service of public debt to a certain percentage of GDP, and by discriminating creditors according to the volume of shares they hold. In fact, very large stockholders (individuals or institutions) must accept a substantial lengthening of the debt profile, and even partial or total cancellation. We must also renegotiate the exorbitant interest rates paid on bonds issued by countries in trouble since the crisis.

On 24 September 2010, ATTAC Spain took the following stand on Greece:

---

35 See http://atterres.org/?q=node/13&page=2

In Greece, the opaque, secret and criminal association between Goldman Sachs and the previous conservative government deceived Greek and European citizens, with the complicity of the French and German banks. The rescue package allowed these German and French banks to make good their losses, while Goldman Sachs and the former political leaders freely enjoy the use of their loot. The fair answer consisted and still consists in the first place of issuing an international arrest warrant for the people responsible so that they be tried for their crimes; then in demanding that an audit of this debt be carried out in order to identify and recognize only the fair part of it, and finally in prioritizing the social interests of the Greeks over the interests of the private international banks by reconsidering the budgets and the commitments made in relation to the purchase of new submarines from Germany.

As far as Ireland is concerned, ATTAC Spain says:

> In this case, there are also many reasons for suing the current leaders and the board members of the private banks for their crimes. Refuse to continue paying the debt without a prior audit and prioritize the people's interests over the interests of the speculators and market fundamentalists who lie and deceive us.[36]

The Irish coalition "Debt and Development" has united several development NGOs and North/South solidarity organizations around a quite moderate platform which essentially focuses on better management of the loans granted to Southern countries. They have produced a 24-page document on the Irish crisis in which they ask for "key reforms in Irish government policy toward the IMF, central to which [is] an end to the IMF's practice of attaching economic

---

[36] "En Grecia la asociación opaca y secreta delictiva de Goldman Sachs con el Gobierno conservador anterior estafó a la ciudadanía griega y a la europea, con el apoyo cómplice de la banca privada alemana y francesa. El rescate articulado con fondos europeos ha ido a garantizar el cobro de sus fondos a estos bancos alemanes y franceses, mientras que Goldman Sachs y anteriores responsables políticos están libres y sin cargos disfrutando de sus botines. La respuesta justa pasaba y pasa primero por imputar a estos responsables y emitir una orden de caza y captura por sus delitos para que sean juzgados; segundo por no reconocer la deuda y exigir su auditoria previa para sanearla y reconocer sólo lo justo y, tercero por anteponer los intereses sociales de los griegos a los intereses de la banca privada internacional replanteándose los presupuestos y compromisos de compra adquiridos como los nuevos submarinos a Alemania." (...) "También allí hay motivos de sobra para juzgar los delitos de los actuales gobernantes y de los miembros de Consejo de Administración de los bancos privados. A negarse a pagar la deuda sin una auditoria previa y anteponer los intereses de la ciudadanía a los espurios de los especuladores fundamentalistas del mercado que nos mienten y engañan.", http://www.attac.es/realidad-contra-incompetencia-de-responsables-economicos-en-la-union-europea/

policy conditions to its loans." [37] As for the main Irish trade union confederation, it demands that a 10% reduction in the value of public debt securities be imposed on their holders. [38]

In a release dated 30 November 2010, ATTAC France put forward six proposals/demands that CADTM can largely subscribe to (even if it is regrettable that the debt audit is not mentioned):

1. Taxing and strictly regulating financial transactions, starting with transactions on the euro; prohibiting speculation on public debts; closing over-the-counter markets;
2. forcing into bankruptcy the banks which are too heavily indebted, without compensating the creditors and shareholders who have accumulated profits by playing with fire;
3. nationalizing the banks which have been bailed out with public funds; these banks will have to be promptly socialized, i.e., placed under the democratic control of workers, citizens and public authorities;
4. prohibiting deposit banks, which manage the savings of private individuals, to take speculative positions and to have subsidiaries in tax havens;
5. restructuring the debt, or establishing a partial default for the States crippled with the public debt burden: debt which has been worsened by tax breaks for the rich, the financial crisis and the bailout of banks, is illegitimate;
6. in addition, partial monetization of the public debt, the ECB buying State bonds directly from the States."

On 5 December 2010, a leading Greek daily published an op-ed by the Greek economist Costas Lapavitsas entitled: *"International Audit Commission on the Greek Debt"*. In his conclusion, the author writes:

> The international commission will have a privileged scope of activity in our country. You only need to think about the debt agreements made with Goldman Sachs's mediation or intended to finance the purchase of weapons to see how badly an independent audit is needed. If they are proved to be odious or illegal, these debts will thus be declared null and our country could refuse to repay them, while taking the people who incurred them to court.

On 17 December 2010, the European ATTAC network published a joint declaration[39] proposing real alternative measures, among which:

---

37   A Global Justice Perspective on the Irish EUI-MF Loans: Lessons from the Wider World ; http://www.cadtm.org/IMG/pdf/EU_IMF_Loan__28_Nov_2010-1.pdf
38   http://www.ictu.ie/download/pdf/prebudget_submission_web.pdf , p. 28
39   See ATTAC France's press release about the common declaration http://www.france.attac.org/spip.php?article12053

> establish a default mechanism by which the States would repudiate all or part of their public debt caused by tax breaks benefiting the rich, the financial crisis and the prohibitive interest rates imposed by the financial markets;
>
> reform taxation so as to restore public revenues and make it fairer, by taxing movements of capital, large fortunes and high incomes, profit made by companies, towards the establishment of a maximum income.

Here again, on the two points above, there are largely converging views between the European ATTAC network and the European CADTM network.

A few days later, Jean-Marie Harribey, former co-president of ATTAC France and a member of its scientific council, published an article titled "Serial killers must be nabbed" in which he proposes "collectivizing-socializing the whole banking system on a European scale."

Two paragraphs to which we can wholly subscribe are dedicated to debt:

> Cancel the illegitimate public debt. Everyone knows that increased public deficits and therefore increased public debt are not due to uncontrolled public spending. They are due to two factors. The first one has been operating pervasively for several decades, the French case being exemplary in this respect: taxation has been reduced on all sides, particularly progressive taxation, without the successive governments managing to make similar, proportional cuts in public and social spending, a great part of which cannot be compressed. The second factor is recent and more violent: it is the endorsement of private debts by the public authorities in the wake of the banking and financial crisis.
>
> It is therefore impossible to justify people being forced to bear the consequences of a situation they are in no way responsible for. Almost all of the public debt is illegitimate.

Conclusion

Unquestionably, the public debt issue erupted in the North on the occasion of the serious global crisis that had its beginnings in 2007-2008. The lessons of thirty years of structural adjustment in the South must be learned and the peoples of Europe must mobilize massively to avoid decisions taken in the North being the mirror-image of decisions imposed on the South over the past three decades.

Many movements are already raising the issue of the legitimacy of this debt and of the need for a comprehensive audit, so as to cancel the part that is illegitimate. This struggle is crucial for laying the basis of a radically different economic and financial logic. The public debt is a stranglehold that must be broken in the interest of the people, not the creditors. To begin implementing an economic and social policy that serves the people and tackles climate change, a radical reduction of the public debt is necessary. But this alone is not enough. It must go hand in hand with a whole series of radical reforms. Only mass mobilization driven by clear objectives can make this possible.

Translated by Francesca Denley, Stéphanie Jacquemont, Christine Pagnoulle in collaboration with Judith Harris

WOMEN'S CRISES

The Spanish economic recession and political responses from a feminist perspective

Sandra Ezquerra

Introduction

Over the past three years there have been numerous debates within the Spanish political and social left about the impact of the current economic crisis on working people and the inefficacy of the measures the government adopted to ameliorate them. However, there has not been much talk about the specific consequences that both the crisis and governmental responses have had on women. As a matter of fact, given the initial decline of male unemployment rates as a result of the enormous job destruction in the industrial and construction sectors, Spanish mass media have often conveyed that the economic crisis has hit men more severely than women. While in early 2007 male unemployment stood at 5.55% and female unemployment was 8.21%, by the end of 2009 the rates reached 18.15% and 15.63% respectively. Spain has not been an isolated case, and during the past few years mass media in other countries have stated that the economic downturn has impacted women less than men in employment (*Daily Mail*, March 2009) and proclaimed not just The Death of Macho (*Foreign Policy*, September 2009) but also the End of Men (*The Atlantic*, August 2010).

A feminist approach

Yet the *masculine crisis discourse* constitutes an uncritical interpretation of official unemployment statistics and masks both women's specific situation in the current economic context and the complexity of processes causing such specificity. The main consequence has been that the government has proven unable to examine the economic crisis from a gender perspective and has failed to notice its real impact on women's lives. The lower unemployment figure has led to trumpeting the achievement of gender equality in the job market. This conclusion is highly counterproductive since it dismisses the need for gender equality policies.

In this article I conduct a reflection on the importance of incorporating the feminist perspective in any critical analysis of current social reality. I do so placing special emphasis on two issues. First, a feminist approach to the crisis in Spain shows important issues such as the important impact that male unemployment has on families and women's quality of life, their real conditions in the labour market, the impacts of the crisis on non-remunerated reproductive work and, among others, the variety of situations looking at other variables such as national origin. Second, the lack of a gender perspective in the Spanish government's responses reproduces and deepens gender inequalities inside and outside the labour market.

Feminist glances...

A gender analysis of the current crisis makes it possible to draw innovative conclusions and proposals that classical and gender blind studies undertaken within sociology and geography have not proven able to offer. During the past few years, authors such as Gibson-Graham (1996), Marchand & Runyan (2000), Holmstrom (2000), Benería (2003) and, among others, Acker (2006), have reflected extensively on the need to analyse global and local economic processes from a standpoint that includes women in all their diversity. The field of economics has received, in turn, numerous criticisms and revisions from feminist economists such as Rubery (1988), Strober (1994), Nelson (1995; 2000; 2006), Waring (1999) that have translated into new conceptualizations of the "economic world". The object of analysis of classical economics had included up to then markets, monetary activities and capitalist accumulation processes therefore disregarding a crucial dimension of women's activities: domestic and care-giving work. Feminist economics, in contrast, has tackled reproductive work deepening into its previously hidden interdependence with the motions of capitalism. The consequences of this eruption, nevertheless, go far beyond a mere revision of the objects of study traditionally assumed by economists and, rather, reside in the vindication of the centrality of human needs fulfilling processes *vis-à-vis* the historical primacy of markets and production.

A reformulation of the concept of "economy" involves in turn a redefinition of the notion of "work", which does not mean just employment any more but also includes non-remunerated work or "all human activity intended to produce goods and services in order to satisfy human needs" (Carrasco et al. , 2007: 5). This redefinition challenges dyads such as employment/unemployment or activity/inactivity, which mask the variety of realities behind and between them and create notions of non-work, non-employment and non-activity from a clearly androcentric bias. Besides stemming exclusively from the experiences of most male remunerated workers, this bias conceals the importance of non-remunerated and non-counted work for the functioning of the system and provides as a result an absolutely distorted portrayal of the social and economic world (Pérez Orozco, 2006).

Therefore, women's social reality in the current context of deep economic crisis is not graspable through the sole use of conventional indicators such as unemployment rates or the evolution of the Gross Domestic Product. Behind the undisputed authority of macroeconomic and labour market official figures, women still suffer a great vulnerability both within and outside the remunerated work market. The cause, but also the justification of this vulnerability, resides in the historical identification of women as the main responsible actors of reproduction. Therefore, the relationship between women's remunerated and non-remunerated work is dialectical and results both in our secondary presence in the former as well as in a persisting invisibility and social, political, and economic devaluation of the latter. One of the consequences of all this in the current context is that when official statistics tell us that men suffer the effects of the crisis more severely than women they embody important gender biases. The results of the calculations are apparently neutral but more complex realities hide behind the numbers.

... at the effects of the crisis

First of all, the increase in male unemployment in Spain has resulted overall in more families depending on the woman's salary, which is usually the lower of the two. It has also forced many women's entry into the labour market to make up for their partner's job loss. However, while many women have important care-giving responsibilities, these are not being redistributed. Thus, the destruction of male jobs has resulted in the increase of women's total working time or, in other words, the number of hours they now have to work both inside and outside the household.

While 2008 was characterized by the bursting of the real estate bubble and a severe decline in the industrial sector, both highly masculine, within a few months the contraction of demand for labour force hit the service sector, where 88.5% of Spanish women work. This made the rate of female unemployment skyrocket, currently standing at 21.94%, slightly higher than the male rate of 20.76%.

Beyond the disturbing evolution of both female and male unemployment rates in Spain, women's labour conditions both before and during the crisis are much less favourable than those of men. First of all, they do not have an egalitarian presence in the labour market. Despite the fact that women are more than 50% of the country's population, they are currently only 44% of the active population. More importantly, 43% of the indefinite work contracts and 77% of the part-time workers are women. Ninety-seven percent of women take part-time work because of their care-giving responsibilities and 94.16% because of other family obligations. Women are in more vulnerable positions in the job market – particularly young women, immigrant women and single mothers (Harcourt, 2009; Larrañaga, 2009; Otxoa, 2009; Pérez Orozco, 2009). The average salary of employed women is 22% lower than that of male workers, and women continue to suffer both vertical and horizontal segregation in the labour market. They also suffer discrimination due to a reduction of working hours during their pregnancy and maternity leave and have a higher presence in the underground economy. The latter has a big impact on their social and labour rights.

Women have higher rates of temporary and part-time jobs as well as underemployment. They are 57.3% of those who receive welfare benefits and 37% of those who get unemployment compensation or retirement benefits. Generally speaking, when women are unemployed, they receive 15% less than their male counterparts and do so for shorter periods of time due to less stable employment patterns. Fully 80% of the "economically active" who do not receive any benefits or compensation are women.

According to numerous feminist authors, in order to cut down on family expenses women's domestic workload has increased (Gálvez & Torres 2010). This increase in their effort and total working hours results from the/a family's diminishing resources to hire another woman to conduct domestic work in the household. Women are constantly juggling their time in order to fulfil their responsibilities in the job market and in the private household. Many others are unable to join the formal labour market because of care-giving responsibilities. This feeds "underground unemployment," where thousands of "unemployed" women are not captured in official unemployment statistics because these only count what is considered "productive" activities. It would be interesting to know what percentage of the 9,392,400 currently "economically inactive" women in Spain (61.13% of the total) have made a choice not to take a remunerated job outside the household, and what percentage are unable to make a formal job compatible with their care-giving and domestic responsibilities.

Lastly, in order to understand the gender impacts of the current crisis we need to incorporate into our feminist and anti-capitalist analysis other social categories. If we examine current unemployment data in relationship to national origin, unemployment clearly affects non-European immigrants more severely than natives: by the end of 2010 the former showed unemployment rates of 30.67%, in contrast to 17.98% for Spanish-born workers. Thus, in clear contrast with the message the mass media has been sending the unemployment figure for Spanish-born men is half that of foreign-born males (34%). The rate for foreign-born women is more than 7% higher than their counterparts. Male unemployment in Spain can be traced to the enormous job losses immigrant men have suffered due to their concentration in the construction sector. Consequently it would be more accurate to state that the economic crisis has affected immigrants, both male and female rather than stating, as the mass media did in the early stages of the crisis, that men in Spain were the most impacted by the economic recession. Moreover, official statistics are not capable of revealing the full force of the crisis on the immigrant population residing in Spain. This is particularly true because immigrant women are concentrated in sectors of the informal economy such as domestic work, care giving and, among others, prostitution, where both their employment and unemployment usually go unrecorded.

In a nutshell, a glance at the crisis from feminist lenses shows several elements hardly noticeable from a conventional approach. Some of these elements are the impact that male unemployment has on families and women's life standards, women's real conditions in the job market, the dialectical relationships between reproductive and "productive" work and the full diversity of the crisis impacts when looking at other variables such as national origin. All this forces us to rethink traditional definitions of "economic", "work" and, among others, "economic activity". It also confirms the need to incorporate the feminist perspective in all critical social and economic analyses.

These analyses should incorporate and use new indicators able to reflect the gender inequalities existing in our society including elements, among others, such as total hours of work (both paid and unpaid), the double presence or double shift, hidden unemployment rates, amount of hours in care-giving work (both paid and unpaid), the number of caregivers according to their gender, immigrant men and women's rates of job permits and their presence in sex work, domestic work and the service sector[1].

Government responses

The lack of a gender perspective in analysing unemployment rates has also be a constant of the PSOE (Socialist Party) government's responses to the crisis, which reproduce and reinforce inequalities between men and women. At the very beginning of the crisis, the publicly funded rescue of banks was followed by a set of measures aimed at creating public employment. While in the government's recovery program (Plan EEE) there was a mention of social investments, its implementation focused on funding infrastructure-building projects that would quickly lead to job creation. The program had a short term approach and proved highly insufficient to solve the structural job destruction following the bursting of the economic and financial bubble. Moreover, while the construction sector had proven to be highly economically, socially, and ecologically unsustainable, it also had a highly masculine profile, since it employed 16% of men in the labour force and only 1.9% of women. During the first year of the crisis most of the €11 billion injected into public employment went to infrastructure (Otxoa 2009). Only 400 million were used for in-home support services. The short-term funding had no target that set aside jobs for women.

In early 2010, the financial and productive crisis yielded leadership and visibility to the fiscal one which, in turn, led to a frantic race toward austerity that still today continues to accelerate. This has resulted in enormous cutbacks in public social spending and a reduction in the salary of government employees. Since women are concentrated in education, social services and health, these "reforms" have had a big impact on them. Thus, women have been the main victims of wage cuts and job elimination. They also suffer more severely as the social services are reduced and disappear. In addition, they are the ones who, through their invisible and altruistic work, end

---

1   For detailed information on the existing studies on non-androcentric indicators see Carrasco, C. et al. (2007) *Estadístiques sota sospita. Proposta de nous indicadors des de l'experiència femenina*. Barcelona: Institut Català de les Dones

up carrying out this work without any compensation or recognition. Women are also more likely to bear the brunt of austerity as retirees who live longer than men and thus rely more on health care and social security and as mothers whose decision to work in the remunerated labour market often depends on the existence of affordable child care.

Beyond its disastrous effects on the working class in Spain, the recently approved Labour Reform erases bonuses for female hires. These have not been replaced by measures that could address the structural factors behind the discrimination women suffer in the labour market. In addition, the Reform keeps and strengthens employers' incentives for part-time hiring, which has been the main cause behind gender stratification in the job market during the past years. The greater internal and geographical mobility that the Reform introduces also affects women disproportionately, since they are usually less flexible than men. In addition, Spanish Labour Reform does not include household service employees in General Labour Law and therefore perpetuates the discrimination of a historically female labour activity, today primarily performed by foreign-born women. In addition, the freezing of pensions and the widening of the time period used to determine the final amount introduced by the recent Pensions Reform again particularly affects women since it increases the amount of formally worked years needed to obtain a full pension. Due to women's concentration in the informal economy and part-time jobs as well as to the frequent interruption of their professional life for motherhood and care-giving, women will face greater handicaps than men in achieving fair retirement benefits after the recently approved Pensions Reform (Ezquerra 2010).

Conclusion

I do not aim to minimize the impact of the economic system and its crises on male workers or other popular sectors. Rather, my purpose has been to shed light on the fact that women continue to be second-class workers and citizens. The current crisis perpetuates and strengthens their secondary presence and their specific exploitation in the job market, continually justified by their responsibility for the care of everyone surrounding them. The vicious cycle of patriarchal capitalism condemns them to a half-way entry into the labour market and a half-way exit out of the household, with both frozen processes permanently reinforcing each other.

The government response shows a lack of interest in transferring and reducing women's vulnerability and subordination.

The measures supposedly adopted to fight the crisis have been designed, debated and approved in order to strengthen the neoliberal obsession of zero-deficit budgets, but whatever gender and equal opportunities policies and programs existed have become its main victims. The recent suppression of the Ministry of Equality, the government's refusal to broaden parental leaves for fathers and the government's support to the European blockage on improving maternal leaves are only a few examples.

To expose and denounce the effects that the systemic crisis and the measures applied by its managers and guardians have on women does not mean we should look away from the totality of the working class. Rather, it constitutes an additional effort to achieve greater rigour and complexity in our everyday work to build a just society. This effort stems from a constant revision of our way of viewing, describing, and understanding the world. Perhaps it could also change our method of transforming it.

Revised, updated and reprinted from Against the Current 151, March-April 2011, International Viewpoint Online magazine, 434 - March 2011, and Viento Sur 114, January 2011

References

Acker, J. (2006) *Class Questions. Feminist Answers.* New York: Rowman & Littelfield Publishers

Benería, L. (2003) *Gender, Development, and Globalization. Economics as If People Mattered.* New York: Routledge

Carrasco, C. et al. (2007) *Estadístiques sota sospita. Proposta de nous indicadors des de l'experiència femenina.* Barcelona: Institut Català de les Dones

Ezquerra, S. "Crisis e igualdad". *Público*, 19/11/2010, pág.9

Gálvez, L. & Torres, J. (2010) Desiguales. *Hombres y mujeres en la crisis financiera.* Barcelona: Icaria

Gibson-Graham, J.K. (1996) *The end of capitalism (as we knew it).* Malden, MA: Blackwell

Harcourt, W. (2009) *El impacto de la crisis en las mujeres de Europa Occidental.* http://www.awid.org/eng/About-AWID/AWID-News/Briefs-The-Impact-of-the-crisis-on-Women

Holmstrom, N. (ed.) (2002) *The Socialist Feminist Project. A Contemporary Reader in Theory and Politics.* New York: Monthly Review Press

Larrañaga, M. (2009) "Mujeres, tiempos, crisis: Combinaciones variadas". *Revista de Economía Crítica*, número 8

Marchand, M. & Runyan, A. (2000) *Gender and Global Restructuring.* New York: Routledge

Nelson, J. A. (1995) "Feminism and Economics". *The Journal of Economic Perspectives*, 8(2)

Nelson, J. A. (2000) "Economics at the Millennium". *Signs*, 25(4)

Nelson, J. A, (2006) "Can We Talk? Feminist Economists in Dialogue with Social Theorists". *Signs*, 31(4)

Otxoa, I. (2009) "Anticapitalismo: algunas razones desde el feminismo". *Viento Sur*, número 104

Pérez Orozco, A. (2006) "¿Hacia una economía feminista de la sospecha?". *En otras palabras.* Nº 13-14

Pérez Orozco, A. (2009) "Feminismo anticapitalista, esa Escandalosa Cosa y otros palabros". Ponencia presentada en las *Jornadas Feministas Estatales* celebradas en Granada en diciembre del 2009.

Rubery, J. (1988) *Women and Recession.* London, Routledge

Sales, L. (2009) *Informe de Recerca. Dones en crisi.* Barcelona: Institut Català de les Dones

Strober, M. H. (1994) "Economics through a Feminist Lens". *The American Economic Review.* 84(2)

Waring, M. (1999) *Counting for Nothing. What Men Value and What Women Are Worth.* Toronto: University of Toronto Press

EASTERN EUROPE FACED WITH THE CRISIS OF THE SYSTEM

Catherine Samary

The project of "European construction" (associated with the redefinition of continental relationships after the fall of the Berlin Wall) aroused popular aspirations, which were radically opposed to the current situation. These were aspirations for a continent that would resist antisocial policies according to a democratic, social, ecological and solidarity-based logic while remaining open to the world. In particular, this was what was hoped for in Eastern Europe, where the populations aimed for greater freedom and a higher standard of living. These hopes were shattered, creating a breeding ground for xenophobic trends. Understanding the turns of history, the specificities of globalisation and "European construction" in which Eastern European countries have been involved, that is, the true framework of the present crisis (versus superficial indicators of "catching up") is essential for the people to be able to re-appropriate their choices and thus their future.

The confrontation of Eastern Europe to the new world order in the 1980s

The 1970s had been a decade marked by a crisis of profitability and of the world order striking the countries of the capitalist centre. The countries of Central and Eastern Europe remained, as exemplified by Czechoslovakia, dependent on the economic "support" of the USSR, backed by its tanks. Their debt towards Moscow, in non-convertible roubles (in the framework of the barter relations within Comecon – the Community of Mutual Economic Aid, governing the exchanges between countries with planned economies) was now coupled with a second debt; this one was denominated in hard currencies, which had become a heavy burden. Still subject to a financial and industrial Cold War boycott that had blocked any imports of cutting-edge technology since 1917, the USSR was not involved in this debt. The opening of borders to Western imports aimed at the acquisition of modern technologies, was thus done (with the agreement of the USSR) by the countries of Eastern Europe that were not subject to the Western boycott. For these regimes, this newly open window also corresponded to the search for imports of Western consumer goods to reduce mass discontent after the stalemate of the economic reforms of the 1960s. Additionally, the process was a question of obtaining certain Western technologies with the aim of improving the quality and the productivity of their own exports: which would then make it possible to repay the debts in foreign currencies. But bureaucratic conservatism did very little to make the technological imports effective and the debt steadily increased, accentuated by rising interest rates in the beginning of the 1980s.

The election of Reagan after the Soviet intervention in Afghanistan launched an extreme phase in the arms race, which weighed heavily on the USSR in the first half of the 1980s. The cold war peak gave the United States the opportunity to take the offensive in several aspects of their own multidimensional crisis: on the domestic level, public spending on military weapons and equipment, strongly supported research and innovation, while re-charging an economy that had started the decade in a recession.

At the same time, on an international level, the United States began the first phase of a broad-reaching resurgence of the Military-Industrial Complex and technological hegemony. This would be enforced by the military interventions of the following decade. The technological revolution that was under way in the United States and in the greater part of the capitalist world was an essential element in the ability of the ruling classes to restructure social relations and the world order. These shifts would widen the gap between the United States and the Eastern bloc; a gap that had been historically reduced between the Second World War and the 1970s.

The 1980s were therefore marked by debt crises in several Eastern European countries – Romania, Yugoslavia, Hungary, Poland and East Germany (the GDR). Incapable of profoundly reforming themselves without major anti-bureaucratic social transformations, these countries had launched imports of Western technologies in the preceding decade, financed by private credit.¹ This debt crisis marked a new historical phase, allowing major external pressures to weigh on the societies of Eastern Europe at the very moment when the USSR of Gorbachev was turning towards an external "disengagement".

This process was aimed at obtaining the Western credit that was necessary for its modernization. The search for hard currency to pay for imports thus resulted in additional pressures and tensions within COMECON at the end of the 1980s. The USSR was, from then on, demanding repayment of debts, and if possible in hard currencies. Moreover, it was making the search for Western finance and technologies a priority in foreign policy. Therefore this phase marked a "withdrawal" from any interventionism, as exemplified by the agreement negotiated with Chancellor Kohl on German unification.

Meanwhile, the five indebted countries of Eastern Europe had experienced different politico-economic trends, which all played a decisive part in the historical turning point of the "transition" towards a change of system at the start of the 1980s:

- The Yugoslav Federation, under pressure from the International Monetary Fund (IMF) in the 1980s, was paralysed by the rise of social and national conflicts and by three-figure hyperinflation, reflecting the loss of overall coherence of the system. The wars of ethnic cleansing which accompanied the dismantlement of the Yugoslav federation and its system, as well as the impasses of the European and U.N. peace plans, were used by the United States to redeploy NATO after the dissolution of the Warsaw Pact. The Yugoslav crisis was a decisive stage in the Euro-Atlantic integration of the region.²

- The Hungarian Communist leaders were unique in deciding to respond to the crisis of the external debt by selling the country's best enterprises to foreign capital. This initially created the opportunity to diminish the internal austerity policy, and made Hungary the principal host country for foreign direct investment (FDI), in the first years of the

---

1   In the 1970s, Western banks sought to use the dollars that came from oil revenues by offering plentiful credit to the countries of the South. But what is less well-known they did the same to the Eastern European countries mentioned above (Yugoslavia, Hungary, Romania, Poland and the GDR). The debt crisis that these countries experienced in the following decade was a decisive vector of the external pressures of Western creditors and of the IMF.

2   See http://csamary.free.fr, for articles relating to these subjects concerning the "world disorder" or the "capitalist restoration."

following decade of "transition." The Hungarian government also did not hesitate (following on the new European relations established by Gorbachev) to help to bring down the Wall (for a price).
- Conversely, the dictator Ceausescu attempted to pay back Romanian debt on the backs of his people – an act that the Romanian *nomenklatura* finally rejected as too explosive for itself. This group subsequently instigated a pseudo "revolution" which included the execution of the dictator at the end of the 1980s.
- Meanwhile, with the agreement of the USSR, the absorption of the GDR by the Federal Republic of Germany was agreed. The USSR received financial resources from Germany accompanying the repatriation of its troops.
- Lastly, after the repression of *Solidarnosc* under the regime of the Polish general Jaruzelski, compromise agreements opened the door for the introduction of liberal shock therapy in Poland. This was backed by the cancellation of the Polish debt, as decided by the United States, at the beginning of the 1990s. Indeed, no expense was spared to win over the new "elites" who came to power in the time of privatizations.

The integration into globalized capitalism and new world order had begun. But what about European construction?

Core and peripheral countries in "European construction"

"European construction" (*i.e.*, the building of a supranational political European Community which became the European Union (EU) in 1993) highlighted the asymmetric relationships between core countries and eastern and southern peripheries.

Analysis in terms of "core/peripheral countries" is necessary to understand how the norms and mode of financing are determined. These structures need to be contextualized: those within the framework of the European Union differ from those between the EU's core countries and non-member peripheral states (for instance, the supposed "free-trade" Euro-Mediterranean zone proposed by the French government). Conflicting policies and economic situations also differentiate core countries like France, Germany, and Great Britain. The EU's architecture, which is now facing a serious crisis, was not a preconceived "project" with a clear-cut political consistency among historical founding members from the Rome Treaty in 1957.

The future EU countries succumbed to the crisis of the Bretton Wood's international monetary system at the beginning of the 1970s. This produced several attempts at building a European monetary system (EMS) among member states, with an official European currency unit (ECU). The ECU-based EMS was confronted with another crisis when the Maastricht Treaty was signed in 1992, thus preparing the way for the euro as a single currency. All these transformations occurred in the context of the neoliberal US-led globalisation and arms race, which had begun in the early 1980s.

French and German choices were key to the political and institutional changes of the European community. Therefore, the social-liberal turn in France in 1982/1983 was the political precondition for a new institutional phase in the European construction. Starting with the White Book in 1986: they radicalised free market competition and ended the control of capital flows. The "economic and monetary Union" was aimed at building a "competitive Europe". German unification was not foreseen in such a project. Moreover, the US, British and French governments did not share the same views on this matter.[3]

The European Community's enlargements to include first southern and then eastern European countries included both similarities and stark differences. All of these countries increased the socio-economic and political heterogeneity of the Community. Also, all the new members came out of dictatorships and were poorer and more rural than the average of the other members.

Last, but not least, in both cases the core countries' vote in favour of the enlargement was more geo-politically motivated than economic. Had what was at stake only been the imposition of market relationships of domination, "usual" means of so-called "free exchange" and financial dependence it would have been easier to implement than the complex constraints of institutional enlargement. Many actors argued in favour of clarifying and "deepening" first the unity and mechanism of decision making before broadening the heterogeneity of the Union. Some voices of the left even opposed the eastward enlargement viewing it as a US project aiming at a "dissolution" of a political rival into a NATO and free market zone. The "reality" is that geo-political issues were involved in a nonlinear and multidimensional "process".

---

3   The opening of the archives 20 years after the fall of the Berlin wall shed new light on the hostility of Margaret Thatcher to German unification, on Mitterrand and Gorbachev's initial projects of "common European House" and on the evolution of Helmut Kohl choices under US pressure. see http://www.timesonline.co.uk/tol/news/politics/article6829735.ece

When Greece, Portugal and Spain began to discuss entering the EC at the end of the 1970s, the Portuguese revolution and Allende's Chile had to be eliminated from popular hopes and memories. At that time, the bi-polar world was threatened by thriving anti-colonialist and anti-bureaucratic movements. This was a period when US imperialism itself was losing its hegemonic strength. Therefore, the integration of the southern European peripheral countries in the European community had to be an attractive socio-economic and political (even if capitalist) alternative: equal status for members and political democracy against dictatorships were stressed. Even if it was more market-oriented than democratic, these included a "regional" approach which could be sensitive to conflicting national issues within the multinational Spain.

Emphasis was put on the need for redistributive funds (therefore for an increased European budget) to decrease inequalities between members. The obvious fact that "pure market competition" between uneven regions and countries simply increases the gaps between them – and therefore produces less cohesion – was clearly recognized. Altogether, slogans and funds were pushed forward in favour of the three new members from Southern Europe and Ireland (called at that time the four *"Cohesion's countries"* – which contrasts with the contemptuous acronym built on their names twenty years later : P.I.G.S.).

But the fall of the Berlin Wall in 1989 opened a more radical historical turning point at the heart of neo-liberal globalisation and European construction. The dismantling of the "Soviet bloc" had, of course, a much wider geo-strategical and ideological stake. This was determined (but not foreseen nor clearly controlled) through the German issue.

From German unification to eastward enlargements - and from NATO to the EU's big bang

Gorbachev's endorsement of German unification was the first step of a "domino effect" favouring the end of the single party and central planning system in the whole region. But it also radically changed the functioning of the European Union and its political, financial and military dimensions.

The final scenario was far from Mitterrand's or Gorbachev's initial projects of "a common European House," a confederated Germany and dissolution of the two cold war's Pacts. Gorbachev's aim was to reduce the arms race and to win western credits and technologies for the internal reforms of the Soviet Union through agreements with Federal Germany. His final signature permitted the repatriation of Russian troops generously financed by Germany, despite the fact that the kind of monetary unification of Germany on the basis of the Deutschmark, and the integration of GDR in NATO were not included in the package deal at all. The unilateral dissolution of the Warsaw Pact was finally accepted with the "promises" that NATO would not extend eastward.

However, the United States' geopolitical aims were (as well as the dismantling of the Soviet Union) to try and define new "functions" for NATO and to prevent the consolidation or establishment of any political and military rival. German unification and its integration into NATO, then NATO's intervention in Kosovo and its extension in Eastern Europe served all those purposes.[4]

Together with German unification, Poland's neoliberal turn and integration in NATO were strategical issues for the dynamics of the whole region. The independent trade union, *Solidarnosc* (Solidarity) had led an impressive democratic mass workers movement mobilized in 1980 against the former regime, but in favour of a "self-managed republic" – far from meeting neoliberal criteria. *Solidarnosc* had already been dramatically repressed after 1981 by the Polish "communist" general Jaruzelski and the former single party's dictatorship. This repression increased the rightist ideological evolution of its members and leaders while sharply reducing the size of the organisation. But for the US-led turn in 1989, any hope or lasting elements of self-management within factories, or any demands in favour of social rights needed to be eliminated or turned towards the illusions of "privatizations". That was the function of neoliberal "shock therapy" in Poland which was combined with the not-very-public cancellation of a broad part of the Polish debt and with a very high level of corruption of trade union leaders.

But what did that mean for the European Community? The US choice to integrate the unified Germany into NATO was paralleled by the French effort to convince the German government to enter the European Monetary Union. In 1992, the Maastricht agreements were established with this purpose in mind. In addition, the "Copenhagen Criteria" established by the European summit in Denmark in 1993, defined the supposed rules for accepting new members.[5]

---

4   These issues are addressed in the articles written by Peter Gowan published by *Labour Focus on Eastern Europe* see http://labourfocus.gn.apc.org
5   Those criteria were supposed to be the rules that define whether a country is eligible to become a member of the Union (it is not the final decision but a precondition): specifically, political institutions protecting democracy and human rights; a

Nevertheless, during a large part of the 1990s, the World Bank, the IMF and NATO – therefore US diplomacy – were much more active in Eastern Europe than was the European Commission. Washington took advantage of the European and United Nation's (UN)'s failures in dealing with the Yugoslav crisis, to define the new role and extension of NATO in Eastern Europe.

The "big bang" of eastward enlargement of the European Union became decisive in 1999. The context of this enlargement was, on one hand, increasing turmoil produced by opaque privatizations; and, on the other, the first NATO war (in Kosovo). Ten years after the fall of the Berlin Wall, the opening of the EU to ten East European candidate countries was again a geo-strategical choice with several dimensions: a way to try to counterbalance (or at least be associated with) the direct US influence in Europe; and an attempt at lessening increasing popular dissatisfaction over the effects of privatizations (with the collapse of all neoliberal coalitions, then of social-liberal parties and of abstentions in the elections and increasing support or the rise of xenophobic nationalist parties). But it was also an ideological argument for the defenders of the neoliberal European construction that were lacking "material" evidence of well-being and real democratic choices for the populations: this new enlargement was presented as an historical and generous "reunification of the continent".

Ideology is built on lies and significant omissions. But it reveals which arguments were useful to win some popular support. This was not the general wild market competition, destruction of social services and the "really existing capitalism." On the contrary, "democracy and freedoms," more peace and cohesion at the continental level, solidarity and sharing the highest "values" on human rights were stressed. Who could be against it?

Joining the Union to become less peripheral?

The EU is not NAFTA (North American Free Trade Agreement between US, Mexico and Canada). Membership of the EU gives a political status. There should be no doubt about the lack of real equality and of real power of popular democratic control within the European institutions: they are dominated by non-elected bodies. But the specificity and attractiveness (even if it is illusionary) of

---

"functioning market economy" and the integration in its legislation of the EU texts and rules.

"European construction" in peripheral countries can be illustrated through different issues which should be taken in account to develop a democratic European alternative.: First, the acute debates (especially in Poland) around the number of votes given to each member states within the European Council, revealing the will of peripheral countries to be respected and treated on equal footing,[6] Second, the relative importance of European funds for the less developed regions and countries - even with a very narrow budget to share – because of their non-market redistributive logic to reduce inequalities. Third, the "image" of a "European social model" explicitly used at a propagandist, ideological level by the European governing institutions (like the European commission – EC) to make people vote in favour of the EU (polls and enquiries made by Eurostats have also confirmed high social popular expectations about the role of the European construction); fourth, the popularity, especially among young people, of the alleged withering away of frontiers – a hope later contradicted by Schengen's anti-immigrant "witch hunts", racism and new walls of poverty.

But all that meant was that one could vote for entering the Union with completely opposing logic. As such, Margaret Thatcher was a champion of the Czech right-wing parties that wanted free market competition against any power for "Brussels." However, on the other hand, entering the EU could be associated with the feeling of easier resistance against relationships of domination from the core countries, national xenophobia and neoliberal competition. The hope of establishing organic links with other European people on a common basis was the dominant logic of the Hungarian left which was involved in European social forums. It could also be summarized by two kinds of "realistic" remarks heard in Eastern Europe at that time. The first one was: "we have already submitted to international and European capital and financial institutions – let us have at least access to some funds and rights." The second was heard in Slovenia, the most developed part of the former Yugoslavia, and the richest of all East European new members of the Union: "better be the last in the town than the first in the village."

With the entry of Spain and Portugal in 1986, the difference in per capita GDP between the poorest and the richest states of the Union was from 1 to 4.9. With the arrival of Romania and Bulgaria in 2007, it increased to 20.1.

---

6   The number of votes is supposed to be according to the size of the population and not to the level of development. Germany, France, Italy and GB have 29 votes each; Spain or Poland has 27 each; Austria has the same number of votes as Bulgaria. Of course all that does not mean "democracy" and real equal power; but it expresses some political constraints within the Union.

> **A look back at the "generous" choices of the "historical" unification of the continent**
> The fall of the Berlin Wall in 1989 began a new historical phase for Eastern Europe. But it also marked a turning point at the heart of neoliberal globalisation and European construction.
> The Maastricht Treaty in 1992 tried to contain the socio-economic and political heterogeneity of the member states by narrowly monetarist criteria without equivalent policies in the richest countries of the planet (Japan, the United States...): limitation of public deficits and debt associated with a veto imposed on the central banks of the eurozone against financing member states. Behind largely arbitrary criteria, what was being negotiated was Germany's abandonment of the deutschmark and its distrust of the "laxness" of the peripheral countries. In fact, since the countries of Central and Eastern Europe were still far from even being part of the EU, it was the southern periphery of the Union that Germany distrusted with regards to the creation of the euro and the future status of the European Central Bank: it was out of the question (and Germany inscribed this in its constitution) that the ECB should assist a member state in difficulty. This stipulation is at the heart of on-going conflicts with Angela Merkel about how to answer the "sovereign debt crisis" today. Therefore while each national budget had to lean towards being balanced, there was no question of an increased European budget to compensate for this constraint.

As already stressed, whereas enlargement towards the countries of Southern Europe and Ireland was accompanied by an increase in the "structural funds" of the European budget the opposite was decided in the EU's "Agenda 2000". Germany had only given up the deutschmark because it had also imposed severe budgetary rules; it did not want to "pay out" for the integration of the countries of Central and Eastern Europe.[7] However enlargement "paid" for Germany: it shifted ("delocalized") many assembly shops or productive units there, exerting downward pressure on German wages and basing its (weak) growth during the 2000s on export surpluses. But the European budget was fixed at a ceiling of 1% of European GDP (versus the 20% ceiling imposed for the US federal budget), whereas the "Growth and Stability Pact" imposed (as a pre-condition to joining the eurozone) limited debts and public deficits,

---

7   German unification involved a transfer of some 100 billion DM per annum towards the new Länder which were formally part of the GDR over more than a decade.

while prohibiting any financing of states by the central banks at reduced or zero rates.

Behind the "norms" and rules European construction covered over large differences in the powers of different states. In particular there was a "German exception" that was codified as such in the draft European Constitutional Treaty: over more than ten years, the budgetary transfers of the Federal Republic of Germany towards the new Länder from former East Germany came to more than 100 billion DM per annum (more, each year, that the entire total of private capital investing in Central and Eastern Europe during this entire period). In the course of the decade, these colossal resources were not used to improve the well-being of the East Germans (as was demonstrated by their political discontent and corresponding voting trends) but to dismantle social provisions, encourage privatizations and to keep wages low under the pressure of competition with the wage levels in neighbouring Eastern Europe.

Transfers of productive units ("delocalisations") were encouraged by the enlargement of the EU. Germany took advantage of its proximity to the new member states of the East to impose drastic wage austerity: between 2000 and 2007, nominal unit labour costs fell by 0.2% per annum in Germany. This can be compared to other European countries: they increased by 2% in France, 2.3% in Britain, between 3.2% and 3.7% in Italy, Spain, Ireland and Greece – in the peripheral countries this was a nominal increase that was augmented by higher inflation.

Another major destabilising element of this construction appeared: (weak) German growth was based on export surpluses, with low inflation and weak domestic demand, as well as a sharp drop in wages helped by the transfer of German factories to Eastern Europe. But the German surpluses corresponded to growing deficits in the periphery of Southern and Eastern Europe, even though they were heterogeneous entities.[8]

Along with France, Germany determined the Maastricht criteria of the Union, but it was one of the first not to respect them. Germany holds the purse-strings of the budget, emphasising how much it contributes without saying what it earns via its exports. And via "imports" within intra-multinational "trade," the final product

---

8   The strategies for growth in the countries of the South differed: Greece financed growth in consumption by debt. Spain based its growth on a scenario close to the real estate bubble of the United States and Britain. In the East the factors behind growth were more diversified (therefore less fragile) in Poland than in the Baltic republics. And, since the countries of Central and Eastern Europe (except Slovenia and Slovakia) are outside the eurozone, the diversity of the kinds of exchange and budget policies was even greater.

"made in Germany" incorporates low-cost inputs and low taxes on profit earned by Eastern Europe subsidiaries.

Therefore, the other side of the coin is the dependence of several Central European countries on Germany's growth.

Altogether, by the time the financial crisis linked to the subprime mortgage sector erupted in the summer of 2007, "Emerging Europe" (as the EBRD, the European Bank for Reconstruction Development, calls it) had received much higher capital inflows than Latin America and "emerging Asia," but for what kind of growth?

The different phases of the capitalist transformation before the crisis in the future "New Member States"[9]

The dominant features of capitalist transformation can be used to classify the history of the NMS (New Member States) between the fall of the Berlin Wall and the crisis of 2008–2009 into two major phases. However, GDP growth rate divides the post-Berlin Wall period into three phases:
- from 1989 to the end of the 1990s: the system's transformation through privatizations – under the dominant form of "mass privatization;"
- then a sub-phase (generally called "systemic crisis") was characterized by overall negative growth rates, more or less up to the middle of the decade;
- finally a "recovery", with uneven positive growth rates.

Overall the 1990s was a decade characterized by destruction of the old system: privatizations, the suppression of planning, and changes in

---

[9] We cannot deal here with the comparative scenarios of capitalist transformation and of the recent crisis in the whole Eastern Europe. Common features do exist between all of them, but also very important differences. Besides the Russian geo-political role, history, and huge resources in commodities – which need of course a specific approach -, one should also distinguish the countries coming out of the former Yugoslav and Balkan conflicts (involved in a process of negotiation to be associated to - or members of - the EU); and the countries coming from the former Soviet Union trying to find their place and interests between Russia, US, China and the EU. We focus here on the New Member States (NMS) of the EU. This common feature does not suppress important historical, socio-economical, political differences that we will certainly not address sufficiently. We shall indicate, at least, some of them for future analysis.

the criteria of economic policy and management were linked to radical changes in the functions of money and the banking system.

Table A: Different phases before the downfall in 2008-2009

	Average rate of growth of GDP and jobs					
	1989-1994		1994-2000		2000-2007	
	GDP	Jobs	GDP	Jobs	GDP	Jobs
Bulgaria	-5.7	-5.8	-0.2	0	5.6	2
Estonia	-1.6	-4.3	5.8	-2.7	8	1.7
Hungary	-3.2	-4.2	3.6	0.5	3.8	0.3
Latvia	-11.2	-5.1	4.3	-2.3	9	2.4
Lithuania	-11.5	-2,0	4.5	-1.2	8	1.3
Poland	-1.6	-3.6	5.7	-0.2	4	0.6
Czech Rep.	-2.3	-2	2.2	-0.8	4.5	0.8
Romania	-4.6	-1.8	0.1	-2.4	6.1	-0.8
Slovakia	-2.4	na*	3.8	-0.6	6.2	1
Slovenia	-2.3	-4.6	4.3	-0.3	4.4	0.9

Source: Eurostats and the online database de WIIW (Viennese Institute of International Economic Studies)

Table B: Life expectancy at birth in the countries of Eastern Europe *compared to the figures for France* **in the same years**

	Average 1970-1975	Average 2000-2005
Bulgaria	98.10%	89.70%
Hungary	95.70%	91.00%
Poland	97.40%	93.50%
Czech Rep.	96.80%	95.40%
Romania	95.60%	89.20%
Slovakia	96.70%	93.30%

Source: United Nations (UNDP), Human Development Report, 2004, New York 2004 – quoted by Jacques Sapir, La fin de l'euro-libéralisme, Seuil, Paris 2006, p.95.

The beginning of what has been called by international institutions, "the transition to market economies," in the first half of the decade, was marked by declines in growth of 20-40 per cent in all branches of the economy, both in the former Soviet Union and Eastern Europe as a whole. Moreover, when recovery took place[10] in an unequal manner, it was in the framework of a radical social transformation, with job losses and widening of income differentials: "inequality increased in all the economies of transition," which "began the transition with levels of inequality that were among the lowest in the world".[11]

Without this data, we cannot understand why within the framework of pluralist elections – the main new positive asset against the former regimes – the popular votes went to the former Communists from the very first years of the 1990s. This was not a question of nostalgia for the one-party state –which was radically rejected – but of the right to employment and access to all to basic goods and services. But the "ex" no longer defended these rights, which were excluded from the kind of growth and "convergence" advocated by the old Europe. From now on, the proclamation of "catching up" was only based on the comparison (East/West) of rates of growth of GDP – which is in no way an indicator of "well-being".[12]

The convergence of systems had privatizations as a benchmark. But with what money? The old system did not make accumulation possible and those who had formerly run the party-state preferred to be the recipients of privatizations. Thus were invented the "mass privatizations" carried out (in various forms) by the legal transformation of enterprises into private limited companies. Their "social capital" was transformed into equities, divided into shares and distributed virtually for nothing, partly to workers and citizens and the remainder to the state. Only Hungary and Estonia chose at the beginning of the "transition" to sell their best enterprises for "real money-capital" – in other words to sell them to foreign capital.[13]

As the functioning and criteria of the former system was not based on market prices and mechanisms, the privatizations were associated with new systems of prices and incomes and therefore

---

10   Poland was the first to return to growth and to catch up with the level of GDP. From 1989, this was enabled by a cancellation of its foreign debt that is seldom mentioned and a decade of repression marking a very low initial level. In 2000, only the countries of Central Europe had got back to the levels of GDP of 1989.
11   The World Bank, *Regional Overview*, 1998. See also World Bank *Ten years of transition*, 2002 Report.
12   You can have "growth" based on the GDP as an indicator (and with the very same criteria "catching-up" of a country in comparison to others if its rate of growth is higher), while at the very same time increasing inequalities, unemployment and destruction of social rights and of environment.
13   I develop the different forms of privatizations in particular in the article "the social stakes of east European Great transformation", *Debatte*, 2009. See also Jean-Pierre Page, "Europe de l'Est: économie politique d'une décennie de transition", *Critique Internationale*, n°6, Winter 2000.

substantial "losses" and "bad loans." There were no commercial banks in the planned economies and very limited deposits or savings. In the middle of the 1990s, the bulk of banks were still state-owned, and the share of foreign banks in the 10 Central and Eastern European countries ranged from 1% to 15% except in Hungary (where 8 out the 10 biggest banks had been sold to foreign owners in 1997) and Slovakia (where their share amounted to 33%).[14] But the real "bank sell-off" began around 1998, in the context of the international General Agreement on Trade and Services opening financial spheres to the free flow of capital.

1999: the "big bang" of the enlargement of the EU to the East

The undertaking by the EU to admit ten countries of Eastern and Central Europe was presented as a "success story" illustrated by a high rate of growth and increasing foreign direct investments (FDI) going to those countries up to 2008. The first eight countries[15] which were admitted in 2004, along with Cyprus and Malta, could vote in the European elections that same year. Romania and Bulgaria were admitted in 2007, and the Council of Salonika (2003) promised that the EU would be open to candidatures from the Western Balkans (Albania and the ex-Yugoslav republics – apart from Slovenia, which is already a member).

In spite of different scenarios and rhythms of reforms, the neoliberal rules for the "transition" from planned to market economies, as well as the heavy involvement of Western banks in the process (especially in New Member States) were generally[16] presented as solid assets: those countries seemed to be protected from the international credit crunch.

---

14   See *Focus on European Economic integration*, special issue 2009, Marianne Kager, "A Banker's Take on Twenty Years of CEE Banking Sector Developments".
15   The first new member states (NMT) were Slovenia, Hungary, Poland, the Czech Republic, Slovakia, and the three Baltic countries (Estonia, Latvia and Lithuania).
16   Özlem Önaran's September 2007 Working Paper n°108 (Vienna University of Economics and Business Administration, Political Economy Research Institute) "International financial market and fragility in eastern Europe : can it happen here?" is in sharp contrast to that dominant "mood." The author stresses the fragilities of that growth associated with increasing current account deficits. Some concerns about that issue were also expressed by the IMF *or* the EBRD's Transition report in 2008 (which one?). But the main "concerns" in such a report – as we will quote later on -, were about the difficulty to "open" the people's mind to privatisations of public services.

The "transitions model" was turned towards private financing because private capital is, according to the (neoliberal dogma, always supposed to be more efficient than public investments and financing. Therefore, decreasing taxes on corporate benefits were implemented to attract private investment flows. In order to reduce the fiscal deficit, the most regressive tax paid by consumers, Value Added Tax (VAT), had to be increased. In fact, at the beginning of the "transition period," such a tax had to be introduced in Eastern Europe, as it did not exist in former regulated economies.

Table C: The unbalanced growth of the Baltic States before the crisis

in 2006	LITHUANIA	ESTONIA	LATVIA
Growth of GDP	7.80%	10.40%	12.10%
Growth of Crédit	35%	53%	52%
Trade balance (as % of GDP)	-9.50%	-14.60%	-21.30%

Source: BIS (Bank for International Settlements), 9/09/2009, "The Baltic Region in the shadow of the financial crisis"

In the whole EU, the rate of corporate tax fell by 8.4% between 2000 and 2009, with the lowest rates established in the East. For example, this rate was 15% in Latvia (compared with an average of 23.5% in the EU 27).[17] The adverse effects quickly became clear: as the fiscal resources were globally being reduced, a balanced budget was to be found in the privatization process and the reduction of social financing of public services.

Table D: Share of foreign banks in total banking assets in new members of the EU (2009)

Bulgaria	Czech Rep.	Estonia	Hungary	Latvia
84%	84%	98,3%	81,3	69,3%
Lithuania	Poland	Romania	Slovakia	Slovenia
91,5%	72,3%	84,3%	91,6	29,5%

Source: European Bank of Research and Development (EBRD) Transition reports 2009 and 2010

---

17   Eurostats, June 22, 2009.

However, we have already mentioned another strategic source of financing under the pressure of capitalist transformation and European integration: the privatization of banks. In Central and Eastern European countries, the years after 2000 saw the onset of an organic banking dependence encouraged by EU membership: in 2008, in the 10 new member states (except Slovenia), the large majority of banking assets were held by foreign banks (between 65% and 80% for Latvia and Poland, and for the seven others between 82% and 100%).[18] Such transitions occurred either through acquisition of shares in the privatization process, or under the form of *de novo* banks that were subsidiary companies of Western European banks. According to the geographical situation of home countries, the majority of banking assets have come from Greece and Italy (in South Eastern Europe), Austria, Belgium, Germany, France or Sweden (in Central European and Baltic countries).

In Slovenia the share of foreign owned banks in total assets was still less than 30% at the end of 2009 whereas the state kept the bulk of its infrastructures (e.g., energy, transport, etc.) under public control; this was highlighted by repeated reproaches of the European Commission, the World Bank, the OECD and the European Bank of Reconstruction and Development.[19] But at the end of 2009, the Slovenian state-owned banks share of the total banking assets was no longer dominant. Therefore, a specific Slovenian structure of ownership appeared. In 2009, the state still kept 16.7% of shares (as opposed to the 0 % in Estonia or Lithuania – but 22% in Poland).[20] But whereas in Poland the majority of banking assets are now foreign-owned, the reluctance in Slovenia towards FDI explains why about half of the total banking assets in 2009 were neither foreign nor state-owned.

A paradoxical scenario has occurred there: in the last decade of the former Yugoslav system, the banks had been integrated in the "collective ownership" as captive financial service of self-managed enterprises. After 1990, they became "privatised" within the juridical transformation of the factories which had become their shareholders. The period of "systemic crisis" in the first half of the 1990s (also associated with the disintegration of Yugoslavia,) produced losses and a large bail-out of the majority of those banks by the central bank, with a formal rehabilitation status. At the end of that rehabilitation (1997) the largest Slovenian banks became state owned. But under the

---

18   Source: EBRD (European Bank for Reconstruction and Development), Annual Transition Reports 2009, 2010 and 2011.
19   The report on Slovenia in the *Transition Report*, 2009, p. 224, cites all these complaints.
20   EBRD Transition report, 2010.

pressure of the European commission, before entering the Union in 2002, Slovenia had to "liberalise" its banking system. Selling the "family silver" to foreigners was not a popular solution. As such, an opaque and lasting process of domestic privatization occurred as the Slovenian economist Joze Menciger commented in 2008, "when the Europeans are nationalising" banks (because of the international banking crisis).[21]

The role of central banks has evolved under the constraint of European treaties for the new members or candidates: in cases of budget deficit, they could not lend money to the government (which they used to do at low or negative rate of interest as national public banks): as such, governmental bonds with sufficiently high rate of interests to attract foreign capital were the answer. In order to respect the "criteria" of balanced budgets, the contraction of revenues from tax was generally accompanied by cuts in welfare expenditure. Under social resistance to such choices, Hungary had to turn to the financial markets to finance its deficit, which increased more than the other countries' deficits (see table G below).From 2000 until the first half of 2008, the economies of Central and Eastern Europe experienced large amounts of FDI from the West, a credit boom and rapid expansion in consumption and investment, with a large share of foreign currency lending and systematic external imbalance of the current account.

Table E: Balance of the current account as percentage of the GDP

	2006	2007	2008	2009	2010 (f)
Bulgaria	-10,5	-13,4	-11,6	-4,5	-5,8
Czeck .Rep	-2,4	-3,2	-0,7	-1,1	-0,7
Hungary	-7,2	-6,6	-7,0	0,2	-
Poland	-2,7	-4,7	-5,1	-1,6	-2,0
Romania	-10,5	-13,7	-11,6	-4,5	-7
Slovakia	-8,2	-5,7	-6,6	-3,2	-2,8
Slovenia	-2,5	-4,8	-6,2	-1,0	-0,8
Estonia	-16,9	-17,8	-9,4	4,6	2,9
Latvia	-22,5	-22,3	-13,0	9,4	4,5
Lithuania	-10,6	-14,5	-11,9	3,8	0

Sources: Etudes du CERI n° 171 Décembre 2010 (WIIW)

---

21 Joze Menciger, Ljubljana, article published in October 2008 in the Newsletter n°9 of the European network PRESOM (Privatization and the European Social Model) http://www.presom.eu/. On that topic, see also "The politics of Europeanization in Europe's Southeastern Periphery: Slovenian banks and Breweries on Sale, Nicole Lindstrom and Dora Piroska, *Queen's Papers on Europeanization* n° 4/2004.

The current account integrates both the trade balance (export minus imports of products), service and income balances. Significant features covered the imbalance : the increase of FDI in Eastern Europe during the 2000s had different dimensions, among which was the ability of multinationals to transfer part of their production to where taxes and wages were low, import the semi-finished products they needed (even if such production existed in the country) and export to the Western markets. So if they contribute to a growth in exports, they also contribute to the imbalance of trade by forced imports and they increase the current imbalance through the outflow of large part of their profits: that also has been behind the crisis of this model in 2009. Another part of the trade imbalance was the increase of consumption of foreign products facilitated by credit: according to the EBRD, the ratio of credit to GDP (beginning with 30% on average) doubled between 2001 and 2007 in "emerging Europe", especially in NMS.

The Hungarian economy showed the first signs of weaknesses with a fall of its rate of growth from 4% in 2006 to less than 1% in 2006 and 2007. Hungary's experience revealed general social tensions behind the "transition model."

People in transition?

Eric Berglöf, Chief Economist of *EBRD* writing the foreword of the *2007 Transition report* had to comment on the chapters devoted to different aspects of "People in transition." On one hand he stressed "an impressive pace" of growth. However, he also stressed "large external imbalances" and significant household borrowing "in foreign currency." Presenting the result of the enquiry (which is worth reading), he could only underline a sharp "contrast" among people themselves: "between strong growth and improving living standards on the one hand", with "most people" recognising "that their lives are better today than before the transition began"; however, "broad dissatisfaction with the outcomes of the transition on the other hand", because "at the same time, people have a profound sense that their household wealth has deteriorated in relative terms [...] This had made them sceptical about how and whether the market can improve their lives and safeguard their livelihoods." The EBRD's chief economist honestly concluded: "It has also eroded their support for reform-minded political parties and had led them to expect more from their governments in terms of tackling social and economic problems and correcting past injustices." It "also undermines support for economic and political reform."

This was before the crisis. The social reality of the "transition" (which is of course not reflected by GDP growth rate) could be read in several polls: they were dealing with inequality, poverty, unemployment and decreasing morale. People were defending social services, especially health care, and this was particularly so in Hungary.[22] It was no big surprise (for us) that in the EBRD's report on "People in transition," that women appeared to be the most radical defenders of social equality and public services. And obviously the EBRD's chief economist was impressed by the people's sense of "well-being."

But his concern was to convince people that "private-sector involvement – through partnership with the public sector" could seriously "address the persistent problems that the government have in upgrading public services (Berglöf, 2007, pp. VI and VII of the Preface)."

The social resistance in Hungary against the privatization of public services and especially the healthcare sector (with several referenda won against the government initiatives) while the best factories had already been privatised in the past decades, combined with neoliberal constraints on fiscal and monetary policy, produced an increase of government deficits.

In comparison, other countries like the Baltic states had been more "disciplined." As can be seen in table G below, the level of government debt (which is the stock of accumulated past annual deficits) was extraordinary low in the NMS in comparison to the "old Europe." This was so even in 2009, the year of a sharp increase in deficits due to the international recession and its effects in Eastern Europe. With the exception of Hungary, generally it was under 50% of GDP, and down to 7.2% in Estonia.

But several countries faced the same problem as Hungary on another topic: private debt in foreign currency through the banking system with increasing imbalances.

At the beginning of the 2000s, the international lowering of interest rates (linked with the US Federal Reserve's decisions, aimed at preventing a recession) had encouraged taking on debt in foreign currencies wherever the exchange rates were favourable. Nearly 90% of Hungarian mortgages since 2006 have been denominated in Swiss francs and the total amount of loans in Swiss francs outside of

---

22   See Newsletter n°9 (October 2008) of the network PRESOM (Privatisation and the European Social Model) the article written in Budapest by Karoly Lorant, "Hungarian doctors and civil organisations try to resist? healthcare privatization."

Switzerland has been estimated to be the equivalent of €500 billion. Of the entire Hungarian market 45% of real estate loans and 40% of all consumer loans are denominated in Swiss francs rather than in the forint, the national currency; this became a trap when interest rates on Swiss francs increased and capital flight made the forint drop in value.

The amount of the loans granted (in particular by Austrian and Swedish institutions) was the equivalent of 20% of GDP in the Czech Republic, Hungary and Slovakia and 90% in the Baltic States. These countries had to refund or refinance the equivalent of $400 billion in 2009.

In 2009, almost the whole of the $1,700 billion of East European borrowing was in fact held by West European banks (between them Austria, Italy, France, Belgium, Germany and Sweden alone hold some 84%). However, private banks gave priority to buying public debt and to consumer credit thereby facilitating the access of the multinationals to the retail sector and to investments in real estate. The frenzy of debt-fuelled consumption (after years of impoverishment) thus provided a base for the leap in growth (in particular in the Baltic States). This was accompanied by profound disequilibrium in the balance of trade, particularly in those countries where foreign exchange rates "were stabilized" by being rigidly pegged to the euro (the Baltic States in particular).

The new Eastern European periphery faced with the test of the crisis

2008–2011: after the boom, the downfall (2008-2009) and the new institutional role of the IMF in the European crisis; and (2010) the beginning of a dominant export-led and uneven recovery.
The fall happened to be the sharpest where the growth had been the most spectacular – in Estonia and Latvia with – 5.1% and – 4.2% negative growth rate respectively, in 2008, and a further slump in 2009. All other Eastern European states (except Poland) were confronted with the most radical recessions of the whole EU in 2009. Their negative rate of growth ranked from -4.2% (for the Czech Republic) to -18% for Lithuania. We will return to the roots of the crisis and the very fragile export-led recovery with some specifics) after a global view about the "European construction" and its core/peripheral relations.

Estonia's entry into the eurozone occurred recently, after more than 40% negative growth in 3 years but with an incredibly low stock of government fiscal debt: 7.2% as share of GDP to be compared with the 60% for Maastricht's "rule". The "worst pupil" has been Hungary with 78.5% government debt combined with a serious private debt in foreign currency which opened a credit crunch in 2008 and a new phase in the history of the IMF/EU relationship: before the unfolding of the Greek crisis within the south periphery, the eastern periphery of the whole Union has demonstrated to the EU its deep lack of cohesion.

Beginning in September 2008, outflows of capital and the contraction of exports started to affect several countries who then called in the IMF. The first to ask for help were those whose growth had been most dependent on external loans and financing (Hungary, Ukraine, and the Baltic States). In 2009 only Poland (and Albania before going into recession at the beginning of 2010) kept a slightly positive growth rate; in the other countries the drop ranged from around 3% to more than 10% and was sharpest in the three Baltic States. This was, accompanied by political and social crises.

Questions began to be raised about the quality of the growth, if not of the model[23]: "the countries of Central and Eastern Europe were ..., even before the crisis affected them, weakened by the imbalances inherent in their model of growth. So the convergence outlined [...] was probably not an intrinsically sustainable process[...]. But it needed what the crisis revealed for that to appear clearly".[24]

Questions began to be raised about the quality of the growth, if not of the model[25]: "the countries of Central and Eastern Europe were ..., even before the crisis affected them, weakened by the imbalances inherent in their model of growth. So the convergence outlined [...] was probably not an intrinsically sustainable process[...]. But it needed what the crisis revealed for that to appear clearly".[26]

In May 2009, we wrote "toward western/eastern European banking and social tsunami".[27] The reality of the social shock is underestimated for the following reasons: the lack of information on social issues and conflicts; the terrible difficulty of resistance under

---

23   See Jason Bush, "Latvia's Crisis Mirrors Eastern Europe's Woes", 03/03/2009, reproduced by *Spiegel* online.
24   *Conjoncture*, January 2010 n°1, « PECO, Alexandre Vincent, 'la convergence à l'épreuve de la crise' ».
25   See Jason Bush, "Latvia's Crisis Mirrors Eastern Europe's Woes", 03/03/2009, reproduced by *Spiegel* online.
26   *Conjoncture*, January 2010 n°1, « PECO, Alexandre Vincent, 'la convergence à l'épreuve de la crise' ».
27   www.europe-solidaire.org/spip.php?article13710 from *International View Point*, May 2009.

the pressure of increasing unemployment and poverty (which is a general issue explaining why the crisis is being used to impose further privatizations and cuts in social benefits); and the ideological strength of neoliberal arguments on the "necessity" of austerity against debts. The social back-lash has, so far, been controlled, and marked by increasing xenophobic right-wing trends with the "left" being viewed as liars and beneficiaries of past privatization.

In November 2009, a report prepared by the EBRD's experts recognized that "Emerging Europe suffered larger output declines during 2008–2009 than any other region in the world". The authors indicate in the introduction of the paper: "Given the high degree of integration of the region with advanced countries at the centre of the crisis, and large pre-crisis financing needs and macroeconomic vulnerabilities, this is not surprising". But they added that in spite of huge social regression, the "policy maker" should maintain the neoliberal tilt.

Several questions will certainly require further analysis and more time; and future discussion will have to specify analyses of different countries. But let us at least raise two sets of questions about the recovery and the effect of European integration, before making a provisional conclusion stressing the instrumentalisation of the "debt crisis"

Resilience and recovery – or social austerity and weak export-led growth?

Real GDP began to increase during the second quarter of 2009 in most countries of Central Europe; while South Eastern Europe has not emerged from recession. With few exceptions, the contribution of net exports (exports minus imports) to growth was positive. Such a recovery in the region is very uneven (see table F) and must be "read" in the context of following the sharpest among the world recessions.

Furthermore, because this growth is mainly export-led, it raises a major contradiction and weakness: First, net-exports as a source of growth are linked in several countries with the fall of imports associated with decreasing internal demand and with "more competitive" wages – therefore poverty. Second, trade surpluses are highly dependent on the EU's growth (whereas the IMF and European institutions are launching a new "austerity pact") and, especially, German growth. Central European countries like Slovakia are the most integrated into Germany's cycles of growth (which has had a positive impact for the last year). For the moment, Slovakia (a member of the eurozone) had increasing capacity in exports, partially supported by the depreciation of the euro providing advantages for export to Eastern European countries.[28]

In Poland, the relatively strong resilience to the crisis (in spite of a sharp shock in late 2008) seems to have several causes: Poland's more diversified economy combines export-led growth with internal sources of growth and different channels of financing. Moreover, investment has been ongoing in Poland: there have been important public and private investments in infrastructure and roads which have been facilitated by European funds in anticipation of the 2012 football championship (which will be held in Poland and Ukraine).

Table F: GDP growth in %

GDP's growth %	2007	2008	2009	2010 (f)	Governme nt déficit *[debt] in 2009 % of GDP	GDP per capita in PPP (US$) - 2010
						UE =30,835
Bulgaria	6,4	6,2	-4,9	-0,1	-3,9 [14,9]	12,052
Czech Rep.	6,1	2,5	-4,1	2,3	-5,2 [35,5]	24,987
Hungary	0,8	0,8	-6,7	1,1	-4,0 (78,4]	18,815
Poland	6,8	5,0	1,7	3,5	-7,1 [50,9]	18,837
Romania	6,3	7,3	-7,1	-1,9	-8,3 [23,9]	11,766
Slovakia	10,5	5,8	-4,8	4,1	-6,8 [35,4]	22,267
Slovenia	6,9	3,7	-8,1	1,1	-5,5 [35,5]	27,889
Estonia	7,2	-5,1	-13,9	2,4	-1,7 [7,2]	18,274
Latvia	10,0	-4,2	-18,0	-0,4	-8,9 [58;0]	14,330
Lithuania	9,8	2,9	-14,7	1,3	-8,9 [29,5]	16,997

Source: Eurostats; and (*) Etudes du CERI, December 2010, WIIW.

Banking integration: a strength?

First, it should be stressed that private domestic banks can have the very same orientation as foreign ones, and governance based on the same kind of "short-termism:" The economic weakness in Slovenia is probably linked with these trends.

Comparisons are made between the crises in Asia and Latin America (characterized by and large outflows of foreign capital at the

---

[28] There are no general rules concerning the impact of belonging (or not) to the Euro: it depends on the structure and importance of trade (with which countries, and in what kind of products).

end of the 1990s), and the crisis in the Central European and Baltic countries (CEB) as well as in the South European countries (SEE). According to the EBRD's *Transition Report 2010,* banking integration has produced, "a much milder, but more persistent outflows from the CEB and SEE compared with other emerging market regions (EBRD, 2010, p.36)."

One of the reasons for this new tendency is the fact "that most banks in the region are subsidiaries of foreign banks": their behaviour was not as "volatile" as "portfolio"-style capital flows. "The need to refinance these subsidiaries may have slowed the pace of outflows"). Political and institutional pressures also came from the European Union to "maintain exposures in the region". That is the positive aspect of the integration. But, there are some problems needless to say.

In addition, "much of the cross-border lending to emerging Europe came from European banks that were faced with similarly sluggish recoveries in their home countries. These banks may have responded by limiting their expansion in both advanced and emerging European markets)." They may? They often have and that is why the "recovery" is no longer based on credit financing internal demands (for housing and consumption).

The EBDR is concerned about "the low share of local currency lending," which has been a feature of domestic bank systems in transition economies for a long time" – in fact this has been the case since the beginning of privatisations. As already discussed, the lending boom mostly took place in foreign currency generally due to lower interest rates. This then turned into a nightmare when exchange rates and interest rates changed. As the European Central Bank and the IMF know the number of persons unable to pay off their debts is increasing in the whole region. Estimates are not transparent and public. But defaults are lasting several years after the credit crisis. This is true both for the sub-prime crisis and for the Eastern European "model." East/West banking integration adds more sources of future default to come. Even in Poland where the growth could be maintained by other sources, 8% of defaults on credits are expected (5.5% in Spain, 9% in Greece, 19% in Latvia, 19.2% in Lithuania, for 2010).[29]

However, it is also true that in Central, Eastern European and Baltic countries, banks seem not to be too concerned about this default risk because of huge profits. In fact, the banks have used the

---

29   *Courrier International* n° 1057, 3-9 February 2011 : "La Hongrie menacée par la crise des subprimes" [A subprime crisis threaten Hungary] translated from *Die Welt*, Berlin.

crisis to increase their profit margin via enormous interest rates imposed on their clients (up to 60% or 70% according to OECD[30]). This is one reason why during summer 2010, a special tax was imposed by the Hungarian government on banks to cover government deficits.

The instrumentalisation of public debt and the recourse to the IMF to impose new austerity plans: from the peripheries to the centre?

The three crises whose effects are augmenting one another (specifically, the crisis of 2007–2009, coming from the US core of the globalised system; the one that threatens the weak links of the Euro; and the one that started to affect Eastern Europe in 2009) have one major point in common. Whether we are talking about the United States, Greece or the Baltic States, these crises are the repercussions of profoundly unbalanced growth where the weakness of earned income and tax revenues was compensated for by creating large-scale indebtedness, the source of financial profits. As in every capitalist crisis since the 19th century, the frenzied increase in this debt was facilitated, by financial and stock-exchange operations that were taken advantage of by free capital.

The recourse to the IMF in the two "peripheries" of the European Union (the South and the East) is aimed at saving this structure. Applied in the middle of European construction, it both reveals the fragile features of the EU and accentuates them. The motivation for this recourse is the reassertion of the monetarist straitjackets of the Treaties by protecting private finance which is both the culprit and the primary beneficiary of the crisis. In the wake of the crisis, the aim is to impose a new radicalisation of the anti-social policies that have been a feature of the system since the 1980s: its purpose is to suppress welfare expenditure, pensions based on solidarity between generations, public sector wages, and the remaining forms of social protection. The extreme flexibility of the labour market,(against any logic of collective rights, incomes and decent status) aims both at generating additional profits and making the unemployed, low-paid workers and those in precarious employment "guilty" of "too many" demands. It hopes to divide

---

30 *Courrier International*, February 2011 (Die Welt).

workers, crush them, and atomise them so as to prevent them fighting back.

In the absence of progressive alternatives, the support for the Far Right, from Hungary to the Netherlands, points to a sad future.

In Central, Eastern European and Baltic countries, like in South-eastern Europe, the sharp recession in 2008–2009 (still not overcome in several countries) has produced fiscal deficits. But the global amount of government debt is low in comparison to the other part of the EU – or developed countries in general. Despite this low debt level, the European commission has expressed warnings to several countries when deficits were exceeding the allowed level. Moreover, new cuts in social benefits and protections, as well as new increases in VAT for consumers, have been introduced, often under the direct demands of the IMF; but also, like in the whole EU, to respect the "rules" as new members of the Union.

Table G: Deficits of EU Member States:

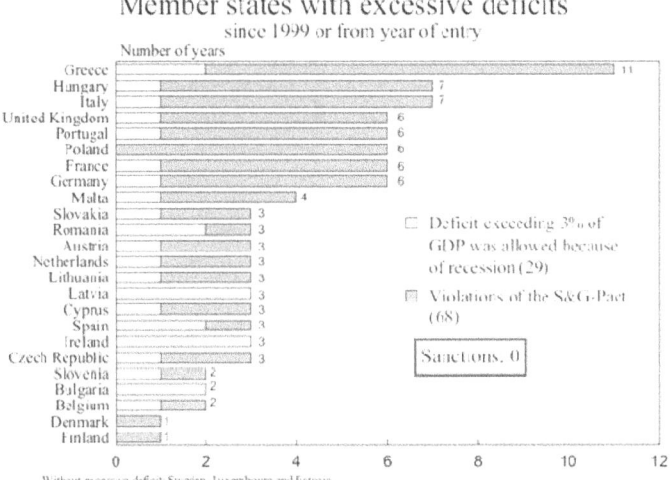

The ideological discourse about public debt seeks on the one hand to camouflage the urgency and "the obviousness" of the necessity of austerity, to what extent this "necessity" is of variable shape; and to obscure the real causes of the debt which are associated with the transformations that have been carried out since the beginning of the 1980s. With wages being treated as costs to be compressed, the change in the share of added value to the detriment of wages has been accompanied by a rise in household debt to sustain consumption. This is particularly so with regard to real estate in the US, as it is in Spain or Hungary.

The Estonian case is an extreme and specific illustration of the dominant "arguments" and social stakes associated with the European integration. There was a collapse of GDP's rate of growth of about 40% in three years; but a full respect of Maastricht criteria permitted Estonia to adopt the euro in January 2011. The Russian issue has since the beginning of the "transition" certainly played a specific role; leading to radicalising the rhythm and trends of privatisation through organic integration in the EU with a rigid link to the euro for the last several years.

The Euro-crisis (and the Greek case) have been instrumentalised in different contexts (Slovakia is member of the eurozone; Poland and Hungary are not; and Estonia decided to join!): the fear of "becoming like Greece," with a "risk of bankruptcy", as a "red flag".

As in each former phase of its installation, European construction is "going forward," because the decision-makers (but also the populations, in the absence of credible alternatives) fear that it is worse to stop than to continue. Nationalist and xenophobic reactions are among the worst possible alternatives. However, the acceptance of the profoundly socially unjust austerity plans being imposed today by the combined action of the IMF and the European institutions will actually prepare the way for the rise of anti-European xenophobes.

This is because it is a particular European construction which is in crisis in the framework of globalised capitalism. The governments that are in power serve the markets (all the European treaties have gone in this direction since the Single European Act of 1986) – and the markets serve the dominant states. These states take refuge behind the anonymous "judgements" of the markets and behind the Treaties (which they signed) in order to "note" with fatalism the right policies to be followed, which are always the same: to reduce welfare spending, to dismantle public services in order to open up new fields of privatisation and financial speculation.

The European Treaties and the economic policies which determined them are bankrupt, and they were established, in variable forms, on the backs of the people and of any democracy worthy of such a name. It is the freedom of movement and the free choice of human beings that is necessary to protect, not the freedom of capital. The criminalisation of poverty and the ethnicisation of social questions are aimed at facilitating the repression of resistance, stopping people from seeing the real causes of the crises and identifying those who are responsible for them.

A real social and democratic European Union would satisfy the demands expressed in polls, strikes and enquiries: social priorities, dignity and cooperative logic as opposed to market competition. Means of financing must be put under public and democratic debate and control, and shifted away from the systematic balance sheet that propelled banking privatisations and European mechanisms and fiscal policies At the level at which decisions are made – in particular the European level – it is necessary to build, from the ground up, a solidarity-based resistance that contests the treaties, the financing, and the finalities with the satisfaction of needs and basic rights and against the logic of scapegoats ("foreigners") and of the law-and-order policies accompanying the destruction of social gains.

CHINA'S RISE AMIDST THE CRISIS

The emergence of a new capitalist power

Jean Sanuk

While North America and Europe were hard hit, China has resisted the international crisis of 2008 thanks to a rescue plan which combined huge public spending, a low interest rate and consumption subsidies. China's growth rate reached 9% in 2009 and 10.3% in 2010. In its wake it dragged Asia and Latin America out of the crisis. It has also managed to maintain unemployment at a sustainable level. China even overtook Japan in 2010 as the second economy in the world in terms of GDP and is closing the gap with the US. On the whole, China's rise seems unaffected by the subprime crisis. A closer look shows that real problems lie ahead.

    Chinese workers do not accept being overexploited any longer. A wave of strikes spread during the summer of 2010. Workers were fighting for wage increases, improvement of working conditions and the right to organize and bargain. The acceleration of inflation since the middle of 2010, especially of food products is adding a new problem for workers and a concern for the government which fears a wave of discontent. Additionally, the government is doing its best to prevent any contagion from the democratic revolutions in Arabic countries. Although the overall situation in China is completely different, these democratic revolutions demonstrate to Chinese workers that it is indeed possible to topple even the worst and powerful dictatorships.

China's resilience in the international crisis

The impact of the crisis on China and Asia has been limited so far (Sanuk, 2008). Unlike European banks, Asian banks were not particularly engaged in subprime loans and toxic products. With the exception of South Korea, Asian countries did not rely on short-term capital and banks loans for financing their economies. They were not caught in a debt trap like Eastern European countries or Greece. Most of them, and in particular China, had accumulated huge amount of currencies reserves and were able to cope with capital flight that occurred at the end of 2008. Asian countries were primarily hit by the fall of their exports because of the slump in demand from North America and Europe.

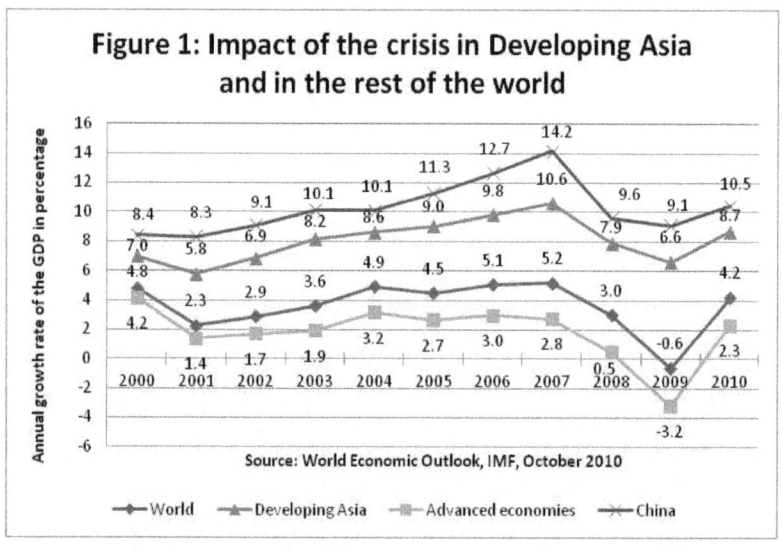

Figure 1: Impact of the crisis in Developing Asia and in the rest of the world

Source: World Economic Outlook, IMF, October 2010

As a general rule, the impact of the recession has been stronger in the most open Asian countries whose exports were concentrated in manufacturing and where the USA was an important customer. For instance, exports of manufactured products represent around 70% in Malaysia, more than 40% in Thailand and Cambodia, around 30% in China, South Korea, Philippines and Vietnam, but less than 10% in India and Pakistan. These characteristics explain why the three biggest and most populous countries in Asia (China, India and Indonesia) have not experienced a single quarter of recession between 2008 and 2009. The resilience of these three countries and primarily China, which is among the biggest, or the biggest trade partner of Asian countries, led to a quick rebound in the second quarter of 2009 and a much stronger "V" shape recovery than in the rest of the world.

Several factors explain the resistance to the crisis of Asian countries and the speed of the recovery.

First, so as to absorb the shock of the fall in exports, Asian countries have launched an unprecedented rescue plan in the region. This is a rather different policy than the "Asian crisis" of 1997-1999 when IMF sponsored structural adjustment plans which worsened the crisis. The Chinese rescue plan is noteworthy in its magnitude: $585 billion amounting to 13.3% of GDP to be spent over a two-year span. On average, the rescue plans announced by Asian countries amounted to 7.5% of GDP against 2.8% of GDP for the G7 countries. Moreover, Asian rescue plans were more focused on public expenses than tax cuts. On average, Asian countries dedicated 80% to increases in public spending as compared with 60% on average in G20 countries. The only exception is Indonesia where tax cuts dominate the policy agenda. Those public expenses were accompanied by expansionary monetary policy.

The median interest rate of Asian central banks has decreased by 2.25 points which is five times more than during the previous crisis. As the banking system continued, this had a positive impact on growth. In countries like Vietnam and China the expansionary monetary policy played a dominant role. In China, public spending has increased by a modest 26% in 2008 (up from 23% in 2007), but it fell back to 21% in 2009 and then to17% in 2010 when the rescue plan officially ended. On the whole, public expenses did not play a crucial role in absorbing the shock. It is, in fact, the expansion of credit which took the lead in 2009 with a spectacular increase of 31% (see figure 2). It also fell back in 2010 to -4% when the Chinese government decided to cool down the economy because easy money induced a new speculative bubble (more on this point below).

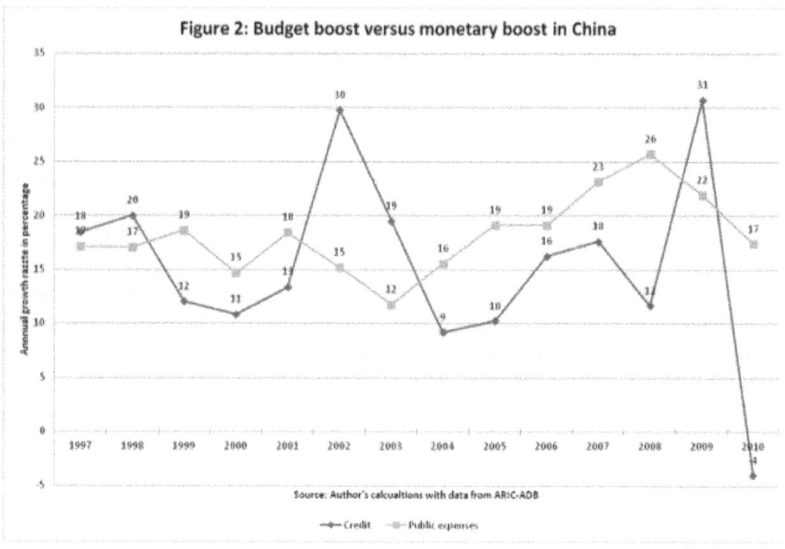

Figure 2: Budget boost versus monetary boost in China

Second, households' consumption kept steady as employment did not collapse during the crisis. In times of crisis, there are usually no strong increases in the unemployment rate in Asian countries, as there are no unemployment benefits except in a few countries. Workers who lose their jobs in industry try to find one in services, or become self-employed or return to the family farm whenever it is possible and where they still exist. This was especially the case in China, where hundreds of thousands migrant workers went back to the interior in the winter of 2008 or stayed there after the end of the new year in February 2009. Following the economic recovery in spring 2009, many returned to the cities to find an urban job which pays more.

Third, defying many sombre predictions, Chinese exports did fall from September 2008 to February 2009 but did not collapse and soon recuperated thanks to the recovery in world trade. Given the high import content component of Chinese exports (about 50%), imports fell in the same proportion so that current accounts stayed almost always positive although by a smaller magnitude (see figure 3). This reveals both the resilience of China to external shocks and its weakness at the same time. It is the processing trade which makes up for the bulk of the Chinese trade account surplus. Classical trade activities are chronically in deficit due to their high-import content of primary products.

Figure 3: Chinese trade through the crisis

To keep the processing trade competitive, the Chinese government has decided to peg the exchange rate of the renminbi to the dollar and to avoid excessive wage increases. This is the reason why new labour laws announced in 2007, have been suspended at the employers' request. Another difficulty with the fixed exchange rate is that the price increases of commodities are fully transferred to the Chinese economy. As we will see, these two contradictions weigh heavily in terms of the manoeuvring room of the Chinese government.

The consequences of the rescue plan: a worsening of previous contradictions

Expansionary budget and monetary policies cannot be extended indefinitely. Officially the Chinese central government is not heavily indebted: its debt to GDP ratio is a modest 19% of GDP. This means that the central government has ample leeway to expand public spending. In fact, the central government made a different choice. Of the RMB 4000 billion public spending programme announced for the years 2008-2009, 1180 billion were actually financed by the central budget, the rest being carried by local authorities. These have competed to make the most spectacular announcements of investment projects for an astonishing cumulated total of RMB 20 000 billion. Most of these announcements have been realised thanks to the expansionary monetary policy. Local authorities have been encouraged to take debt indirectly because they are not officially allowed to take debt directly. Special financial vehicles have been created at the local level to bypass this prohibition.

Local authorities pump capital into the financial vehicles which then use it as collateral to take loans from banks. Different kind of capital have been brought by local authorities: land; cash obtained by the sale of financial assets sold by investment funds controlled by local banks; disguised short-term loans which are then used to get a bigger and medium-term loan which serves to reimburse the first ones. These fragile financial set-ups have multiplied in 2009. Local authorities had on average 2 to 4 special vehicle funds before 2008. In 2009 after the launch of the rescue plan, they controlled 10 on average. Most of the investment projects financed in this way were in real estate and in infrastructure and operated by state companies. This had several perverse effects.

First, it has fuelled speculation in real estate and housing. One quarter of investment growth in 2009 comes from investment in real estate where prices have soared by 24% in 2009 and 11% in the first five months of 2011.

Second, it has created a vast amount of potential non-performing loans since many projects are not profitable. Banks, which finance 90% of investment, are becoming fragile - not for the first time. In 1999, non-performing loans had reached 36% of total loans. Four asset management companies had been formed by the state to buy them from banks in order to clean their balance sheets. At the end of 2007, non-performing loans still accounted for 6.7% of the total. The monetary authorities would like to avoid a repetition of the same story.

Third, it has increased public debt. According to Victor Shih (2010), the consolidation of local authorities' debt into the national public debt led to a debt-to-GDP ratio of 71% in 2009 compared with a ratio of 19% for the sole central government. It is still manageable but it means that either local or national taxes will have to increase.

The problem is that once a speculative bubble has formed it is very difficult to deflate it without damage. Local authorities depend on real estate for around 20% of their fiscal revenues. The value of the land they expropriate from farmers to use as collateral or to sell to developers depends on real estate market prices and hence on speculation in this market. Raising the interest rate of the Bank of China is a powerful instrument to reduce bank loans and cool down the economy in a country where local politicians and powerful leaders of the Communist Parties do not always agree with the central power. But it would reveal a lot of non-performing loans and put local finances at risk.

Most of all, in a country where investment is the major component of growth, raising interest rates too much could have a too strong recessionary impact. Instead of raising interest rates, the Bank of China has preferred to increase the reserve obligations that banks must maintain at the central bank. Between January 2010 and January 2011, the Central Bank increased the reserve obligations seven times while interest rates were raised modestly in October and December 2010 only. The monetary authority has also re-established a quota system for credit. The problem is that banks have to find ways to circumvent the quota by multiplying off-sheet balance operations.

On the whole, it seems that bank loans have maintained the same pace in 2010 in comparison with 2009 - which already was a record year. The difficulty in controlling bank credit is compounded by the exchange rate policy. China decided in July 2008 to re-establish a fixed exchange rate between the yuan and the US dollar. But because the trade account is always in surplus, the Bank of China has to buy dollars with yuans. This pumps more yuan into circulation in the Chinese economy that the Bank of China tries to take out by issuing bonds. This so-called sterilisation is proving even more difficult due to the huge amounts involved. The result is that there is more money in circulation which adds another source of speculation and inflation. In particular, investors have speculated in the market for food products thereby contributing to rising food prices these last months.

Inflation has turned into a political problem because the population is complaining about the cost of living and starts to protest. Having in mind that the democratic revolutions in Arabic countries have started as a protest against food price hikes, the Chinese government is sensitive to the subject. In November 2010, the State Affairs Council has published a series of measures aimed at stabilising the prices of food products. If these measures are not sufficient, the government will have to resort to a more significant interest rate increase in order to cool down the economy, and it is reluctant to do for the reasons outlined above.

Whether it will do it or not and to what extent will depend much on the political situation and the intensity of workers protests. This may be the reason why the government has tolerated the wave of workers strikes in the summer of 2008, first in Honda and Excon and then in tens of other, mostly foreign companies. Workers were demanding wages increases, an improvement of their working conditions, respect for basic rights and the right to bargain. The government which is usually quick in repressing workers especially when they claim the right to self-organise, instead decided to let the workers strike. It tried to distract workers from the real problems by emphasising that most of the companies were foreign so as to encourage the nationalism of the population implying that somehow workers were better treated and paid in Chinese firms, a tale that nobody believes. A more serious reason is that it was a way to loosen the social pressure mounting around the question of inflation and to pave the way for a rebalancing of growth in favour of the domestic market in a context of uncertain foreign demand for Chinese products.

Rebalancing growth in favour of the domestic market

Rebalancing growth is a recurrent topic in most East Asian countries that tied their fate to an export-promotion strategy. After the Asian crisis of 1997-1999, there were already discussions about the need to reduce the dependence of growth on massive exports to western countries. But the export-led recovery of the most stricken countries (Thailand, Malaysia, South Korea, and Indonesia) plus the success of Chinese products on foreign markets in the 2000 decade put an end to the debate. It is now reviving because there is a consensus that the recovery from the crisis in the US, Europe and Japan will be slow and tentative.

There will be a prolonged period of reduced demand for Asian export products. As a consequence East and South-east Asia are now more seriously confronted with the necessity to reorient their growth strategy towards their domestic market. Western countries are in favour of this reorientation because they would benefit from it. They hope to export more to Asian markets. This is why they insist so much on the necessity for China to revalue the yuan. This would give a boost to western exports to China and would reduce the price competitiveness of Chinese exports. This is why many official reports from the World Bank, the IMF and the Asian Development Bank are discussing the best way to rebalance growth by boosting internal demand and reducing the importance of exports.

Both due to the importance of its domestic market and also because China is the biggest trade partner of many Asian countries and the central hub of international and regional production networks, China is the country where rebalancing growth is of the utmost importance. It is true that China combines the most blatant imbalances. It is the country where trade surplus (and its corollary, foreign reserves), are massive, where savings as a proportion of GDP are the highest and households consumption the lowest. In 2007, the last year before the crisis, the share of households consumption in the GDP had reached an historic low point at 35%, while the share of investment was very high at 40% of GDP and the current account surplus registered a record level of 10% of GDP (see figure 4).

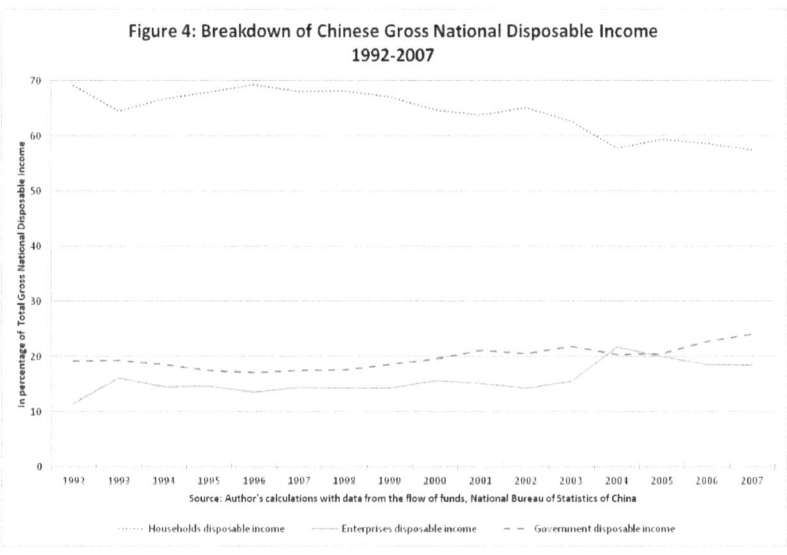

Rebalancing growth obviously means reducing the importance of investment and of the current account surplus, and increasing household consumption. The crux of the matter is how? The economic proposals made, under their false appearance of technical neutrality, have social and political consequences. For instance, abandoning the peg of the yuan to the dollar to revalue the exchange rate of the yuan would benefit the Chinese bourgeoisie and the middle class which has the purchasing power to buy imported consumption goods at a lower cost. However, the vast majority of Chinese workers cannot have access to them because they are too expensive.

Another topic at the centre of the debate is the question of the high savings rate in China. Reducing savings is considered by many mainstream economists as the best way to increase consumption. Behind this simple and apparently neutral proposal lie social and political stakes. The first question is to determine who saves the most in China?

The most frequent explanation is that the high saving rate of households is the primary cause of the high saving rates in general [Blanchard and Giavazzi (2005); Modigliani and Cao (2004)]. Some economists add the importance of the saving rate of the state (Wiemer, 2009), while others insist on the importance of corporate savings and of the state [Prasad, Eswar (2009), Jha, Prasad and Terada-Hagiwara, (2009) and (Hofman, and Kuijs (2008)], or even the sole importance of corporate savings (Anderson, 2009). More generally, the growing importance of corporate savings would not be a unique feature of Chinese capitalism, but a common feature of many East Asian countries [Chandra, Nabar and Porter (2010)].

Those who stress the importance of households' savings conclude that it is necessary to create or strengthen a "social safety net." Chinese households save too much for precautionary reasons: they have to save to pay for their health expenses, for the education of their children, to buy a house or a flat and because of the absence of a significant pension system. They need more public spending in education, health, social housing and pension. For instance, a permanent increase of one percentage point of public spending equally shared between education, health and pension would lead to an increase of households' consumption by 1.25 percentage point of GDP (Baldacci, et al, 2010). According to the same authors, a one percentage point increase of public spending in pensions only would have a higher impact on consumption of, 1.6 point because the reduction of precautionary savings would be higher. These proposals move in the right direction because there is an urgent need for a better education and health system and because the majority of Chinese do not have pension benefits.

But what is proposed is a "social safety net" not the creation of a full social security system whereby citizens are guaranteed social rights. Furthermore, it does not say anything about the kind of institutions to be created. To give just one example, the creation of pension funds could be proposed as the best solution. This is what the World Bank has proposed or imposed in many countries. It would increase the power of finance in China, where it is still not dominant as in advanced capitalist countries.

What is at stake are the final steps in the complete conversion of China to capitalism. Those studies also do not explain how these social spending would be financed. If the bulk is financed by households' income tax increases, the positive effect on consumption will be diminished.

The Chinese government announced a "social plan" in January 2009 to complete the stimulus plan. Education, health and pensions are supposed to be improved or established with a special focus on rural population. But it remains to be seen how comprehensive these measures will be. The budget dedicated to these measures is small in proportion and the government has not explained how they will be financed. Its impact on consumption is uncertain. In any case, it will take time. Chinese people will have to experience the reality of these announcements before starting to change their behaviour so as to save less and consume more.

Regarding corporate savings, the social and political issues are also very important. Corporate savings are in fact non-reinvested profits. The fact that corporate savings are high in China means that a high share of labour-value does not accrue to workers in terms of higher wages but goes to profit which is only partly invested. The fact that this feature is encountered not only in China but also in many Asian countries tells us a lot about the overexploitation of Asian workers. One simple way to increase consumption and rebalance growth is to reduce excessive corporate savings by increasing wages. But it is not the proposal made by many economists, in particular those of the World Bank (Chandra, Nabar and Porter, 2010). Instead, they propose to develop and improve financial markets so that more companies would get listed on the stock markets. The Chinese government could change the law to improve corporate governance so that firms would pay dividends to their share owners which as yet is not the case. Finally, workers would become share-owners of their firms' capital and receive dividends instead of wage increases. The conversion to Anglo-Saxon capitalism would be complete.

We believe that these proposals are not serious and credible. Wage increases are a much simpler, more equitable and more certain way to boost consumption, in particular in China where the wage share of total income has decreased these last years as in many countries [IMF, (2007), Ellis and Smith (2007), (European Commission (2007)]. In the Chinese case, the portion of labour income as part of GDP has lowered to 57.5% in 2007 down from 69.2% in 1992 (see above figure 4).

This fall of 11.7 points has benefited firms (whose profit has increased to 18.4% in 2007 up from 11.5% in 1992) and to the state (whose revenues have increased to 24.1% up from 18.4%). The impact of this decline in the wage share is often neglected in the debate on rebalancing growth in China and in Asia in general. In the case of China, following a simple calculation made by Aziz and Cui (2007), one can show that if the wage share of households had stayed at the level reached in 1992 during the whole period of 1992-2007, and if households' savings had followed the same evolution as the one actually observed, consumption would have stayed constant at around 46% of GDP in 2007 (see figure 5).

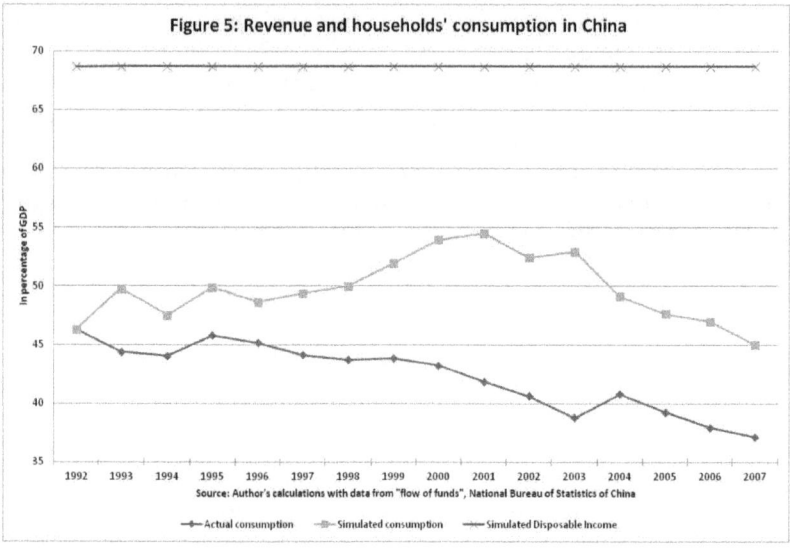

Instead, consumption has lost nearly 10 percentage points and reached 36.4% in 2007, which is very low by international standards. One may conclude that the fall of the wage share (and the corollary profit increase) is a much more serious factor in explaining the fall of household consumption than the increase of household savings.

Conclusion

Rebalancing Asian growth can only be achieved by a concerted wage increase and the establishment of a social security system in Asian countries, although China is powerful enough to do it on its own. This would pave the way for a more self-centred economy at the regional level which would be less dependent on export and therefore less sensitive to international crises. It would also be a measure of social justice for Chinese and Asian workers that have suffered for decades from low wages, dirty and dangerous jobs for the sake of export competitiveness. The recent wave of strikes in China (and also Vietnam, Bangladesh and Pakistan) demonstrate that there are social forces available even in countries where the political context looks at first unfavourable. This is an element of hope.

References

Anderson, Jonathan. 2009. "The Myth of Chinese Savings." *Far Eastern Economic Review*.

Aziz, Jahangir and Cui Li. 2007. "Explaining China's Low Consumption: The Neglected Role of Household Income." *IMF Working Paper*: 38. IMF: Washington DC.

Baldacci, Emanuele, Callegari Giovanni, Coady David, Ding Ding, Kumar Manmohan, Tommasino Pietro, and Woo Jaejoon. 2010. "Public Expenditures on Social Programs and Household Consumption in China." *IMF Working Paper, Fiscal Affairs Department*: 28. IMF: Washington DC.

Blanchard, Olivier and Giavazzi Francesco. 2005. "Rebalancing Growth in China: a Three handed Approach." *MIT Department of Economics* 37. MIT: Washington D.C.

Cai, Fang and Wang Meiyan (2010). "Growth and structural changes in employment in transition China". Journal of Comparative Economics, Vol. 38, p 71-81.

Chandra, Sonali, Nabar Malhar, and Porter Nathan. 2010. "Corporate Savings and Rebalancing in Asia," in *Asia and Pacific. Building a Sustained Recovery*. IMF ed. Washington D.C.: IMF, pp. 55-70.

Ellis, Luci and Kathryn Smith. 2007. "The global upward trend in the profit share." *BIS Working Papers Monetary and Economic Department*: 29. BIS: Basle.

European, Commission. 2007. "The Labour Income Share in the European Union," in *Employment in Europe*. European Commission ed. Brussels.

Hofman, Bert and Kuijs Louis. 2008. "Rebalancing China's Growth," in *Debating China's Exchange Rate Policy*. Morris Goldstein and Lardy Nicholas R. eds: Peterson Institute for Economics, pp. 401.

IMF. 2007. "The Globalization of Labor," in *World Economic Outlook 2007*. Washington D.C.: IMF.

Prasad, Eswar. 2009. "Rebalancing Growth in Asia." *Discussion Paper Series*: 36. Institute for the Study of Labor (IZA): Bonn.

Jha, Shikha, Prasad Eswar, and Terada-Hagiwara Akiko.2009. "Saving in Asia: Issues for Rebalancing Growth." *ADB Economics Working Paper Series*: 54. Asian Development Bank: Manila.

Prasad, Eswar. 2009. "Rebalancing Growth in Asia." *Discussion Paper Series*: 36. Institute for the Study of Labor (IZA): Bonn

Sanuk Jean (2008). "The Way Out of the Crisis in Asia: Rebalancing Growth Without Income Hikes?"

Downloadable at Asia Left Observer: http://daniellesabai1.wordpress.com/2009/10/04/the-way-out-of-the-crisis-in-asia-rebalancing-growth-without-income-hikes/

Wiemer, Calla. 2009. "The big savers: households and government." *China Economic Quarterly*, pp. 25-30.

LATIN AMERICA'S CRISIS
Comparisons and explanations

Claudio Katz

The impact of the global crisis in Latin America has been less than in the developed countries and sharper than in the rising economies of Asia. It affected Central America more seriously than the southern hemisphere. The external origin of the tremor explodes the myth of home-grown responsibility. But that does not let the local ruling classes off the hook.

The crisis has not so far acquired the same dimensions as the other collapses experienced in Latin America in the last two decades. This difference reflects the limited character of the financial transmission and the effects of massive restructuring of the region's banking sector. Paradoxically, this very counterweight attracts short term capital, which in turn threatens fresh speculative bubbles.

The key fact in all this has been the recovery in foreign trade, which nonetheless confirmed the precarious nature of the region's dependence on primary commodity exports. Unemployment and poverty also returned to centre-stage with the fall in remittances, while the exodus from the countryside is deepening the social divide and the problem of urban exclusion.

Heterodox economists slid from a diagnosis of catastrophe to another that shrugged off the crisis as irrelevant. They now attribute the reduced impact of the quake to opportune state intervention, while forgetting that the whole world did the same. They also conceal the aid given to the ruling classes, and fail to note that the efforts to prop up purchasing power resulted from the fear of popular resistance.

The relief felt in Latin America after the initial, sharp impact of the crisis, reflects a worldwide trend. It was in mid-2008 that recession burst onto the scene. Unemployment rose and trade shrank in spite of all the governments' improvised efforts to rescue companies.

But by the middle of the following year, the financial system was moving once again and the drop in credit and commodity prices had been contained. Gross domestic product was significantly down, but was set to recover in 2010. So what was the scale of this crisis, compared with others that have shaken the region in recent decades?[1]

Magnitudes and comparisons

Latin America's GDP grew 4.1% in 2008, fell 1.8% in 2009, but recovered again in 2010. The growth rate climbed back to more than 5% and it seemed that the expansive cycle of 2003 to 2008 might return. Exports were growing again and so was foreign investment. This fluctuation is broadly in line with international trends, with better percentages than in the developed countries but worse than in the rising economies of Asia. This intermediate result confirms that the impact in the region was less than in the core countries, but not as little as in China or India.

This time the break-down did not begin in Latin America, but in the epicentre of capitalism. It did not follow any foreign debt collapse, fiscal crisis or sharp devaluation, of the sorts that periodically afflict the region. This external cause destroyed the myth that all our calamities are of our own doing. No one could blame this storm on "the corruption of civil servants", the "population's lack of discipline" or "the poor productivity of our workers". The neoliberals had to forego their favourite arguments to explain this crisis in the region.

So now the external cause is used to absolve the local ruling classes of any responsibility, forgetting that capitalism does not operate in a separate galaxy. Latin America is part of a system that suffers periodic, global convulsions; the same ones that this time brought down US banks, had on several previous occasions devastated the finance systems of the periphery. Crises move from place to place, but always have the same capitalist cause.

---

[1] This continues our initial analysis in: Katz, Claudio, "América Latina frente a la crisis global," *Crisis capitalista, economía, política y movimiento*, Espacio Crítico Ediciones, Bogotá, 2009.

In so far as it confirmed the system's structural instability, the new crisis shook the Latin American establishment which had grown used to five years of growth and was banking on doing good business for another similar period.

However, the effects of the crisis have been very uneven. While Mexico's GDP plunged by 7%, Brazil suffered only a moderate drop of one or two points. Central America was hit immediately by the recession in the US, while the more diversified economies in South America could offset this impact.

So far the US origins of this crash and its relatively lesser impact in Latin America are its only points of similarity with the depression of the 1930s. Comparisons with the more recent collapses of the last few decades are much more instructive.[2]

The latest recession has been sharper that those of 1990 and 2002 (when GDP fell by less than one percent), but not as grave as that of 1983 (with a fall of 2.6%). It has been a profound shock, but with less impact than the "lost decade" of the 1980s or the "lost half-decade" from 1998-2003.[3]

In those periods, various countries suffered more dramatic collapses in their GDP: 17% in Chile (1983-84), 10% in Mexico (1994), 11% in Argentina (2001-2002), as well as big falls in Brazil (1998). The present crisis has so far been quantitatively slighter than those earlier ones.

Only in Mexico has the scale of this crash been comparable to that of the "Tequila Crisis" of 1994, in terms of both industrial contraction and rising unemployment. But the current turbulence has not included bank or currency collapses of the kind that then led to an unprecedented bail-out by the Federal Reserve.

The sharp brake put on Argentina's economy this time around bears no comparison with the historic catastrophe of 2001. This crisis put a temporary end to five years of high growth, but did not produce the collapse of a model (that of "convertibility"), nor did it trigger the suspension of debt payments, the confiscation of bank deposits or monetary meltdown.

The same holds for Brazil. The biggest economy in Latin America was hit hard in 2009; but the initial devaluation was not followed by capital flight, further currency collapse, resurgent

---

2   Although the crisis lasted until 1939 in the US, in most of Latin America it had ended between 1932-35. Maira (confirm that is Maira rather than Maria) Luis, "¿Cómo afectará la crisis la integración regional?", *Nueva Sociedad*, no. 224, November-December 2009.

3   This is the judgement of Ocampo, José Antonio, in "La crisis económica global," *Nueva Sociedad* no. 224, November-December 2009.

inflation or astronomical increases in interest rates.⁴ On the other hand, all of these did accompany the demise of the cruzado currency (1986), the end of the Collor plan (1990) and the previous balance of payments crisis (1999). The latest crisis has been characterized by a very different kind of linkage.

More impact on trade than on finance

Unlike the 1980s and 90s, the financial effect of this crisis in Latin America has not been significant. International issues of government bonds have maintained high yields, while early falls on the region's stock markets were followed by steady recovery. Already in the second half of 2009, the bourses in Brazil, Chile, Peru and Colombia saw increases of 100%.

On the other hand, the volume of reserves is higher than in earlier crises and the weight of foreign debt has fallen. These debts (net of international reserves) amounted to 6% of GDP in 2008, compared with the 30% that prevailed at the time of the earlier crises.⁵

The lesser significance of financial imbalances has meant that interpretations centred on this sector are of limited interest. There has also been less interest in monetary aspects, given the limited damage done this time to the banking system.

Yet this shift is not a work of nature. It reflects the huge transformation of the financial institutions following the string of failures that resulted from the previous crises. Latin American banks were hit less hard than their equivalents in the core countries because they had already undergone the kind of shake up now under way in the United States and Europe.

However, this greater post-crisis resilience is double-edged, as it attracts new speculative bubbles to the region. With interest rates low and risks high in the metropolitan banks, short-term capital has flowed into Latin America to make gains on the ups and downs of shares, property prices and currencies. This stream of hot money contrasts with the 35-45% drop in long-term foreign investment that was registered in 2009.

---

4   Although by the end of 2010 the rising value of the Real was fuelling inflation and Dilma Rousseff felt obliged to raise interest rates after assuming the Presidency in January 2011.
5   Ocampo, La crisis.

The well-known destabilizing effects of such speculative capital flows have led governments to impose restrictions (especially in Brazil). But as long as such operations retain high levels of profitability, these short-term funds are likely to find ways around any barriers.

This time around, the traditional financial expression of the crisis has been replaced by its impact on trade. The sudden fall in the prices (29%) and volume of exports, seen after the beginning of the crisis in September 2008, has few precedents. Even though this bottomed out by June of the following year and was followed by a new rise in commodity prices, the final outcome of these fluctuations remained uncertain.

Renewed demand in China, India and other intermediate economies had driven these prices back up, making for an unprecedented influence of Asian imports on the Latin American trade cycle. However such a change in buyer does not alter the region's heavy dependence on the ups and downs of prices for its export commodities. Their recent surge has provided a lifeline, but an uncertain one.

Social retreat – the people bear the brunt

The outbreak of the crisis caused an immediate increase of 1% in the region's unemployment. At least three million people lost their jobs in the first few months of 2009, reversing the modest growth in employment seen during the previous five years of growth.

The most recent estimates suggest an increase of between 7.4 and 8.3% (or 9%) in the average unemployment rate, with variations between the various economies (8.8% in Argentina, 10.7% in Chile, 6.12% in Mexico). The lay-offs began with wage-earners in the most internationalized industries and ended up affecting those in precarious and informal work. Among youth, unemployment reached double the overall average. 50 million young people in Latin America are completely outside the educational system, while 20 million children work inhuman conditions.[6]

---

6   Rojas Aravena, Francisco, "Siete efectos políticos de la crisis internacional en América Latina," *Nueva Sociedad* no 224, November-December, 2009. Fazio Hugo, "Las grandes crisis latinoamericanas de los últimos 15 años," La explosión de la crisis global, LOM, Santiago, 2009. Also Página 12, 8-12-09.

This worsening unemployment coincides with an increase in acute poverty, affecting between 6 and 10 million individuals. The proportion of Latin Americans without the means to satisfy their basic needs continues to hover around 40%, with peaks during recessions and limited improvements during periods of recovery. This ocean of the poor feeds into precarious forms of labour in all countries[7].

In the most vulnerable countries, the eruption of crisis brought with it the scourge of hunger. This is the direct result of the neoliberal restructuring of agriculture, which increased the concentration on exports, the rural exodus and the shortage of food. Latin America now contributes some 53 million individuals to the world figures of undernourishment[8].

Another consequence of the crisis has been the sharp fall in remittances. This drop in the amount sent by relatives abroad has especially hit the Central American countries which have undergone massive demographic shifts. One in ten Mexicans now lives in the United States and the funds they transfer have taken on a vital role – they increased from $7.5 billion in 2000 to $26 billion in 2007.[9]

The last few months of 2009 saw the unprecedented phenomenon of reverse remittances, with families in the South sending money to relatives who had lost their jobs in the North. Yet returning home did not seem to be an option at a time when the recession was aggravated by swine flu and the slump in tourism.

The crisis also saw a worsening of income distribution, widening the social divide that had closed slightly during the preceding cycle of growth. The Gini coefficient (which measures this inequality) rose from 0.47% to 0.51%.

For a region with the greatest levels of inequality on the planet, the consequences of any regression in this respect are dramatic. You only have to look at the numbers for the region's biggest economy to see the scale of the imbalance. In Brazil, the richest 10% owns 75% of the total wealth, and 45% of this is in the hands of 5000 families, living in four cities[10].

The social disintegration caused by such high levels of inequality translates into an explosive rise in crime rates. Gangs are recruited among unemployed youth experiencing urban exclusion, aggravated by the destruction of agricultural communities. Countless individuals with no job, no skills and no prospects, have been pushed

---

7   *La Nación*, 11-11-09, 6-9-09.
8   *La Nación*, 15-10-09.
9   CEPAL Report, 15-7-09, *La Nación*, 22-11-09
10   *La Nación*, 6-9-09, Página 12, 26-12-09. Pochman Marcio. "El país de los desiguales". *Le Monde Diplomatique*, December 2007.

into this informal existence by the last few decades of capitalist restructuring.

Such crime is also fed by the culture of conspicuous consumption which neoliberalism promotes, at the same time that it is demolishing the living standards of working-class families. The capitalists who caused this tragedy, now howl in protest at its effects, especially when they personally suffer the kidnappings and violent robberies that characterize this new crime wave. Those responsible also complain about the low levels of education, as if the retreat on this front had nothing to do with the dismantling of state education.

The explanation for intervention

The spokespeople for CEPAL (the UN's Economic Commission for Latin America) have followed the swings in interpretation of the crisis offered by the most eminent economists. First they called it the biggest crash since the war, then promptly declared it had come to an end. They pondered, approvingly, on the maturity and capacity for resistance that Latin America had shown in the face of these tremors.[11]

Not once did they explain how this miraculous shift from economic catastrophe to passing hiccup had arisen. Rather, they attributed the region's new-found capacity to deal with a global crisis to the heterodox policies of state intervention. Some authors contrasted these measures to the paralysis and ineffectiveness imposed on previous occasions by orthodox subordination to the dictates of the market.

State intervention has indeed been a generalised feature this time around, expressed in a range of measures. Some sought to avoid interest rate rises and others sought to sustain demand by expanding the money supply. This approach prevailed, with variations, in almost all countries, giving the lie to neoliberal dogmas about the self-correcting qualities of the market. But this was no Latin American invention. It followed a worldwide tendency, expressed with greatest intensity in the United States and Europe.

Such intervention was possible in Latin America because of the reserves accumulated in the years of prosperity from 2003-2008. That period saw growth rates of 5% a year and improvements in the terms of trade of 100%. As a result, governments had much greater room to manoeuvre than in earlier crashes. They took advantage of a

---

11   CEPAL, "Panorama de la inserción internacional de América Latina y el Caribe," 10-12-2009, Santiago de Chile. Also, *La Nación*, 11-11-09.

situation created by the first period since the war when Latin American growth was higher than in the economies of the core countries. In particular, the export boom brought tax revenues that made it possible to avoid any repetition of the Mexican crisis of the 80s or the Argentinean collapse of 2001.

Nonetheless, the intervention extolled by CEPAL was not neutral. It used public funds to rescue big companies and banks, through aid that excluded any income redistribution. The increase in public spending benefited the ruling classes and included social compensation of only secondary importance.

The attention devoted to avoiding a collapse of purchasing power, reflects the fears left by the big popular revolts of recent decades. The still fresh memory of those social uprisings has been much stronger among the upper echelons of power than any new commitment to heterodox economics.

The explanation for adjustment

Orthodox economists attribute the limited impact of the crisis in Latin America to strict adherence to policies of fiscal surplus, monetary constraint and limited debts. They argue that such sobriety made for a solid shield against the storm outside.[12]

This description takes account of what is indeed a distinct fiscal and monetary context compared with the recent past. The region's debts, which in 1987 amounted to 53% of GDP and 365% of the value of total exports, had fallen by 2008 to 21% and 87% respectively. The banks were also less leveraged, as both public and private debt was less[13].

However this was not the result of administrative moderation. It was brought about by a brutal social adjustment, that included the liquidation of debts, the devaluation of capital and the concentration of incomes, all paid for by the majority of the population.

The neoliberals forget to mention this surgery, which also led to a reorganisation of finances in favour of a more select group of institutions. Such shake-ups turned Brazil, for example, into a favourite of the global establishment. The country has been given a high investment grade by the bankers and even lends money to the IMF. After an increase in bankruptcies (1994) that concentrated the whole system in fewer hands, the main survivors have specialised in trading with derivatives and options. In a context of greater monetary

---

12   This thesis is advanced by Arriazu, Ricardo, "América Latina logró ser menos vulnerable," *Clarín*, 21-9-09. Also, Sturzenegger, Federico, in *Página* 12, 2-2-08.
13   *Clarín*, 21-9-09.

stability, just 25 financial institutions control 81% of assets and make large profits as intermediaries.

Something similar happened in Mexico after the crash of 1994. However, in that case the banking concentration went hand in hand with a foreign take-over of the whole system, especially after Banamex was bought by Citigroup and Bancomer by BBVA. Moreover, the entire credit system has become closely connected to the whole economy's subordination to the United States.

In Argentina, the reorganisation of the banks followed the extraordinary collapse of 2001-2. Here it was not just a question of bank closures and takeovers, but also the confiscation of deposits, compulsory debt-swaps, the forced exchange of dollar assets into pesos and bond defaults. The scale of the collapse ended up limiting the hegemony that the financial sector had achieved in the 1990s, but it didn't alter a profoundly retrograde and highly concentrated banking system. Just 10 institutions control 77% of deposits.[14]

A similar (or more violent) processes of bank restructuring took place in Ecuador, Venezuela and other countries, the recent crisis hit Latin America just as it had reorganised the sector following those earlier collapses. Nonetheless, this situation is precarious and would offer little protection should there be another external tremor or fresh erosion from within. The underlying causes of the disintegration suffered by the banks in the 1980s and 90s still exist and a repetition of those collapses remains a latent possibility.

The two factors that put off such an outcome – high prices for export commodities and a degree of control over the fiscal deficit and inflation – are both open to sudden and unpredictable changes. Orthodox economists sense this fragility and warn against the dangers that the region faces. But they invariably forget how much *they* are responsible for this vulnerability.

From industrialisation to basic exports

The fluctuating international prices for exports have more impact than ever on the Latin American economy. Mexico depends on its income from oil sales. Argentina finds itself chained to the ups and downs of the soya market, and the same holds for Brazil with the various basic commodities it sells. Such dependence on the prices of

---

14   *Página* 12, 27-1-09.

metals, foodstuffs and fuel is even greater for the other countries of the region.

Debate: a new dependency on primary exports

There is no doubt that the export model has returned to the centre-stage in the region. Big infrastructure projects aim to secure foreign outlets for commodities produced in the mining and oil extraction sectors. The main conglomerates focus their activity in the primary sector, recreating the kind of specialisation that historically pushed Latin America into a peripheral status.

Between 1985 and 1996, 2,706 million tons of produce were extracted, 88% of which were made up of minerals and oil. Latin America is highly prized by the mining companies, which exploit the immense reserves of copper and iron ore and large deposits of lithium and uranium. It also has the biggest concentrations of fresh water and biodiversity on the planet.

For most of the 20th century, development economists opposed the concentration on exports promoted by liberals. But this rejection has diminished in the last few decades and this has now led to the paradox of CEPAL promoting primary commodity exports.

Once the main proponent of the now heterodox, "industrialisation" school, CEPAL can now be found singing the praises of the "potential offered by activities based on natural resources," pointing out its technological contribution and defending the signing of free trade agreements to facilitate the delivery of basic goods to the developed economies.[15]

Not only do such positions stand in sharp contrast to the industrialist tradition embodied by CEPAL between 1950 and 1980. They also sweep aside the arguments it developed over decades against the pernicious consequences of the primary-extractive model; it argued that it was, a system that had generated foreign dependence, the plunder of resources and lasting obstacles to accumulation.

Today, it perpetuates poverty and expels the rural population from their land, without creating equivalent numbers of jobs in the cities. All the classic objections to the primary export model remain valid; the new characteristics of transnational companies,

---

15 CEPAL, "Panorama de la inserción internacional de América Latina y el Caribe", 10-12-2009, Santiago de Chile. A more apologetic version of this model is put forward in Castro, Jorge, "Los países exportadores de alimentos adquieren mayor relevancia", *Clarín*, 6-9-09.

globalization and the emergence of Asia do not lessen the negative features of this model.

In fact, the old problems of reliance on exports are intensified by the new consequences of environmental devastation. Technical experts at CEPAL itself have evaluated the dramatic social cost of climate change for Latin America, in terms of pests, disease and the deterioration of water and soil resources.[16]

But they divorce such effects from their root causes in the primary-extractive model. In particular, they forget that the most important source of toxic gases in the region comes from opencast mining, deforestation and the irrational use of the soil to expand monocultures.

This profound damage to the environment in Latin America will not be corrected with energy-saving light-bulbs or hybrid motor vehicles. It demands policies to conserve nature which are radically opposed to the continued centrality of primary commodity exports.[17]

The United States' priorities

Latin America still occupies a strategic position for the United States as a great repository of natural resources. It plays a vital part in supplying metals and oil used by the Pentagon and the industrial complex of the north. The United States has sought to secure these supplies through bilateral free-trade agreements, at the same time as it increases its exports of finished goods and its manufacture of parts in the region's free-trade zones.[18]

North American imperialism sees this as a way of overcoming the crisis of domination that it has suffered in an area it traditionally treated as an extension of its own territory. The Bush administration was marked by the failure of its FTAA (Free Trade Area of the Americas) initiative and by the reappearance of a wave of popular, anti-imperialist struggles, which also produced new governments at loggerheads with the State Department. Obama has sought to reverse

---

16   *La Nación*, 17-12-09.
17   Acosta, Alberto has made a sharp critique of this model: "Los gobiernos progresistas no han puesto en tela de juicio la validez del modelo extractivista". 10-9 2009 www.ecoportal.net/content/view/full/88404. See also, Gudynas, Eduardo, "Inserción internacional y desarrollo latinoamericano", *Observatorio de la Globalización*, no 7, December 2009.
18   These policies are described by Saxe, Fernández John, ¿"América Latina: reserva estratégica de Estados Unidos"?, OSAL no. 25, April 2009. Delgado Ramos, "América Latina como reserva minera," *Memoria* 238, October-November 2009.

this loss of US influence, which was much stronger in the South America than in Central America.[19]

The United States is also trying to make up ground lost to European capital ever since Spain made major inroads into Latin America's banking and service sectors. Europe makes no bid for military or political pre-eminence in the area, but it promotes free-trade deals to benefit its own companies. It remains to be seen whether the severe impact of the crisis on Spanish firms will allow them to hold onto their position as the second biggest investors in the region.

The arrival of China in a part of the world historically removed from its sphere of activity represents a much bigger challenge for the United States. The eastern giant's demand for oil, soya and copper has increased greatly. Its trade with Latin America rose from $10 billion in 2000 to $140 billion in 2008.

What is more, the Chinese economy inundates its new partners with products, turning Brazil, for example, into one of its top clients. Bilateral trade between these two countries is on the verge of outstripping Brazilian-US trade, and similar tendencies are at work in Peru, Chile and Argentina. But big brother in the North has already responded by signing a transoceanic free-trade agreement with Vietnam, Singapore and Australia, which also includes its Pacific-coast partners in South America. It is here that the fight to control the region's treasure chest of natural resources is unfolding.

The demise of the national bourgeoisie

The old industrial structures that produced limited goods for the domestic market have been reshaped by the successive crises affecting Latin America. Now they have become a part of the export-led model, especially in the three countries that had developed a significant manufacturing sector.

The new emphasis on raw materials has not destroyed Latin-American industry, but it has reduced its importance in comparison with the post-war period. The character of manufacturing has changed with the growing weight of foreign corporations. On the other hand, some Latin-American multinationals have also emerged, occupying niches not already taken by big international firms.

---

19   We have analysed this in Katz, Claudio, *"El rediseño de América Latina, ALCA, MERCOSUR y ALBA"* Ediciones Luxemburg, Buenos Aires, 2006.

The relative retreat of the region's industry is most clearly visible when you compare it with growth of Asian companies. The overall share of world trade for the two regions has developed in very different directions. While Latin America has held onto its traditional share (from 4% of the total in 1980 to 5% in 2008), Asia has jumped from 6% to 23% in the same period. But the difference in the kinds of product sold is even more significant. While the former remains centred on raw materials, the latter is exporting manufactured goods.[20]

This shift in recent decades has also changed the profile of the ruling classes. The old national bourgeoisies that promoted the domestic market have been replaced by new, local bourgeoisies that prioritise exports and relations with transnational companies. Neoliberalism consolidated this change in the three main economies of the region.

Brazil's old industrial bourgeoisie, forged in the heat of developmentalist policies, has lost its ascendancy. Since the 1980s it has been replaced at the helm of the state by the current block of bankers, agri-businessmen and industrial exporters. In Mexico, the unanimous support of capitalists for the free-trade agreement with the USA shows even more categorically the decline of the old, industrial protectionism. In Argentina, the jump from one model to the other took the dramatic form of factory demolitions and the destruction of old, formal employment generated during the import-substitution period.

These changes in the ruling classes also gave rise to a growing preference for short-term financial gain, in tandem with the ever stronger links to foreign companies. Both aspects can be seen in the flight of capital and its investment abroad given the lack of opportunities to make similar returns in the sphere of domestic accumulation.

But the disappearance of those old national bourgeoisies does not mean that the local capitalist class has been eliminated; it continues to act according to its own interests and to dispute segments of the market with foreign firms. To point to the decline of the national bourgeoisie is simply to recognise that one sector of the ruling class (and its particular strategy for accumulation) has lost importance. There has not been a complete foreign take-over or submission to the transnational corporations. Latin-American capitalists continue to dominate the state machinery in these

---

20   *La Nación*, 11-11-09.

countries, although they are ever keener to deepen their ties to global finance capital.[21]

One example of this change was the attitude of the Mexican, Brazilian and Argentine governments to the latest crisis. All three countries were brought into the G20 meetings to back up the international bail-out of the failed banks. As was to be expected, Mexico's neoliberal administration signed up unquestioningly to all the Federal Reserve's initiatives. What was more surprising was that the more autonomous presidents of Brazil and Argentina did exactly the same.

All three governments backed the worldwide support for the dollar and the failed banks. They reiterated this support at the meetings held in Chile in mid-2009, with the US Vice President and the British Prime Minister – a gathering that was, quite absurdly, dubbed a "meeting of progressive leaders" by the international media.

To use this label to describe such a regional convergence with Anglo-US leaders is just as ridiculous as giving the Nobel Peace Prize to the main exponent of imperialism. In these meetings that agreed to socialize the bankers' losses, there was not the slightest drop of anything progressive. Mexico, Brazil and Argentina took on this agenda as a way of demonstrating that their ruling classes shared the priorities of global capitalism.

"Post-liberalism?"

Another expression of the same thing has been the support given to the IMF to reorganise international finances. Nations that only recently have themselves suffered the adjustments imposed by this body, now support its relaunch.

Mexico immediately asked for a new IMF loan. Brazil raised the stakes by itself contributing fresh capital to the Fund, while Argentina began the long road back to the body it had only recently repudiated when it cancelled its illegitimate debts with the IMF.

This new validation of the IMF is often justified by reference to its role in compensating for international financial imbalances. It is argued that the IMF's support for under-developed regions in times of crisis will be strengthened by the injection of greater resources.[22]

---

21   This view is further developed in Katz, Claudio, "Burguesías imaginarias y existentes", *Enfoques Alternativos*, n 21, February 2004, Buenos Aires.
22   This is argued by Frenkel, Roberto, and Rapeti, Martín, "La crisis mundial desde la perspectiva de los países en desarrollo," *Nueva Sociedad* no. 224, November-December, 2009.

However, the current credibility of such a tale is very limited. The IMF always helps banks by hitting states, and imposing adjustments that are invariably paid for by the oppressed. Any "more active role for the Fund" simply means placing more drastic demands on those it makes loans to.

We often hear that the IMF has suddenly changed, that it has "learnt the lessons of the past", "no longer demands sacrifices" and "respects the sovereignty of nations". But it is hard to find any evidence of this strange conversion from aggressor against peoples to conduit for development.

In fact, the IMF continues to implement the same policies with the same ultimatums. You just need to look at the agreements brokered with Ireland and Greece, not to mention the earlier ones signed with El Salvador, Iceland and Pakistan, to see this continuity. It is true that the body's resources increased threefold, and its lines of credit have been renewed to include loans that are more flexible than the traditional Stand By facility. But its agreements include the same demands as before. Serbia and Bosnia had to accept wage cuts for public employees, while Ukraine and Belorussia had to introduce strict, zero-deficit legislation. The only thing that has changed is the language used to legitimise such adjustments.[23]

The new illusions in the IMF have a political objective. They aim to isolate the governments and social movements that have criticised the institution, pressing them to abandon these criticisms, and they aim to build alternatives to what had become the main emblem of neoliberalism.

The current vogue for rehabilitating the IMF is shared by many developmentalist currents, which are hostile to the primacy given to foreign capital ("external saving") and to the obstacles put in the way of industrial development by high interest rates. So these approaches diverge from conventional neoliberalism; but they accept the priority given to exports, wage constraint and the close association with transnational corporations. Like CEPAL, they have renounced the combative stance of the old developmentalism and they oppose any radical redistribution of income, or its corollaries in terms of nationalisations or land reform.[24]

Only the application of these last three measures could lead to a real "post-liberal" situation. It is a mistake to apply this category to governments that maintain the privatization of basic resources,

---

23 There are detailed accounts in Nemiña, Pablo, "El nuevo FMI," *Página* 12, 20-9-09, and Wesibrot, Mark, "Jubilar al FMI," *Página* 12, 7-5-09.
24 One example is in Bresser Pereira, Luiz Carlos, "Globalizacao e competicao," Folha de Sao Paulo, 2,11.09

regressive tax regimes and the increased concentration of land and capital in agriculture.

Progressive changes in these three areas are indispensable starting points for beginning a break with the neoliberal legacy that is currently preserved by so-called progressive governments. In this respect they differ from their nationalist predecessors, who in the middle of the last century clashed with the oligarchy and with foreign capital, in their efforts to develop independent industries and introduce social reforms.

Translated by Iain Bruce

IN THE EYE OF THE STORM: THE DEBT CRISIS IN THE EUROPEAN UNION

Eric Toussaint
(interview by the CADTM[1])

In July-September 2011 the stock markets were again shaken at international level. The crisis has become deeper in the EU, particularly with respect to debts. The CADTM interviewed Eric Toussaint about various facets of this new stage in the crisis.

Greece

CADTM: Is it really true that Greece has to commit to paying about 15% interest rates to be allowed to contract ten year loans?
Eric Toussaint: Yes, it is; markets are only ready to buy the ten-year bonds Greece wishes to issue on condition it commits to paying such extravagant rates.
CADTM: Will Greece contract ten-year loans on such conditions?
Eric Toussaint: No, Greece cannot afford to pay such high interest rates. It would cost the country far too much. Yet almost every day we can read in both mainstream and alternative media (the latter being essential to develop a critical opinion) that Greece must borrow at 15% or more.

In fact, since the crisis broke out in spring 2010, Greece has borrowed on the markets for 3 months, 6 months or 1 year, no more, at interest rates ranging between 4 and 5%[2]. Note that before

---

1   CADTM is the Committee for Cancellation of Third World Debt, www.cadtm.org.
2   *Hellenic Republic Public Debt Bulletin*, n° 62, June 2011. Available at www.bankofgreece.gr

speculative attacks against Greece started, it could borrow at very low rates since bankers and institutional investors (pension funds, insurance companies) were eager to lend.

For instance, on 13 October 2009, it issued three month Treasury bonds also called T-Bills with a very low yield of 0.35%. On the same day it issued six month bonds at a 0.59% rate. Seven days later, on 20 October 2009, it issued one year bonds at 0.94%[3]. This was less than six months before the Greek crisis broke out. Rating agencies had given a very high rating to Greece and the banks that were granting one loan after another. Ten months later, it had to issue six month bonds at a 4.65% yield – in other words, 8 times more. This denotes a fundamental change in circumstances.

Another significant fact points to the banks' responsibility: in 2008 banks demanded a higher yield from Greece than in 2009. For instance in June-July-August 2008, before the crash produced by the Lehman Brothers bankruptcy, rates were four times higher than in October 2009. They were at their lowest (below 1%) in the fourth term of 2009[4]. This may seem irrational, since a private bank is certainly not supposed to lower its interest rates in a context of major international crisis, least of all with a country such as Greece, which is prompt to borrow; but it was perfectly logical from the point of view of bankers out to maximize profits while relying on public rescue in case of trouble. After the Lehman Brothers bankruptcy, the governments of the US and European countries poured huge amounts of cash to bail out banks, restore confidence and boost economic recovery. Banks used this money to lend to countries such as Greece, Portugal, Spain and Italy, convinced as they (rightly) were that if there were any problem, the ECB and the European Commission would help them out.

CADTM: You mean that private banks deliberately pushed Greece into the trap of an unsustainable debt by offering low interest rates, then demanded much higher rates that made it impossible for Greece to borrow beyond a one year term?

Eric Toussaint: Yes, exactly. I don't mean that there was some sort of plot but it is obvious that banks literally threw capital into the arms of countries such as Greece (notably by lowering the interest rates they demanded) since they considered that the money they so generously received from public authorities had to be turned into loans to eurozone countries. We have to bear in mind that only three

---

3   Hellenic Republic Public Debt Bulletin, n° 56, December 2009.
4   Bank of Greece, Economic Research Department – Secretariat, Statistics Department – Secretariat, *Bulletin of Conjunctural Indicators*, Number 124, October 2009. Available at www.bankofgreece.gr

years ago States appeared to be the more reliable actors while the capacity of private companies to repay their debts was questionable.

To go back to the concrete example mentioned above, on 20 October 2009 the Greek government sold its three-month T-Bills with a 0.35% yield in an attempt to raise 500 million euro. Bankers and other institutional investors proposed about five times this amount, i.e. 7,040 million. Eventually the government decided to borrow 2,400 million. It is no exaggeration to claim that bankers literally threw money at Greece.

Let us also go back to the time sequences in the increase of loans granted by West European banks to Greece between 2005 and 2009. Bankers of Western European countries increased their loans to Greece (to both public and private sectors) in several stages. Between December 2005 and March 2007, the amount of loans increased by 50%, from just under $80 billion to $120 billion. Although the *subprime* crisis had broken out in the US, loans increased again, this time by 33%, between June 2007 and summer 2008 (from $120 to $160 billion), then they stayed at a very high level (about $120 billion). This means that Western European private banks used the money they received at very low rates from the European Central Bank (ECB), the Bank of England, the US Federal Reserve and the US money market funds (see below) in order to increase their loans to countries such as Greece[5] without taking risk into consideration. Private banks thus bear a heavy responsibility for the crushing debts of Greece. Greek private banks also loaned huge amounts to public authorities and to the private sector. They too have a significant responsibility in the present situation. Consequently the debts claimed from Greece by foreign and Greek banks as a result of their irresponsible policy should be considered illegitimate.

The great Greek bond bazaar

CADTM: You say that since the crisis broke out in May 2010 Greece has stopped issuing 10-year bonds. Why then do markets demand a yield of 15% or more on Greece's 10-year bonds?[6]

---

5   The same can be observed in the same period with Portugal, Spain, and the countries of Central and Eastern Europe.
6   On 25 August 2011 the Greek rate for 10 years reached 18.55%, on the day before, 17.9%. The rate for 2 years was a staggering 45.9%. http://www.lemonde.fr/europe/article/2011/08/25/les-taux-des-obligations-grecques-a-dix-ans-atteignent-un-nouveau-record_1563605_3214.html (accessed 26 August 2011)

Eric Toussaint: This has an influence on the sale price of older Greek debt bonds exchanged on the secondary market or on the Over The Counter (OTC) market.

There is another much more important consequence, namely that it forces Greece to make a choice between two alternatives:

Either depend even further on the Troika (International Monetary Fund (IMF, ECB, EU) to get long-term loans (10-15-30 years) and submit to their conditions;

Or refuse the diktats of markets and of the Troika and suspend payment while starting an audit in order to repudiate the illegitimate part of its debt.

CADTM: Before we look at these alternatives, can you explain what the secondary market is?

Eric Toussaint: As is the case for used cars, there is a second-hand market for debts. Institutional investors and hedge funds buy or sell used bonds on the secondary market or on the OTC market. Institutional investors are by far the main actors.

The last time Greece issued ten-year bonds was on 11 March 2010, before speculative attacks started and the Troika intervened. In March 2010, to get 5 billion euro, it committed itself to an interest rate of 6.25% every year until 2020. By that date it will have to repay the borrowed capital. Since then, as we have seen, it no longer borrows for ten years because rates blew up. When we read that the ten-year interest rate is 14.86% (on 8 August 2011 when the 10-year Greek rate, which had been as high as 18%, was again below 15% after the ECB's intervention), this indicates the price at which ten-year bonds are exchanged on the secondary or OTC markets.

Institutional investors who bought those bonds in March 2010 are trying to sell them off on the debt secondary market because they have become high risk bonds, given the possibility that Greece may not be able to refund their value when they reach maturity.

CADTM: Can you explain how the second-hand price of the ten-year bonds issued by Greece is determined?

Eric Toussaint: The following table should help us understand what is meant by saying that the Greek rate for ten years amounts to 14.86%. Let us take an example: a bank bought Greek bonds in March 2010 for 500 million euro, with each bond representing 1,000 euro. The bank will cash €62.5 each year (i.e. 6.25% of €1,000) for each bond. In security market lingo, a bond will yield a €62.5 coupon. In 2011 those bonds are regarded as risky since it is by no means certain that by 2020 Greece will be able to repay the borrowed capital. So the banks that have many Greek bonds, such as BNP Paribas (that still had €5 billion in July 2011), Dexia (€3.5 billion), Commerzbank (€3 billion), Generali (€3 billion), Société Générale (€2.7 billion), Royal

Bank of Scotland, Allianz or Greek banks, now sell their bonds on the secondary market because they have junk or toxic bonds in their balance sheets. In order to reassure their shareholders (and to prevent them from selling their shares), their clients (and to prevent them from withdrawing their savings) and European authorities, they must get rid of as many Greek bonds as they can, after having gobbled them up until March 2010. What price can they sell them for? This is where the 14.86% rate plays a part. Hedge funds and other vulture funds that are ready to buy Greek bonds issued in March 2010 want a yield of 14.86%. If they buy bonds that yield 62.5 euro, this amount must represent 14.86% of the purchasing price, so the bonds are sold for only 420.50 euro.

	Nominal value of a 10-year bond issued by Greece on 11 March 2010	Interest rate on 11 March 2010	Value of the coupon paid each year to the owner of a EUR 1,000 bond	Price of the bond on the secondary market on 8 August 2011	Actual yield on 8 August 2011 if the buyer bought a EUR 1,000 bond for EUR 420.50
Example	EUR 1,000	6,25%	EUR 62,5	EUR 420,50	14,86%

To sum up: buyers will not pay more than €420.50 for a €1,000 bond if they want to receive an actual interest rate of 14.86%. As you can imagine, bankers are not too willing to sell at such a loss.

CADTM: You say that institutional investors sell Greek bonds. Do you have any idea on what scale?

Eric Toussaint: As they tried to minimize the risks they took, French banks reduced their Greek exposure by 44% (from $27 billion to $15 billion) in 2010. German banks proceeded similarly: their direct exposure decreased by 60% between May 2010 and February 2011 (from €16 billion to €10 billion). In 2011 this withdrawal movement has become even more noticeable.

CADTM: What does the ECB do in this respect?

Eric Toussaint: The ECB is entirely devoted to serving the bankers' interests.

CADTM: But how?

Eric Toussaint: Through buying Greek bonds itself on the secondary market. The ECB buys from the private banks that wish to get rid of securities backed on the Greek debt with a valuation haircut of about 20%. It pays approximately €800 for a bond whose value was €1,000 when issued. Now, as appears from the table above, these bonds are valued at much less on the secondary market or on the OTC market. You can easily imagine why the banks appreciate being paid €800 by the ECB rather the market price. This being said, it is another example of the huge gap between the actual practices of private bankers and European leaders on the one hand and their discourse on the need to allow market forces to determine prices on the other.

The ECB: ever loyal to private interests

CADTM: On 8 August 2011 the ECB started buying bonds issued by European States that had run into trouble. What do you think of this?
Eric Toussaint: A first important point to remember: the media announced that the ECB would start buying bonds without specifying that this would only occur, as usual, on the secondary market.

The ECB does not buy bonds on the Greek debt directly from the Greek government but from banks on the secondary market. This is why banks were pleased on 8 August 2011.

Indeed, between March 2011 and 8 August 2011 the ECB claims that it did not buy any bonds on the secondary market. This was a source of aggravation for the banks since, as they wanted to get rid of the Greek bonds and the bonds of other states experiencing difficulties, they had had to sell them at knock-down prices on the secondary market. Most of them only sold a few because prices were really too low.[7] This is why they insisted that the ECB start buying again.
CADTM: The ECB's return to the secondary market raises the price of Greek bonds, is that it?
Eric Toussaint: Yes, but only for a while, and what matters is that the ECB buys in huge quantities and at a higher value than the market price. Between May 2010 and March 2011 it bought Greek bonds from bankers and other institutional investors for 66 billion euro. Between 8 and 12 August, i.e. within five days, it bought Greek, Irish, Portuguese, Spanish and Italian bonds for 22 billion euro. Over the following week it bought another 14 billions' worth. We do not know the proportion of Greek bonds but we can see that the purchase was massive. What is clear is that the ECB's practice of buying bonds makes it possible for institutional investors to speculate and make juicy profits.

---

7   In the *Hellenic Republic Public Debt Bulletin*, n° 62, June 2011, p. 4, we clearly see that the secondary market literally dried up from May 2010 when the ECB started buying bonds.

Indeed, banks can buy bonds at cut prices on the secondary market or much more unobtrusively on the OTC market that is outside any regulation (42.5% of their face value in the days following 8 August 2011 and even lower a few weeks later) and sell them to the ECB at 80%. The volume of this kind of transaction may be marginal, it is difficult to know exactly. But they certainly are most profitable and I cannot see how the ECB or market authorities could prevent this, even if they wanted to.

We have to remember that transactions on the secondary market are barely regulated, and that next to the secondary market there is the OTC market that is not regulated at all by the public authorities. On a regular basis, debt bonds are sold and bought as 'short sales', i.e. a buyer, for instance a bank, can buy bonds for dozens of millions without having to pay for them when receiving them. Buyers promise they will pay, they get the bonds, sell them on, and pay what was owed with the proceeds of the resale. This proves that the purchase was never intended to be used for its own yield, but was bought to be sold on immediately to maximize profit (speculation).

Of course if they cannot sell these bonds on at a good price or at all, they cannot foot the bill. This can lead to a crash, since hundreds of institutional investors play the same game and the amounts at stake are astronomical. Transactions on securities backed on the public debt of States facing problems amount to tens or hundreds of billions of euros on a liberalized market.

CADTM: Why doesn't the ECB buy directly from the States that issue the bonds instead of buying on secondary markets?

Eric Toussaint: Because the governments concerned wanted to preserve the monopoly of the private sector on providing credit to public bodies. Direct lending to member States is prohibited by the ECB's own statutes as well as by the Lisbon Treaty, and this also applies to central banks in the EU. The ECB therefore lends to private banks which in turn lend to States with other institutional investors.

As mentioned above, French, German and other banks sold Greek bonds massively in 2010 and in the first term of 2011. The ECB has so far been their first buyer and it buys above the secondary market price.[8]

As you can see, this makes for all sorts of manipulations by the banks and other institutional investors, since bonds are warranted

---

8   By the end of 2009 before the Greek crisis broke out, French financial institutions (mainly banks) held 26% of Greek bonds sold abroad, German banks held 15%, 10% for Italy, 9% for Belgium, 8% in the Netherlands, 8% in Luxembourg, 5% in Britain. In short, financial institutions, especially banks, of seven EU countries held no less than 81% of Greek bonds sold abroad.

to the holders and the markets are liberalized. Clearly the private banks put pressure on the ECB for it to buy bonds at a higher price, claiming that they needed to get rid of them to clean up their balance sheets and so prevent another large-scale financial crisis.

July and August were good months for such blackmail, as the stock markets went through a fall of 15% to 25% in their indexes between 8 July and 18 August 2011. Share prices of those banks that lent money to Greece, French banks in particular, literally plummeted. Panic-stricken, the ECB gave in to the bankers' and institutional investors' pressure and started buying bonds again. The ECB's intervention saved the day (at least for a while) for a number of major banks, particularly French ones. Once again public institutions helped out the private sector. But there is an even more outrageous aspect to the ECB's behaviour.

CADTM: Can you explain?

Eric Toussaint: It's very easy. It lends money at a very low rate to private banks, 1% from May 2009 to April 2011, 1.5% today, merely asking banks that receive the loans to provide a financial guarantee. Now what the banks provide as guarantee are the very bonds (called 'collaterals') on which they receive, if they are Greek, Portuguese or Irish bonds, interest rates ranging from 3.75 to 5% if they were issued for less than a year (see above), and more if they are bonds maturing after 3, 5 or 10 years.

CADTM: Why do you call this outrageous?

Eric Toussaint: Here is why. Banks borrow at 1% or 1.5% from the ECB to grant loans to some States at 3.75% at least. Once they have bought the bonds and cashed their interest, they win twice over: they leave these bonds as collateral to borrow again at low rates from the ECB and loan this money to States at high interest rates. The ECB makes it possible for them to make even more juicy profits.

Moreover, from 2009-10 the ECB has changed its safety and security criteria and agreed to banks using high-risk bonds as collateral, which obviously encourages those banks to make inconsiderate loans since they are sure to be able either to sell the bonds to the ECB or to use them as guarantee.[9] It seems logical to consider that the ECB should behave differently and lend directly to States at 1 or 1.5%, without lavishing gifts to bankers as it does.

CADTM: But does it have a choice since this is prohibited by its statutes and the Lisbon Treaty?

Eric Toussaint: A number of dispositions in the Treaty are not adhered to anyway (the debt/GDP ratio that should not be over 60%,

---

9   Just try to get a major loan from a bank with high risk bonds as evidence of your solvency, and see where it gets you!

the government deficit/GDP ratio that should not be over 3 %), so considering the circumstances we can forget about that one too.

For the next stage we need to be aware that various EU treaties have to be abrogated, that the ECB statutes have to be radically changed, and that the EU has to be founded on other premises.[10] Yet to achieve this, the balance of power has first to be changed through massive street mobilizations.

A European Brady deal: austerity for life

CADTM: After the European summit of 21 July 2011 it was announced that the Greek debt was to be reduced by calling upon bankers. Was this a good move?
Eric Toussaint: Not at all. Those decisions do not provide countries facing financial problems with a favourable solution. The decisions taken on 21 July, supposing they are ratified by the parliaments of the member States in September-October 2011, will only slightly loosen the noose that strangles those countries and particularly their populations.

Moreover, in the case of Greece (soon followed by other countries), European governments have relied on bankers, who are largely responsible for the disaster, to devise a policy tailored to their own needs. They set up an *ad hoc* cartel of the major creditor banks under the grand but misleading name of Institute of International Finance (IIF), which has drafted a menu with various options offering four possible scenarios.[11]

As recalled by Crédit Agricole, one of the main French banks (it owns a bank in Greece, 'Emporiki,'[12] stuffed full of Greek bonds), the IIF clearly found its inspiration in the Brady Plan that was implemented in the 1980s-90s to face the debt crisis in 18 emerging countries (see below). Heads of State, the EC and bankers, relayed by the media, announced that this would reduce the debt by 21%, which is wrong. Actually, at best, the Greek debt would be reduced by 13.5 billion euro, i.e. 4% of the current principal, which amounts to €350

---

10   See our Eight key proposals for another Europe (particularly proposal n°8 on the issue of the EU), http://www.cadtm.org/Eight-key-proposals-for-another
11   They are summed up in an article in *The Financial Times* on 26 July 2011, p. 23, and in the Crédit Agricole's bulletin Perspectives Hebdo 18-22 July 2011.
12   http://www.lesechos.fr/entreprises-secteurs/finance-marches/actu/0201589122728-les-metiers-de-credit-agricole-compensent-le-fardeau-grec-210653.php (accessed 26 August 2011).

billion (which will further increase in the coming years). The 21% figure is the haircut bankers are ready to apply to the value of the Greek bonds they hold. It is just a bookkeeping operation. Indeed it does not affect at all what the Greek government has to pay. Bankers are so pleased that their proposal should have been accepted by the Heads of State and the ECB that several of them announced as early as late July-early August that they provisioned 21% losses on Greek bonds maturing in 2020. For instance, BNP Paribas provisioned €534 million, and Dexia €377 million.[13] By doing that, banks that play a leading part in the IIF hope to get parliaments in the EU countries to ratify the agreements made with the Heads of State and the ECB. Besides, such expected loss provisioning can be offset from their profits to reduce taxation. So far, however, there is one trouble-maker among the bankers, namely the Royal Bank of Scotland (RBS), which withdrew from the IIF and announced that it would apply a 50% haircut instead of 21% and provision losses for £733 million, which shows that the 21% cut is far from sufficient. Moreover, according to the *Financial Times* and the Belgian financial daily *L'Écho*[14] the International Accounting Standards Board (IASB) sent a letter to the European Securities and Markets Authority which regulates the European financial markets, calling into question banks that apply a 21% cut on their Greek bonds when the market to market value is less than 50%.

CADTM: The 21 July 2011 agreement is also said to mean that the Troika's loans to Greece, Ireland and Portugal would be extended over a longer period with lower interest rates. Is this the case?

Eric Toussaint: European governments did announce that they intended to reduce the interest rates they charge Greece, Ireland and Portugal by 2 or 3 points.[15] Announcing a reduction of 3.5% in interest rates for 15 or even 30 year loans amounts to acknowledging that the rates they had demanded so far were prohibitive. The move is motivated by the obvious disaster they have contributed to bring down on those countries and by the risk of the crisis spreading to other countries. The measures announced by European governments on 21 July 2011 are a clear acknowledgement of the 'unjust enrichment' they are responsible for and of the fraudulent nature of their policies.

CADTM: What is unjust enrichment?

---

13   *Financial Times*, 6-7 August 2011.
14   *L'Écho*, 31 August 2011. See also TF1 "La BNP a-t-elle sous-estimé son risque grec?" http://lci.tf1.fr/economie/entreprise/la-bnp-a-t-elle-sous-estime-son-risque-grec-6663932.html
15   See the official declaration of the EU Council: http://www.consilium.europa.eu/uedocs/cms_data/docs/pressdata/en/ec/123978.pdf

Eric Toussaint: Unjust enrichment is abusive enrichment, profit gained through unlawful means. It corresponds to a general principle in international law defined in article 38 of the statutes of the International Court of Justice.[16] States such as Germany, France and Austria borrow at 2% on the markets and lend the same money to Greece at 5% or 5.5%, to Ireland at 6%. Similarly the IMF borrows from its members at low interest rates and lends to Greece, Ireland and Portugal at much higher rates.

CADTM: What is the fraudulent nature of the Troika's policies?

Eric Toussaint: Fraud[17] is an important notion in international law. It refers to an intentional deception made to damage another individual. If a State were led to contract a loan through the fraudulent behaviour of another State or an international organization that is party to the negotiation, it may invoke fraud as grounds for declaring the contract void, since it was agreed to through deceit. Now the Troika uses the plight of Greece, Ireland and Portugal to enforce measures that go against citizens' social and economic rights, challenge collective conventions, and contravene the country's sovereignty and in some cases also its constitution. Thanks to some Italian newspapers, we know that in early August 2011 the ECB benefited from speculative attacks against Italy forcing its government to implement the same kind of antisocial measures as Greece, Ireland and Portugal. If the Italian government did not comply, the ECB said it might not help Italy at all.

What the members of the Troika are doing can be compared to the odious behaviour of someone who, while claiming to help a person in a difficult predicament, would actually make it worse and benefit from it. We can also consider that it is a criminal act planned collectively by the IMF, the ECB, the EU, and the governments that are supporting their action. Associating in order to plan and carry out a criminal act increases the responsibility of the aggressors.

There is more: the economic policies enforced by the Troika will not allow the affected countries to improve their situation. For three decades this kind of damaging policy has been implemented on behalf of large private companies, the IMF and the governments of industrialized countries, in indebted countries of the South and in a number of countries of the former Soviet bloc. The countries that complied most diligently have had to face terrible times. Those that refused the diktats of international bodies and their neoliberal

---

16   It is also mentioned in several national civil codes, for instance in those of Spain (articles 1895ff) and France (articles 1376ff).
17   Article 49 of the Vienna Convention of 1969 and of the Treaty of Vienna of 1986.

doctrine have fared much better. This has to be recalled for we have to make it known that the results of the policies demanded by the Troika and institutional investors are a foregone conclusion. Neither today nor tomorrow will they ever have the right to claim they did not know what their policies would result in. We can already see what is happening in Greece.

CADTM: For over a year now, the CADTM has been warning against a debt reduction led by creditors, namely the Troika, bankers and other institutional investors. Is this justified?

Eric Toussaint: Of course. The current operation is led by creditors and geared to their own interests. As indicated above, the current plan is a European version of the Brady plan.[18] Let us remember the context in which this plan was implemented at the end of the 1980s.

In the early years of the crisis that broke out in 1982, the IMF and the governments of the US, the UK and other major powers helped private bankers in the North that had taken huge risks as they granted loan after loan to countries of the South, particularly in Latin America (as was to happen later with subprime mortgages and loans to countries such as Greece, Eastern European countries, Ireland, Portugal and Spain). When developing countries, starting with Mexico, were close to defaulting, the IMF and countries of the Paris Club agreed to lend them capital, provided they further repay private banks of the North and implement austerity plans (the notorious structural adjustment policies). Next, as the debt of the South was snowballing, they set up the Brady Plan (after the name of the US Treasury Secretary of the time) that involved a restructuring of the debt of the main indebted countries with bond exchanges. The participating countries were Argentina, Brazil, Bulgaria, Costa Rica, Côte d'Ivoire, the Dominican Republic, Ecuador, Jordan, Mexico, Nigeria, Panama, Peru, the Philippines, Poland, Russia, Uruguay, Venezuela and Vietnam. At the time, Nicolas Brady announced that the amount of the debt would be reduced by 30% (actually, when there was a reduction it was much less than that, and in several major cases the debt even increased, see below) and the new bonds (the Brady bonds) guaranteed a fixed interest rate of about 6%, which was very favourable to bankers. It also ensured that austerity policies would continue under the supervision of the IMF and the World Bank. Today, under other latitudes, the same logic produces the same disasters.

It is most interesting to look at *a posteriori* assessments by two well-known US neoliberal economists, Kenneth Rogoff, former chief economist with the IMF, and Carmen Reinhart, university professor

---

18 See Éric Toussaint, *The World Bank: the never-ending coup d'État*, Mumbai: Vikas Adhyayan Kendra; (2007), chapter 15.

and advisor to the IMF and the World Bank. Here is what they wrote in 2009 about the Brady bond. They first assert: *"Conspicuously absent from the large debt reversal episodes were the well-known Brady restructuring deals of the 1990s."*

They then base their negative assessment on the following elements:
- In fact, in Argentina and Peru, three years after the Brady deal, the ratio of debt to GDP was higher than it had been in the year prior to the restructuring!
- By the year 2000, seven of the seventeen countries that had undertaken a Brady-type restructuring (Argentina, Brazil, Ecuador, Peru, the Philippines, Poland and Uruguay) had ratios of external debt to GDP that were higher than those they had experienced three years after the restructuring, and by the end of 2000, four of those countries (Argentina, Brazil, Ecuador and Peru) had debt ratios that were higher than those recorded before the deal.
- By 2003, four members of the Brady bunch (Argentina, Côte d'Ivoire, Ecuador and Uruguay) had once again defaulted on or rescheduled their external debt.
- By 2008, less than twenty years after the deal, Ecuador had defaulted twice. A few other members of the Brady group may follow suit[19].

The European version is true to the original Brady Plan down to its finest details. In the context of the plan, participating states had to buy US treasury zero coupon bonds[20] as guarantee in case of defaulting. The European plan devised by the banks, the EU and the ECB (with the full support of the IMF) proposes four options. In the first three, Greece, through the European Financial Stability Facility (EFSF), buys zero coupon euro bonds as a guarantee that it will repay the principal on thirty-year bonds.[21]

CADTM: What do you think of this plan?

Eric Toussaint: It will not help Greece to clear its debts for two essential reasons. Firstly, the debt reduction is completely insufficient; and secondly, the economic and social policies implemented by Greece to meet the Troika's demands will further

---

19   Carmen M. Reinhart, Kenneth S. Rogoff, *This Time is Different: Eight Centuries of Financial Folly*, Princeton University Press, 2009, pp. 84-85. Accessed online as googlebook.
20   These are bonds that do not give a right to periodic interest payments or coupons, hence their name. They are bought at a discount price from their face value, which is paid when the bond reaches maturity. Zero-coupon bonds are usually inflation indexed.
21   See Crédit Agricole, *Perspectives Hebdo 18* - 22 July 2011, p. 3.

weaken the country. As a consequence the new loans granted to Greece in the context of this plan as well as the former, now restructured, debts can be defined as odious.[22]

CADTM: The ECB is said to be against a strong haircut of the Greek debt.

Eric Toussaint: Correct. The ECB is trapped by its own policy: as it bought lots of Greek bonds on the secondary market and agreed to banks, including Greek banks, depositing Greek bonds as guarantee on the loans it grants, the assets in its balance sheet consist of huge amounts of Greek bonds (plus Irish, Portuguese, Italian and Spanish bonds). If a 50 or 60% haircut were to be applied to Greek bonds, its balance sheet would be unbalanced. That being said, it is still quite feasible since this is merely a matter of book-keeping.

The ECB's opposition to a strong haircut coincides once again with the interests of private bankers who do not agree to their assets being devalued either. The ECB has put pressure on EU Heads of State and on the EU for them to strengthen the European Financial Stability Facility so that it can buy high risk bonds. It wants to get this over with as soon as possible.

CDS and rating agencies: factor(ie)s of risk and destabilization

CADTM: You haven't talked about Credit Default Swaps (CDSs) yet.

Eric Toussaint: CDSs are a derivative financial product which is not submitted to any form of public control. They were created in the first half of the 1990s in the middle of the era of deregulation. Credit Default Swap literally means permutation of unpaid debts. Normally, it should allow the holder of a loan to obtain compensation from the CDS seller in the case of default by the bond-issuer, whether a government or a private company. I use the conditional for two main reasons. Firstly, a CDS can be bought as protection against the risk of non repayment of a bond that the buyer **does not have**. This is the same as taking out insurance for the house next door, hoping that it will catch fire so that one can get the money. Secondly, CDS sellers do not begin by banking enough funds to indemnify victims of defaults. If a whole lot of private companies having issued bonds should go

---

22   On the odious and consequently void nature of debts claimed by the Troika from Greece, Ireland and Portugal (to which we can add debts claimed by the IMF from Romania, Latvia, Bulgaria and Hungary, i.e. countries that are all members of the EU) see Renaud Vivien and Éric Toussaint, 'Greece, Ireland and Portugal: why agreements with the Troika are odious' http://www.cadtm.org/Greece-Ireland-and-Portugal-why

bankrupt, or if a major lender State should default on payments, it is quite certain that CDS sellers would be incapable of indemnifying as promised. In 2008, the collapse of the North-American company AIG, the biggest international insurance company (which was actually nationalized by Bush to avoid the consequences of bankruptcy) and that of Lehman Brothers were directly linked to the CDS market. AIG and Lehman had both been very active in this sector.

The CDS enables all sorts of manipulations. I had the opportunity to observe closely an attempt at manipulation when I was a member of the audit commission for the internal and external debts set up by the government of Ecuador in 2007, which delivered its report in September 2008. While we were auditing the Ecuadorian debt and President Rafael Correa was threatening to stop paying the illegitimate part of the debt to the international money markets, a private North-American company contacted the Ecuadorian government with a most edifying proposal. The company suggested that President Correa should let it be known that he was going to suspend payments just before the next due-date three weeks later. This would enable the company to sell CDSs for a value they had calculated at $300 million. The final outcome was supposed to be as follows: in reality, Ecuador would pay what it owed as usual. This would mean that the company would not need to indemnify the CDS holders and it would give half the proceeds to the Ecuadorian government. The company claimed that this operation was completely free of any risk of prosecution as it would be an over-the-counter transaction outside US government control. It claimed to have already carried out similar transactions on several occasions. In the end, the Ecuadorian government refused the offer, opting for another strategy which produced good results. The point about this true-life story is that it illustrates that issuers and buyers of CDSs can carry out all sorts of manipulations.

Let us not forget that right up until the AIG disaster and the collapse of Lehman Brothers, the IMF, the US Federal Reserve and the ECB repeatedly claimed that CDSs were a new product that offered excellent guarantees against risks (see the box on CDSs). Since then, their discourse has changed, but nothing, absolutely nothing, has been done to regulate the CDS market. Meanwhile, in view of the size of the phenomenon, CDSs constitute a huge time-bomb hanging over the international finance system. The fact is that CDS should be outlawed.

CADTM: How much responsibility do rating agencies bear for the crisis?

Eric Toussaint: The North-American Standard & Poor's and Moody's and the Franco-American Fitch are the three private agencies which rule the roost regarding credit ratings and the credibility of bond issuers, whether they be State or corporate.[23] They have existed for almost a century but it was not until the 1970s-1980s, with the financialisation of the economy, that their business took a sudden leap.

However they are constantly in a situation of conflict of interests. Until the 1970s, it was the prospective buyers of bonds issued by the State and by companies who paid rating agencies for their advice on the quality of the issuers. Since then, the situation has been

---

Monetary and financial authorities have encouraged the creation of a time-bomb composed of CDSs (2)

In 2007 the IMF issued the following declaration referring to the health of the United States and particularly CDSs, labelled new risk-transfer markets:

> Although complacency would be misplaced, it would appear that innovation has supported financial system soundness. New risk transfer markets have facilitated the dispersion of credit risk from a core where moral hazard is concentrated to a periphery where market discipline is the chief restraint on risk-taking. (...)Although cycles of excess and panic have not disappeared — the subprime boom-bust being but the latest example — markets have shown that they can and do self-correct.
> *(IMF, 2007 Consultations Report, article 4 with the United States).*[1]

Clearly, certain supposedly reputable banks are still covering themselves against defaults through CDSs. Thus the Deutsche Bank announced at t`he end of July 2011 that it had reduced its exposure regarding the Italian debt by 88%. The principal German lender claims to have reduced its exposure in Italy from €8 billion to €997 million. According to the *Financial Times*, the Deutsche Bank achieved this not by selling over €7 billion worth of Italian bonds, but by a stroke of book-keeping wizardry, buying up CDSs to hedge its investments against possible default on the part of Italy.[2] On another level, hedge funds, particularly active on the OTC and CDS markets, are worried at the perspective of the Greek debt being partly written off. They are wondering whether they will retain enough street cred to continue selling CDSs once they have failed to indemnify CDS holders of the Greek debt.[3]

1   See http://www.imf.org/external/pubs/ft/scr/2007/cr07265.pdf. For more on the IMF's errors of judgement concerning the USA and Ireland, see: François Sana *'Zéro de conduite pour le FMI'* http://www.cadtm.org/Zero-de-conduite-pour-le-FMI
2   *Financial Times*, 'Deutsche hedges Italian risk', 27 July 2011, p. 13.
3   *Financial Times*, 'Greek rescue plan worries hedge funds', supplement FTfm, 8 August 2011.

---

23   There are others, such as the Chinese Dagong, but they have little influence.

completely reversed: now it is the issuers of bonds who pay the agencies to rate them. What motivates the government and the companies is of course to get good ratings so that they can pay the lowest possible interest rates to those who buy their bonds. Let us recall: that until the eve of the collapse of Enron in 2001, highly paid rating agencies attributed top marks to the power supplier; again, in 2008, it was the same story with the investment banks, Merrill Lynch and Lehman Brother;. and again with Greece in 2009-early 2010. These are ample demonstrations of the harm they do. They should be sued for the damage caused by the results of the ratings they hand out. Risk assessment is a task which should only be entrusted to public bodies.

Eric Toussaint: The North-American Standard & Poor's and Moody's and the Franco-American Fitch are the three private agencies which rule the roost regarding credit ratings and the credibility of bond issuers, whether they be State or corporate.[24] They have existed for almost a century but it was not until the 1970s-1980s, with the financialisation of the economy, that their business took a sudden leap. However they are constantly in a situation of conflict of interests. Until the 1970s, it was the prospective buyers of bonds issued by the State and by companies who paid rating agencies for their advice on the quality of the issuers. Since then, the situation has been completely reversed: now it is the issuers of bonds who pay the agencies to rate them. What motivates the government and the companies is of course to get good ratings so that they can pay the lowest possible interest rates to those who buy their bonds. Let us recall that until the eve of the collapse of Enron in 2001, highly paid rating agencies attributed top marks to the power supplier. Again, in 2008, it was the same story with the investment banks, Merril Lynch and Lehman Brothers. And again with Greece in 2009-early 2010. These are ample demonstrations of the harm they do. They should be sued for the damage caused by the results of the ratings they hand out. Risk assessment is a task which should only be entrusted to public bodies.

Has the crisis peaked yet?

CADTM: Has the crisis peaked yet?
Eric Toussaint: The crisis is far from over. Even if we only consider the financial aspects, we must be aware that private banks have continued to play an extremely dangerous game which profits them as long as nothing goes wrong, but which is prejudicial to the majority of

---

24 There are others, such as the Chinese Dagong, but they have little influence.

the population. The amount of bad assets on their balance-sheets is enormous. If we look at only the top 90 European banks, the fact is that over the coming two years, they will have to refinance debts to the tune of an astronomical 5,400 billion euro. That represents 45% of the wealth produced annually in the EU. The risks are colossal and the policies adopted by the ECB, the EC and the member States of the EU will not solve anything – indeed quite the contrary.

A central aspect of the risks taken by the European banks needs to be emphasized. They finance a significant part of their operations by making short-term loans in dollars from the North-American lenders known as 'US money market funds' at a lower rate than the ECB's. Furthermore, to return to the case of Greece, how could the European banks possibly settle for 0.35% over 3 months if they had to borrow from the ECB at 1%? They have always financed their loans to European States and companies using loans they themselves took out from the US money market funds – and they continue to do so. Now those money market funds were scared by what was happening in Europe and also by the dispute over the US public debt between Republicans and Democrats. So by June 2011, that source of low-interest finance had just about dried up, which has hurt major French banks most. This was what precipitated the tumble they took on the Stock Exchange and led to the increase of pressure on the ECB to buy back their bonds and thus provide them with new money. In short, this demonstrates the extent of the knock-on effect between the economies of the USA and the EU. It further explains the continual contact between Barack Obama, Angela Merkel, Nicolas Sarkozy, the ECB, the IMF ... and the major banks from Goldman Sachs to BNP Paribas and the Deutsche Bank. A breakdown in the flow of dollar-loans to European banks could cause a very serious crisis in the Old World, just as difficulties encountered by European banks in repaying their US lenders could trigger off a new crisis on Wall Street.

Since 2007-2008, banks and other institutional investors have displaced their speculation activities from the property market (where they had created a bubble which burst in nearly a dozen countries, including the USA) to the public debt market, the currency market (where the equivalent of $4,000 billion changes hands every day, 99% purely for speculative purposes) and the primary resources market (petroleum, gas, minerals, food commodities). These new bubbles can burst at any moment. A possible trigger could be if the US Federal Reserve decided to raise interest rates (followed by the ECB, the Bank of England, etc.). In this respect, in August 2011 the Fed announced its intention to maintain its base rate near zero until 2013. However other events could trigger off a new bank crisis or a crash on the Stock Exchange. The events of July-August 2011 show us it is time to muster our energy in order to prevent the private financial institutions from doing any further damage.

The extent of the crisis is also determined by the volume of the US public debt and the way it is financed in Europe. European bankers hold more than 80% of the total debt of an array of European Union countries in difficulty such as Greece, Ireland, Portugal, the Eastern European countries, Spain and Italy. In volume, Italian public debt paper amounts to 1,500 billion euro, more than twice the combined public debt of Greece, Ireland and Portugal. Spain's public debt comes up to 700 billion euro, i.e. about half of Italy's. The arithmetic is simple: the public debts of Spain and Italy added together represent three times the sum of those of Greece, Ireland and Portugal. As we saw in July-August 2011, while each country continued to pay off its debts, several banks almost collapsed. The ECB had to intervene to save the day. The financial scaffolding of the European banks is so fragile that an attack through the Stock Exchange is enough to bring them down... Not to mention what would happen if the Stock Exchange crashed, which cannot be ruled out.

So far, with the exception of Greece, Ireland and Portugal, the States have managed to refinance their debts by taking out new loans as and when the borrowed capital fell due. The situation has worsened significantly over the last few months. By July/early August 2011, the interest rates demanded by the institutional investors to enable Italy and Spain to refinance their public debt as it fell due with 10-year loans had literally exploded to reach 6%. Once again, the ECB had to intervene, buying up massive amounts of Spanish and Italian debt paper to satisfy the bankers and other institutional investors and bring down interest rates. For how long, though? Italy will have to borrow about €300 billion in August 2011 and July 2012 as that is how much they will require to honour bonds that fall due over that short period. Spain's needs will be considerably lower, at about €80 billion, but that is still a hefty sum. How will the institutional investors behave over the coming twelve months and what will happen if their borrowing conditions on the North-American money market funds become stiffer? Many other events could aggravate the international crisis. One thing is certain: the present policies of the EC, the ECB and the IMF cannot result in a favourable outcome.

CADTM: On several occasions you have written that the private debt was far greater than the public debt. So far you've been talking about public debt.

Eric Toussaint: There is not a shadow of a doubt that the private debts are much higher than the public debts. According to the last report by the McKinsey Global Institute, the sum total of private debt worldwide comes to $17,000 billion, i.e. about three times the sum of all public debts, which is $41,000 billion. There is a great risk that private companies, including banks along with the other institutional investors, will not be able to repay their debts.

Bankers, chief executives of other companies, the traditional media and governments only discuss public debt and use its increase as a pretext to justify new attacks on the social and economic rights of the majority of the population. Austerity and the reduction of public deficits by axing social budgets and civil service jobs have become the only way of raising funds, along with privatizations and more consumer taxes. For appearances' sake in Europe, some governments have added a tiny tax for the rich and talk of taxing financial transactions.

Obviously the increase of public debt is the direct result of 30 years of neoliberal policies. They have used loans to finance fiscal reforms in favour of the wealthy and of large private companies. They have rescued banks and large companies by getting the State budget to take on part of their debt or other losses. Due to the recession, there have been new falls in tax revenues and an increase in some public spending to help victims of the crisis. The combined effect of these different factors has been to increase the public debt. It all comes down to deliberately unjust social policies which aim systematically to favour one social class only. A few crumbs are tossed to the middle classes to keep them quiet. On the other hand, the great majority of the population have been hit by these policies and seen their rights trampled underfoot. That is why the public debt has to be seen as globally illegitimate. And that is why I have been focusing on the public debt in this interview, because we absolutely must find a positive solution to this problem.

Alternative ways out of crisis

CADTM: During this talk, you have claimed that Greece is forced to choose between two options: either to eat humble pie, resigning itself to turning to the Troika; or to refuse the dictates of the markets and the Troika by suspending repayment and calling an audit in order to be able to repudiate the illegitimate part of the debt. You have described the first option. Could you now explain the second in more detail?

Eric Toussaint: We talked about the case of Greece. It is important to mention that other countries are now being confronted with the same choices – Ireland, Portugal, not forgetting Hungary, Bulgaria, Romania, or even Latvia – to mention ones in the European Union. There is every reason to believe that tomorrow it will be the turn of

Italy and Spain. And we should not be surprised to see yet other EU countries in a similar predicament the day after tomorrow, because the crisis is accelerating rapidly. Outside the EU, Iceland is another high risk case.

The best thing would be for these countries, subject to blackmail by speculators, the IMF and other organizations such as the European Commission, to resort to a unilateral moratorium on public debt payments. Commitment to such a unilateral sovereign act would completely transform the balance of power to the detriment of the creditors. Whether they are banks, insurance companies or pension funds, they would be in such haste to sell off their bonds that interest rates would plummet to almost nothing. As for the Troika, it would be obliged to seek to negotiate concessions. Russia in 1998, Argentina in 2001 and Ecuador in 2008 all declared unilateral moratoria on their debt payments, and they all came out of it very well.[25]

It is important to take stock of these recent experiences and to see how to apply the best strategy so that the population can see improvements in their living conditions and make a tangible break with the capitalist system.

CADTM: What other immediate measures are needed alongside a unilateral suspension (moratorium) of debt payments?

---

25   See Damien Millet, Éric Toussaint (eds), *La dette ou la vie*, Aden-CADTM, 2011, chapter 19. On 19 July 2011, the Financial Times (p.7) devoted a whole page to the relative success Argentina had had after refusing to repay a substantial part of her debt. Referring to Argentina and Russia, Joseph Stiglitz, winner of the Bank of Sweden's prize for economics in memory of Alfred Nobel in 2001, who presided over President Bill Clinton's council of economists from 1995-1997 and was Chief Economist and Vice-President of the World Bank from 1997 to 2000, argues strongly in favour of suspending repayment of public debt. In a collection of essays published in 2010 by Oxford University Press (Barry Herman, José Antonio Ocampo, Shari Spiegel, *Overcoming Developing Country Debt Crises*, OUP Oxford), he claims Russia in 1998 and Argentina in the 2000s demonstrated that unilateral suspension of debt payment could be beneficial for countries who decide to take that course of action. 'Both theory and practice suggest that the threat to turn off the credit tap has probably been exaggerated' (p.48). In an article published in the *Journal of Development Economics* entitled 'The elusive costs of sovereign defaults'. Eduardo Levy Yeyati and Ugo Panizza, two eonomists who have worked for the InterAmerican Development Bank, present the results of their meticulous research into cases of default of payment in about forty countries. One of their main conclusions was: 'Periods of default of payment mark the end of economic recovery' (in Journal of Development Economics 94, 2011, p. 95-105). For more on Russia and Argentina, see also: C. Lapavitsas, A. Kaltenbrunner, G. Lambrinidis, D. Lindo, J. Meadway, J. Michell, J.P. Painceira, E. Pires, J. Powell, A. Stenfors, N. Teles: 'The Eurozone between Austerity and Default', September 2010, http://www.researchonmoneyandfinance.org/media/reports/RMF-Eurozone-Austerity-and-Default.pdf. About lessons for Greece from Argentina , see Claudio Katz : http://www.cadtm.org/IMG/pdf/Lecciones_de_Argentina_para_Grecia__CADTM_-1_-_Claudio_Katz.pdf

Eric Toussaint: A unilateral moratorium should be combined with an audit of public loans (with the participation of civil society). The audit must allow the necessary proofs and arguments to be brought before the government and popular opinion to justify the cancellation/repudiation of the part of the debt identified as illegitimate. International law and each country's domestic laws offer a legal basis for the sovereign unilateral act of cancellation/repudiation.[26]

For countries who resort to suspension of payments, there needs to be a moratorium without delay interest on the part not paid.

In other countries, such as France, Belgium, Great Britain, it is not necessarily imperative to decree a unilateral moratorium while the audit is made. The audit is required to determine the extent of cancellation/repudiation to be effected. Should the international conjuncture deteriorate, suspension of payments could become a necessity, even for countries that claim to be safe from the blackmail of private creditors.

CADTM: And how can civil society participate?

Eric Toussaint: The participation of civil society is imperative to guarantee that the audit is carried out both efficiently and transparently. The audit commission should be composed of, for example, different bodies of the State concerned, so that they can report on its work. In any case, it is the participation of the social movements, of grassroots civil society, that will be the key to the audit's success. Social movements can designate their own experts in public finance auditing, economists, jurists and constitutionalists. Obviously the different social movements affected by the debt crisis must also be represented. The audit ought to help determine the different responsibilities in the indebtedness process and demand that those responsible, nationally and internationally, be brought to justice.

CADTM: In most cases, the ruling class has no interest in seeing an authentic audit carried out under the auspices of civil society. In other cases, it may resign itself to the idea in order to circumvent the problem.

Eric Toussaint: That is quite true. The case I mentioned earlier corresponds to a situation where strong popular mobilization brings left-wing forces into government who will adopt policies in the interests of the people or go even further. I am reminded of something Arthur Scargill, one of the main leaders of the Miners' Strike in Britain in the mid-eighties, said. Basically he said that they needed a government as true to the interests of the workers as

---

26   See Damien Millet, Éric Toussaint (eds.), *La dette ou la vie*, Aden-CADTM, 2011, chapters 20 and 21.

Margaret Thatcher was to the interests of the capitalist class. In the present situation in Europe, we are still far from achieving that. We are confronted with governments who are hostile to the idea of an audit and unwilling to call debt repayment into question. That is why we need to constitute proper citizens' audit commissions without government participation.

CADTM: Who will have to foot the bill of debt cancellation?

Eric Toussaint: Whatever happens, it is only right and proper that the private institutions and high-earning individuals who hold the debt paper should bear the brunt of cancelling illegitimate sovereign debt since they are largely responsible for the crisis, and furthermore, they have largely profited from it. Making them bear the cost of cancellation is only fair, if there is to be a return to greater social justice.

CADTM: Will small stock-holders or salaried workers who hold public debt paper through pension savings also have to pay up?

Eric Toussaint: A proper survey of debt-stock holders needs to be drawn up so that citizens of modest or middling means among them can be indemnified.

CADTM: What will happen to those responsible for illegitimate or odious debt?

Eric Toussaint: If the audit proves the existence of offences linked to illegitimate indebtedness, the offenders will be severely condemned to make reparation and should not escape prison sentences in accordance with the seriousness of their felony. As for government authorities that have instigated illegitimate borrowing, they must be held accountable.

CADTM: What about the part of the debt that cannot be declared illegitimate, illegal and/or odious?

Eric Toussaint: For debts that are not deemed illegitimate, creditors should be made to contribute through reduction of stock and interest rates, as well as by rescheduling payments over a longer period. Here too, positive discrimination should be adopted in favour of small public debt holders, allowing them to be repaid on normal terms. Moreover, the amount of funds in the State budget earmarked for debt repayment should be limited as befits the state of the economy, the government's capacity to repay and the incompressible nature of social spending. Such practices will emulate what was done for Germany after the Second World War. The 1953 London Agreement on the German debt, which consisted, for example, of reducing the debt stock by 62%, stipulated that the ratio of debt service to export revenues should not exceed 5%[27]. A ratio of the following type might be defined: the sum allocated to debt repayment may not exceed 5% of State revenues. A legal framework is also required to avoid a repetition of the crisis that started in 2007-2008: socializing private debts should be prohibited; a permanent audit of public debt policy with citizens' participation should be mandatory; there should be no prescription for offences linked to illegitimate indebtedness; illegitimate debts should be ruled null and void... and so on.

CADTM: Debts can be cancelled, but what could be done about the rest?

Eric Toussaint: A whole panoply of further measures are needed. Austerity programmes must be stopped; banks should be transferred to the public sector; radical tax reforms are required ; sectors privatized during the neoliberal era should be socialized there must be a radical reduction of working hours[28]. All these measures have to be implemented, as debt cancellation, however necessary, will not suffice if the logic of the system remains intact.

---

27   See Éric Toussaint, *The World Bank : the Never-ending coup d'état*, Mumbai: Vikas Adhyayan Kendra; (2007), Chapter 4.
28   See Eight Key Proposals for Another Europe, http://www.cadtm.org/Eight-key-proposals-for-another

For more on the debt crisis in the EU by the same author, see the following papers:

- *'Greece, Ireland and Portugal: why agreements with the Troika are odious'* (with Renaud Vivien), published 9 Aug. 2011 http://www.cadtm.org/Greece-Ireland-and-Portugal-why

- *'Il faut annuler les dettes illégitimes'*, Eric Toussaint interviewed by Sébastien Brulez in *Le Courrier*, Geneva, published 3 Aug. 2011 http://www.cadtm.org/Il-faut-annuler-les-dettes

- *'Facing the Debt Crisis in Europe'* (with Damien Millet), published 10 July 2011, http://www.cadtm.org/Facing-the-debt-crisis-in-Europe

- *'Pourquoi la crise frappe l'Union européenne davantage que les Etats-Unis'*, published 6 July 2011, http://www.cadtm.org/Pourquoi-la-crise-frappe-l-Union

- *'Core vs Periphery in the EU'* , published 13 June 2011, http://www.cadtm.org/Core-vs-Periphery-in-the-EU

- *'Aides empoisonnées au menu européen'*, published 17 April 2011, http:/ http://www.cadtm.org/Aides-empoisonnees-au-menu

- *'Eight key proposals for another Europe'*, published 7 April 2011, http://www.cadtm.org/Eight-key-proposals-for-another

About Resistance Books and the IIRE

Resistance Books

Resistance Books is the publishing arm of Socialist Resistance, a revolutionary Marxist organisation which is the British section of the Fourth International. We publish books jointly with the International Institute for Research and Education in Amsterdam and independently under the name of Resistance books. Socialist Resistance also publishes a bi-monthly magazine of the same name and occasional pamphlets.

Socialist Resistance is an organisation active in the trade union movement and in many campaigns against the war, in solidarity with Palestine and with anti-capitalist movements across the globe. We are ecosocialist – we argue that much of what is produced under capitalism is socially useless and either redundant or directly harmful. Capitalism's drive for profit is creating environmental disaster – and it is the poor, the working class and the global south that are paying the highest price for this.

We have been long standing supporters of women's liberation and the struggles of lesbians, gay people bisexuals and transgender people. We believe those struggles must be led by those directly affected – none so fit to break the chains as those who wear them. We work in antiracist and anti-fascist networks, including campaigns for the rights of immigrants and asylum seekers.

Socialist Resistance believes that democracy is an essential component of any successful movement of resistance and struggle. With Britain and the western imperialist countries moving into a long period of capitalist austerity and crisis, deeper than any since the Second World War, Socialist Resistance stands together with all those who are organising to make another world is possible.

Further information about Resistance Books and Socialist Resistance can be obtained at www.socialistresistance.org.

International Viewpoint is the English language on-line magazine of the Fourth International which can be read at www.internationalviewpoint.org.

The International Institute for Research and Education

The International Institute for Research and Education (IIRE) is an international foundation, recognised in Belgium as an international scientific association by Royal decree of 11th June 1981. The IIRE provides activists and scholars worldwide with opportunities for research and education in three locations: Amsterdam, Islamabad and Manila.

Since 1982, when the Institute opened in Amsterdam, its main activity has been the organisation of courses in the service of progressive forces around the world. Our seminars and study groups deal with all subjects related to the emancipation of the world's oppressed and exploited. It has welcomed hundreds of participants from every inhabited continent. Most participants have come from the Third World.

The IIRE has become a prominent centre for the development of critical thought and interaction, and the exchange of experiences, between people who are engaged in daily struggles on the ground. The Institute's sessions give participants a unique opportunity to step aside from the pressure of daily activism. The IIRE gives them time to study, reflect upon their involvement in a changing world and exchange ideas with people from other countries.

Our website is constantly being expanded and updated with freely downloadable publications, in several languages, and audio files. Recordings of several recent lectures given at the institute can be downloaded from www.iire.org - as can talks given by founding Fellows such as Ernest Mandel and Livio Maitan, dating back to the early 1980s.

The IIRE publishes Notebooks for Study and Research to focus on themes of contemporary debate or historical or theoretical importance. Lectures and study materials given in sessions in our Institute, located in Amsterdam, Manila and Islamabad, are made available to the public in large part through the Notebooks.

Different issues of the Notebooks have also appeared in languages besides English and French, including German, Dutch, Arabic, Spanish, Japanese, Korean, Portuguese, Turkish, Swedish, Danish and Russian.

For a full list visit http://bit.ly/IIRENSR or subscribe online at: http://bit.ly/NSRsub. To order, email iire@iire.org or write to International Institute for Research and Education, Lombokstraat 40, Amsterdam, NL-1094.

Resistance Books and IIRE publications

Resistance Books and the IIRE would be glad to have readers' opinions of this book, and suggestions for future publication. Our books are available at special quantity discounts to educational and non-profit organizations, and to bookstores.

To contact us, please write to:

Resistance Books
PO Box 62732, London, SW2 9CQ
Email at contact@socialistresistance.org

International Institute for Research and Education
Lombokstraat 40, Amsterdam, NL-1094 AL
Email at iire@iire.org

Forthcoming books

The united front & the Transitional Programme, Leon Trotsky, Daniel Bensaïd, John Riddell.

The Delusion of Green Capitalism, Daniel Tanuro

Struggles of Indigeneous People in Latin America, Hugo Blanco.

Marxism and Anarchism, Marx, Engels, Totsky and others

Fascism and the far right in Europe.

Introduction to Marxist Economic Theory (Third Edition), Ernest Mandel, Özlem Onaran, Raphie de Santos.

The thought of Leon Trotsky, Denise Avenas, Michael Löwy, Jean-Michel Krivine.

Dangerous relationships: marriage and divorces between Marxism and feminism, Cinzia Arruzza.

Palestine in crisis, Camile Dagher, Cinzia Nachira, Roland Rance

Titles from Resistance Books

Militant years - car workers' struggles in Britain in the 60s and 70s, Alan Thornett, February 2011 (£12, €14, $19).

The Global Fight for Climate Justice – Anti-capitalist responses to global warming and environmental destruction, Ian Angus ed., June 2009 (£10, €14, $18).

Ireland's Credit Crunch, Kearing, Morrison & Corrigan, October 2010 (£6, €8, $10).

Foundations of Christianity: a study in Christian origins, Karl Kautsky (£12, €18, $25).

The Permanent Revolution & Results and Prospects, Leon Trotsky (£9, €15, $18).

My Life Under White Supremacy and in Exile, Leonard Nikani, February 2009 (£10, €12, $15).

Cuba at Sea, Ron Ridenour, May 2008 (£8, €12, $15).

Ecosocialism or Barbarism (new expanded edition), Jane Kelly ed., February 2008 (£6, €9, $12).

Cuba: Beyond the Crossroads (new expanded edition), Ron Ridenour, April 2007 (£10, €15, $20).

Middle East: war, imperialism, and ecology – sixty years of resistance, Roland Rance & Terry Conway eds. and Gilbert Achcar (contributor) et al., March 2007 (£12, €14, $19).

It's never too late to love or rebel, Celia Hart, August 2006 (£8, €15, $20).

Notebooks for Study and Research

New Parties of the Left – Experiences from Europe, Daniel Bensaïd, Alain Krivine, Alda Sousa, Alan Thornett et al., May 2011 (€8, £7, $11), NSR 50, IIRE and Resistance books pub.

Revolution and Counter-revolution in Europe from 1918 to 1968, Pierre Frank, May 2011 (€10, £9, $14), NSR 49, IIRE and Resistance books pub.

Women's Liberation & Socialist Revolution: Documents of the Fourth International, Penelope Duggan ed., October 2010 (€8, £7, $11) NSR 48, IIRE pub.

The Long March of the Trotskyists: Contributions to the history of the International, Pierre Frank, Daniel Bensaïd, Ernest Mandel, October 2010 (€8, £5, $8), NSR 47, IIRE and Resistance books pub.

October Readings: The development of the concept of Permanent Revolution, D. R. O'Connor Lysaght ed., October 2010 (£5, €6, $8), NSR 46, IIRE and Resistance books pub.

Building Unity Against Fascism: Classic Marxist Writings, Leon Trotsky, Daniel Guérin, Ted Grant et al., October 2010 (€6, £5, $8), NSR 44/45, IIRE and Resistance books pub.

Strategies of Resistance & 'Who Are the Trotskyists', Daniel Bensaïd, November 2009 (€8, £6, $10), NSR 42/43, IIRE and Resistance books pub.

Living Internationalism: the IIRE's history, Murray Smith and Joost Kircz eds., January 2011 (€5, £4, $7), NSR 41, IIRE pub.

Socialists and the Capitalist Recession (with Ernest Mandel's 'Basic Theories of Karl Marx'), Raphie De Santos, Michel Husson, Claudio Katz et al., March 2009 (€9, £6, $12), NSR 39/40, IIRE and Resistance books pub.

Take the Power to Change the World, Phil Hearse ed., June 2007 (€9, £6, $12), NSR 37/38, IIRE and Resistance books pub.

The Porto Alegre Alternative: Direct Democracy in Action, Iain Bruce ed. (€19, £13, $23.50), NSR 35/36.

The Clash of Barbarisms: September 11 & the Making of the New World Disorder, Gilbert Achcar (€15, £10, $16), NSR 33/34.

Globalization: Neoliberal Challenge, Radical Responses, Robert Went (€21, £14, $21), NSR 31/32.

Understanding the Nazi Genocide: Marxism after Auschwitz, Enzo Traverso (€19.20, £13, $19.) NSR 29/30.

Fatherland or Mother Earth? Essays on the National Question, Michael Löwy (€16, £10.99, $16), NSR 27.

Resistance Books
London

International Institute for Research & Education
Amsterdam, Islamabad & Manila

Lightning Source UK Ltd.
Milton Keynes UK
UKHW010923090822
407057UK00001B/23